Indian Art Traditions of the Northwest Coast

Indian Art Traditions of the Northwest Coast

Roy L. Carlson, Editor

Archaeology Press
Simon Fraser University
Burnaby, B.C.

Department of Archaeology
Simon Fraser University
Burnaby, B.C.   V5A 1S6

Canadian Cataloguing in Publication Data

Main entry under title:

Indian art traditions of the Northwest Coast

Based on papers of a symposium titled: The
    prehistory of Northwest Coast Indian art,
    held at Simon Fraser University in 1976.
Bibliography: p.
ISBN 0-86491-031-2

1. Indians of North America—Northwest Coast
of North America—Art—Congresses. I. Carlson,
Roy L., 1930-   II. Simon Fraser University.
Dept. of Archaeology.
E78.N78I52   709'.01'109711 C83-091291-6

Design and production: Barbara Hodgson Graphic Design
Typesetting: Baseline Publication Trades Cooperative
Printed and bound in Canada.

CONTENTS

ILLUSTRATIONS

This book is dedicated to
Erna Gunther

PREFACE

The chapters in this book originated from a symposium entitled *The Prehistory of Northwest Coast Indian Art* organized for the Northwest Studies Conference at Simon Fraser University in 1976. The prehistoric background to this art tradition had not really been explored since Harlan I. Smith's *An Album of Prehistoric Canadian Art* published in 1923, and Wilson Duff's *Prehistoric Stone Sculpture of the Fraser River and Gulf of Georgia* published in 1956, both of which predate the period of extensive archaeological excavations on the coast. In some minds there still lingered the question of whether the art tradition was prehistoric and not dependant on the introduction of iron and steel tools in quantity. Indeed, it is only now with the accumulation of archaeological information over the last twenty-five years from dated archaeological contexts that this question can be answered with confidence. The symposium concentrated on the contexts of both *time* and *meaning* for the Northwest Coast Art Tradition, and the chapters in this book are the expanded and re-written results of this concentration.

Many things have happened since the original symposium. Two of the participants have died, Wilson Duff in August, 1976 and Charles Borden in December, 1978. While Duff had agreed to prepare a written version of his paper from the conference tapes, this task was not done prior to his death, so the task of transcribing fell to me. His presentation was well prepared, and he had written a lengthy abstract, so this work was not as formidable as it might have been. An abbreviated transcription was given to the British Columbia Provincial Museum at their request for inclusion in the memorial volume to Duff, but the full text has not previously been published. Borden completed the revisions to his chapter the morning of his death, leaving only two illustrations to be pasted into his manuscript.

Erna Gunther, to whom this volume is specifically dedicated, as was the symposium which preceded it, has also died, in August, 1982. Her particular specialization was art and material culture and she not only inspired those of us who were her students (Suttles, Holm, Daugherty, Duff, Carlson) to investigate this fascinating subject area, but created the conditions at the university which made such study and research possible. Some of our students (Stryd, Friedman, Lundy) have continued this interest. For this we all thank her. Wilson Duff expressed his wish that his chapter also be dedicated to Viola Garfield, another of our professors from whom we learned so much about Northwest Coast Indian cultures. It is my understanding that a volume dedicated specifically to her is in preparation.

Bill Reid (Haida artist), Knut Fladmark and Philip Hobler (Simon Fraser University), Astrida Onat (Seattle Community College) and Patricia Severs (then, University of Alberta) served as discussants at our original symposium. Perhaps it is now time to get together again.

R.L.C.
Burnaby, B.C.

CHAPTER 1

Prehistory of the Northwest Coast

ROY L. CARLSON

In the beginning there was ice... in the end there were approximately 100,000 Indian people living along the Pacific coast from southeast Alaska to the mouth of the Columbia River in Oregon... in between is the prehistoric period, the time span of the unknown, between the retreat of the last continental glacier and the arrival of the first Europeans with their notebooks and artist's sketches who ushered in the period of written history. The prehistoric period here lasted from perhaps 12,000 years ago to the late 1700's when Cook, Vancouver, Mackenzie and others began writing about the area and its inhabitants. Glacial geology suggests that the coast was ice free by 12,000 years ago, but there remains the possibility of even earlier movements of peoples whose traces were wiped out by the last glacial advance. The beginning date is not actually important; what is important is that there was such a date and we can conceive of it as during or just after the last period of deglaciation.

Imagine yourself on the coast north of the Strait of Juan de Fuca some 15,000 years ago when what are now forested shores and snow capped mountains were hidden under a cover of glacial ice many thousands of feet thick. Neither man nor other land animal was present to break the icy stillness. By 13,000 years ago this massive blanket of ice had begun to melt, and as this melting continued, a barren land, free of vegetation, free of animal life, and free of human culture emerged. This freedom of the land was shortlived. Even as the ice turned to water, and rushed downstream to the sea, first alder, birch, and pine, and later fir and cedar and other trees and plants spread onto the land from adjacent unglaciated regions. The mantle of white was now replaced by one of green. As the infusion of ice water caused the level of the sea to rise, the land also rose, freed from the weight of glacial

ice. Sub-arctic and then temperate fauna spread into this new found land. Man was part of this fauna; he preyed on the other animals for food and used their hides for clothing. He arrived by different routes, and brought with him different cultural traditions. By 10,000 years ago ice only existed in the mountain top remnants we still see today.

The Northwest Coast *(Fig. 1:1)* is a ribbon of green, wet forested land which hugs the Pacific coast of North America from the mouth of the Copper River in Alaska to just below the mouth of the Klamath River in northwest California. It was part of the "Salmon Area" of early ethnographers and its cultures were clearly different from those of the California acorn area, the agricultural Southwest and East, and the buffalo-hunting Plains. The Northwest Coast was less clearly differentiated, however, from its immediate hinterland, the Columbia-Fraser Plateau, where the rivers also ran with salmon. South of the Columbia River, little in the way of graphic or plastic art was produced by the aboriginal Indian peoples. From the Columbia River northward however, there was considerable art in materials which preserve archaeologically. It is to this portion of the Northwest Coast, the part from the lower Columbia River northward, that is emphasized in this chapter.

Whereas the historic Indian cultures encountered by the explorers and colonists were truly spectacular with their potlatches, totem poles, masks and huge dugout canoes, the most obvious surface evidences of the prehistoric cultures are uninspiring middens of clam shells, the discarded remains of food-gathering enterprises. Nowhere were there spectacular stone ruins as, for example, in the Southwest which stimulated early intensive archaeological work. Difficulty of access to this remote, wet land also

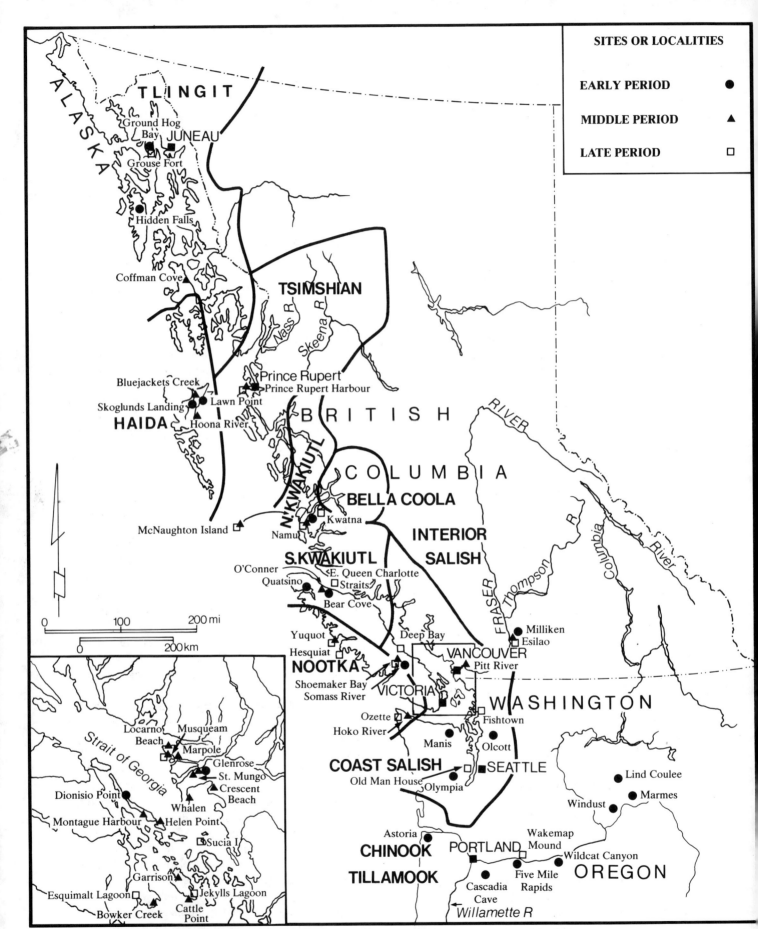

Fig. 1:1. **Map of the Northwest Coast showing cultural and geographic divisions mentioned in the text.**

contributed to the slow pace of archaeological research. Thirty years ago the only chronology of prehistoric cultures for the whole of the Northwest Coast was limited to the last 2500 years, and was applicable only to the southern end of the Strait of Georgia. By twenty years ago, the situation had changed to the extent that two 9000 to 10,000 year long sequences had been discovered, one at Five Mile Rapids on the lower Columbia River (Cressman et al 1960), and a second at the mouth of the Fraser Canyon (Borden 1960). Today, after some twenty years of research by a great many archaeologists, the prehistoric period is less mysterious than it used to be, but is still far from being a "squeezed lemon" suffering from archaeological exhaustion. The decline in mystery is the result of the archaeological research of the 1970's, a decade which witnessed about ten times more archaeological research and publication than in all previous decades combined. New discoveries provided a chronological framework for most regions of the coast, and new interpretations can now lay to rest some of the older ideas of the events of that unknown prehistoric period. It is now possible to look at the past in terms of a framework of Early, Middle and Late periods *(Fig. 1:2)*, and to glimpse both culture content and change that took place during these segments of prehistoric time.

Early Period 12,000 - 5500 Years Ago

The Early Period is the period of initial settlement of the Northwest Coast. Everyone knows that the ancestors of coastal Indians and all other New World aborigines crossed Bering Strait and eventually reached all parts of North and South America. Although there is no reasonable alternative to Bering Strait, there are alternative routes south. Once this side of the strait, according to one older model, man followed the Pleistocene fauna south down an ice free corridor just east of the Rockies and rapidly became dispersed throughout both North and South America. Following extinction of the Ice Age animals, man then gradually spread from interior to coastal areas and settled in to exploit local subsistence resources. For the Northwest Coast the latter meant fish. Kroeber (1939) considered the ethnographic coastal culture as ". . . originally a river or river mouth culture, later a beach culture, and only finally and in part a sea going one." The hinterland to this coastal strip, the Columbia-Fraser Plateau, was conceived as a survival of the earlier riverine stage of cultural development influenced both by ideas spreading from the coast and from interior North America, and by a late intrusion or Athabascan speaking peoples from Asia. This model was based on almost no real archaeological data, and when examined in the light of the results of archaeological research of the 1970's requires considerable modification. The maritime coastal cultures were not the result of a simple evolutionary development from interior hunters to riverine fishermen to coastal exploiters of fish and sea mammals. The evidence suggests that at least some of the peoples arrived in the area already with a maritime adaptation, that migration routes were coastal as well as interior, and that the subsistence system based on salmon spread up the river from the coast rather than the reverse. These points are not as precisely documented as one would prefer, and must be viewed as hypotheses, but together they do form a consistent picture of events during the Early Period. Within the Pacific Northwest there is archaeological evidence for at least four early basal cultures or cultural traditions by 10,000 years ago: the Pebble Tool Tradition; the Microblade Tradition; the Fluted Point Tradition; and the Lind Coulee or Stemmed Point Tradition. Each of these cultures is characterized by a slightly different tool kit *(Fig. 1:3)* and a slightly different way of life.

The Fluted Point Tradition is well known archaeologically. Fluted points, which are its hallmark, extend from this side of Bering Strait south through Alberta and on into the continental United States, Mexico and South America. Where dated the earlier part of this tradition (Clovis) is about 11,500 years old and usually associated with mammoth remains, and the younger part (Folsom) about 10,000 years old and usually associated with extinct species of bison. Dating of this tradition is not sufficiently reliable to demonstrate whether it originated and spread south from Alaska (there are no fluted points in Siberia) via the ice free corridor, or north to Alaska from interior North America as the Pleistocene fauna and their glacio-pluvial environment retreated with the waning of the last ice sheet. Fluted points are very rare on the Northwest Coast, and are only known from surface finds south of the area covered by the glaciers. One point was found just west of Olympia, Washington (Osborne 1956), and another west of the Cascades in the Willamette drainage, Oregon (Alley 1975). This tradition seems to have contributed nothing to later cultural development on the Northwest Coast.

The Lind Coulee Tradition is characterized by large stemmed projectile points, chipped stone crescents, and large steep scrapers. Rice (1972) has shown that it is an early hunting tradition, exploiting bison, pronghorn, elk and smaller mammals. Its dates range from 8500 to 13,000 years ago with most dates in the 8500 to 10,000 year period. This tradition centers in the Columbia-Snake drainage of interior Washington and Oregon, and around the pluvial lake areas of Oregon and Nevada to the south, but did reach the coast at the mouth of the Columbia. It is present in interior British Columbia in the Kootenai and south Thompson, upper Columbia areas, and possibly on the upper Fraser, but the evidence is meagre and consists of undated surface finds of projectile points similar to those from dated contexts further south. The

YEARS AGO	PERIOD	Prince Rupert Skeena R. TSIMSHIAN	Southeast Alaska TLINGIT	Queen Charlotte Islands HAIDA	North Central B.C. Coast BELLA BELLA BELLA COOLA	S. Central B.C. Coast SOUTHERN KWAKIUTL	West Coast Vancouver I. NOOTKA
0	LATE	Prince Rupert I	Grouse Fort / Ground Hog Bay I		Transition / Kwatna Phase / Anutcix Phase	Sites in E. Queen Charlotte Strait	Late Yuquot / Shoemaker Bay I / Hesquiat
1000							
2000	MIDDLE	Prince Rupert II / Kleanza Complex / Prince Rupert III / Skeena Complex	? / Coffman Cove / ?	Transitional Complex / Bluejackets Creek / Graham Tradition	McNaughton II / McNaughton I / Cathedral Phase / Namu IV / Namu III	Bear Cove II	O'Conner II / Middle Yuquot / Shoemaker Bay I
3000							Early Yuquot
4000		Gitaus VI / Hagwilget A	Bay II				
5000					Namu II		
6000	EARLY	?	Ground Hog III / Hidden Falls	Moresby Tradition / Early Skoglund's Landing (?)	(Zone IIb) / Namu I (Zone IIa) / Moresby Beach Complexes (?)	O'Conner I / Bear Cove I / Quatsino Beach Complexes (?)	Somass River
7000							
8000							
9000							
10,000				MICROBLADE TRADITION		P E B B L E	
11,000							

Northwest Washington Coast	Puget Sound		Georgia Strait and Lower Fraser	Gulf and San Juan Islands	Fraser Canyon	Lower Columbia	B.C./A.D.
MAKAH	C O A S T		S A L I S H			CHINOOK	PRESENT
Ozette	Old Man House	Penn Cove Phase	Stselax Phase	San Juan Phase	Esilao	Wakemap Mound	
			Belcarra II Whalen II	Late Marpole Phase	Emery		1000 A.D.
	Marpole Phase		Marpole Phase	Marpole Phase	Skamel		1 A.D.
Hoko River			Locarno Beach Phase	Locarno Beach Phase	Baldwin	Five Mile Rapids, Late	1000 B.C.
	Cornet Bay I		St. Mungo Phase	Mayne Phase	Eayem		2000 B.C.
	Rosario Beach I						
			Maurer				3000 B.C.
					?	Five Mile Rapids, Transitional	4000 B.C.
			Glenrose I	Dionisio Point I	Mazama		5000 B.C.
						Five Mile Rapids, Full Early	
Olcott	Olcott				Milliken		6000 B.C.
						Five Mile Rapids, Initial Early (Windust)	7000 B.C.
							8000 B.C.

O O L   T R A D I T I O N   STEMMED POINT TRADITION

| Manis Mastodon | Clovis (?) FLUTED POINT TRADITION | | | | | | 9000 B.C. |

Fig. 1:2. Regional Chronology of the Northwest Coast. This chart summarizes the current state of knowledge concerning the temporal and spatial extent of prehistoric cultures of the Northwest Coast. Some of the names used are for well defined and well dated cultural phases such as the Marpole phase, whereas others refer to single sites such as Maurer or to different components at the same site such as McNaughton I and II where the geographic extent of the cultures or phases of which these components were a part is either unknown or poorly defined. The validity of the assigned time placement of such components varies from *well dated* such as for Glenrose I, Namu and Milliken with solid C^{14} dates, to *estimated* such as for Somass River, the various beach complexes, and the single Clovis point from near Olympia whose chronological positions are suggested by geology or typology. Other names, the Graham Tradition for example, refer to temporal continuities of culture based on data from a number of sites. The largest data gaps are for the Early Period in the Tsimshian and Nootkan regions, and the Middle Period in S.E. Alaska and Puget Sound. In spite of these and smaller gaps throughout the sequence, the overall picture is of settlement during the Early Period by bearers of the Mircroblade Tradition, the Pebble Tool Tradition, and the Stemmed Point (Lind Coulee) Tradition followed by biological continuity with cultural change brought about by inter-regional trade and acculturation, adaptation to the environment, and diffusion of cultural complexes from other parts of the world. There is so far no evidence that the fourth early culture, the poorly represented Fluted Point Tradition, contributed anything to subsequent developments on the Northwest Coast.

distribution of this tradition correlates with the distribution of the northern segment of the Macro-Penutian language phylum which includes Chinook and Sahaptin and other Oregon languages. If this correlation is meaningful, then some traces are expectable at or near the present distribution of the Tsimshian languages on the Skeena River, as Tsimshian has been considered (although not demonstrated) to be a Macro-Penutian outlier (Voegelin and Voeglin 1966). Otherwise, this early cultural tradition was more affected by the coastal cultures than it was effective in influencing them. It existed before the spread of salmon up the Columbia.

The Pebble Tool Tradition centres in southwestern B.C. It is an early coastal and river tradition with sites both at the major rapids on the Fraser in B.C. and the Columbia in Oregon, and on the sea coast in B.C. as far north as Namu. Its hallmarks are the unifacial pebble tool and leaf-shaped biface. The earliest unequivocal dates are between 10,000 and 8000 years ago. The pebble tools are thought to be partly indicative of wood working, an adaptation to the post glacial forest environment. Site locations at the main fisheries on the Columbia and the Fraser indicate salmon utilization, and other site locations along the rugged B.C. coast indicate knowledge and use

of marine resources. In 1977 a property owner near Sequim, Washington uncovered mastodon bones in a bog when he started to excavate a duck pond. Archaeologists from Washington State University (Gustafson *et al* 1979) were called, and excavated these remains. The most exciting find was the tip of a bone point embedded in one of the mastodon's rib bones. X-rays showed that healing had taken place around the wound, and indicated that the animal had not died of this injury. Two radiocarbon dates of 12,000 ± 310 B.P. and 11,850 ± 60 B.P. were obtained from samples of vegetal remains preserved in the wet deposit. The skull was badly crushed, and bones from the right side were broken and scattered and bore cut marks and scratches suggestive of butchering. The only associated stone artifact was a crudely flaked cobble spall (a leaf-shaped point was found in more recent layers at the site). This site is the only evidence so far which suggests earlier dates for the bearers of the Pebble Tool Tradition and that they were originally elephant hunters rather than fishermen. Perhaps the fact that this elephant got away at least once and didn't succumb until he had reached a ripe old age, tells us something of the hunting abilities of these earliest people. At other sites the subsistence base of Pebble Tool Tradition peoples seems to have been fish, although some of the evidence for this activity is indirect, and these sites are 2000 to 4000 years younger than the Manis Mastodon.

Excavated sites on the Northwest Coast which have Early Period components of the Pebble Tool Tradition are few and far between: 1) the Milliken site near the mouth of the Fraser Canyon two miles above Yale with occupation beginning by 9000 years ago (Borden 1968a); 2) the Glenrose Cannery site on the lower Fraser in Surrey with earliest dates about 8000 B.P. (Matson 1976); and 3) the site of Bear Cove at the entrance to Hardy Bay on the northeastern end of Vancouver Island (C. Carlson 1979). The earliest strata at all three of these sites have pebble tools, foliate bifaces and various casually flaked stone tools, and lack types of tools known from more recent sites. In addition, all are situated in locations for taking fish or marine animals. Bone tools and bone faunal remains are rare in these early components because of acidic conditions of the soil. Mollusc shells are also rare to absent.

Two other sites have yielded early components which are best conceptualized as interfaces between the Pebble Tool Tradition and other early basal cultures. The Early Stage at the Five Mile Rapids site on the Columbia River in Oregon (Cressman *et al* 1960) represents an interface with the Lind Coulee Tradition, and the Namu site (R. Carlson 1979) at the mouth of Burke Channel on the central coast of British Columbia, an interface with the Microblade Tradition. Both sites are clearly oriented toward fishing. Five Mile Rapids is at the main Indian fishery on the Columbia during ethnographic times, and no one could have reached Namu on the rugged central coast without a good knowledge of watercraft and a marine adaptation. The occupation begins at both Namu and Five Mile Rapids by 9700 years ago on the basis of C¹⁴ dates. No bone was preserved in the acidic soil of Namu before 6000 years ago, but at Five Mile Rapids thousands of salmon bones and a number of bone tools were preserved through the fortuitous formation of a layer of opality.

A number of types of bone or antler tools preserved at Five Mile Rapids may be added to the list of flaked stone tools typical of the Pebble Tool Tradition: antler flakers and cylindrical hammers for making stone tools, antler wedges usable in woodworking and in fleshing hides, bone awls for basket making or sewing, hooks which were part of the spear thrower used in sea or land hunting, notched elk teeth for use as pendants, a small curved unilaterally barbed point which is probably part of a fish spear, a numerous unfinished and broken fragments.

At Glenrose (Matson 1976) the lower levels did contain some clam and mussel shell whose alkaline content helped in the preservation of bone. Antler wedges and punches, a tooth pendant from an unidentified animal and a strange barbed bone point were recovered. Bones of seal, beaver, deer and elk indicate hunting. Salmon, sturgeon, eulachon and bones of a few other fish were also found. Small girdled stones used as either bolas or net weights occur at both Five Mile Rapids and Namu and further up the Columbia in sites of the Stemmed Point Tradition. The lowermost two components at the Milliken site which Borden (1968a) calls the Milliken and Mazama phases have no bones preserved, but the site location in the steep canyon would only have been useful if salmon were being taken. These components are dated between 9000 and 7000 years ago, and underlie a layer of volcanic ash spewed from the eruption of Mt. Mazama in Oregon some 6700 years ago. Red ochre is in these components, and obsidian traded from Oregon. Charred choke cherry pits suggest use of the site in late summer when this fruit ripens which is also the time of major salmon runs.

At Bear Cove (C. Carlson 1979) initial occupation occurred by 8000 years ago. The artifactual assemblage is typical of the Pebble Tool Tradition with pebble choppers, leaf-shaped points and retouched flakes which may have served as cutting and scraping implements. No shell was present in the early deposit and bones were found only in the upper part of the early stratum. Some fish bones were recovered there and consisted mostly of rockfish with smaller amounts of salmon, cod, sculpin, greenling, dogfish and ratfish. Most of the mammal bones were from sea mammals: porpoise and dolphin, northern fur seal, sea lion, sea otter and harbour seal. Although the sample is small, this assemblage of bones and the site location certainly indicate a primary marine adaptation.

At Namu, the early component lies in a layer devoid of shell in which the soil is so acidic that no bone has been preserved, below a three metre deep shell midden accumulation. Artifacts are typical of the Pebble Tool Tradition, but in addition there are microblades which are not present in sites to the south until more recent times. The bottom of the Namu site is dated by radiocarbon to 9720 ± 140 B.P.

Other than the Manis Mastodon site, Pebble Tool Tradition sites are rather clearly associated with marine or riverine subsistence patterns, although certainly deer and elk were not ignored. Cascadia Cave (Newman 1966), for example, may well represent a hunting camp of this culture. However, the history of this basal culture seems to be tied in mostly with the history of salmon. In the aftermath of glaciation as the rivers warmed and lost their loads of ice, and up-river habitats become suitable for spawning, the lake-spawning species of salmon spread further and further up the rivers. It seems likely that peoples followed this spread up the Fraser, Columbia and smaller rivers where they may well have met other peoples expanding from other areas. The distribution of the Pebble Tool Tradition suggests that it is ancestral to the Salish and Wakashan speaking peoples.

Where the Pebble Tool Tradition came from originally is unknown. Possibly the bearers of this culture were already adapted to coastal and river areas south of the glaciers along the coasts and river valleys of southwest Washington, western Oregon and northern California, and spread north following the retreat of the glaciers. Alternatively, these peoples may have arrived coastwise in the immediate post-glacial from Asia or Beringia. Hopkins (1978:17) who has studied the glacial and sea level changes notes that the relevant Asian and North America coasts were deglaciated early, and that peoples with the requisite technology and coastal adaptation could have reached Puget Sound from Beringia as early as 12,000 years ago. At the Ushki Lake sites in Kamchatka in Layer VI salmon bones have been found as well as artifacts similar to those of the Pebble Tool Tradition dating between 10,000 and 11,000 years ago (Dikov 1979:289). The Aleutian Islands are an obvious route for marine oriented peoples between the two continents. Unfortunately, most of the evidence necessary to support either of these hypotheses regarding origins has either been washed away by rising sea levels or if still present is submerged on the narrow continental shelf.

The last early basal culture is the Microblade Tradition. Microblade technology is a different system of making cutting and piercing tools than that employed by the bearers of the other early cultures. In Microblade technology, small nodules of stone called micro-cores are carefully prepared so that a number of sharp-edged, parallel-sided flakes called microblades can be struck or pressed from these nodules. These microblades were then presumably inset into a wooden or bone point to produce

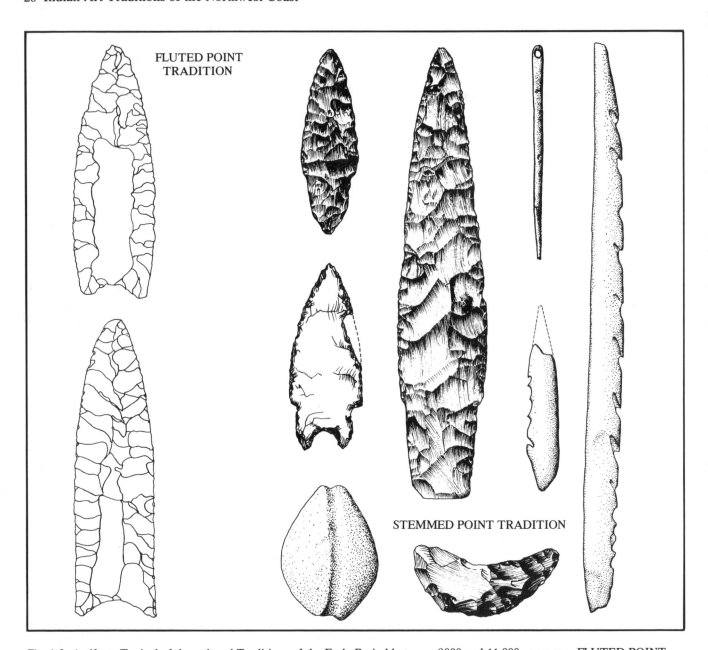

FLUTED POINT TRADITION

STEMMED POINT TRADITION

Fig. 1:3. Artifacts Typical of the cultural Traditions of the Early Period between 9000 and 11,000 years ago. FLUTED POINT TRADITION: Fluted points from the Willamette drainage (upper), and southern Puget Sound (lower). STEMMED POINT TRADITION: Chipped stone points and crescent, grooved bolas or sinker, bone needle and barbed harpoon and point from the Lind Coulee, Marmes, and Wildcat Canyon sites in eastern Washington and Oregon.

sharp cutting edges on this piercing implement, or into a handle to form a knife. In the other cultural traditions bifaces performed much the same function. Microblade technology begins in North China or Siberia about 30,000 years ago and is found in younger sites in the far north. Microblades appear in Alaska by 11,000 years ago, and on the Northwest Coast between 10,000 and 9000 years ago. Early components of this basal culture are present at the Ground Hog Bay Site near Juneau, Alaska (Ackerman *et al* 1979) the Hidden Falls Site in the Alexander Archipelago (Davis 1979), at Kasta and Lawn Point in the Queen Charlotte Islands (Fladmark 1979) and at Namu where there is an interface with the Pebble Tool Tradition. Little else is known about this culture other than what can be gleaned from site geography. Site locations on islands and steep fjords clearly indicate a marine subsistence pattern with watercraft and those tools necessary for survival in coastal waters. Site distribution suggests that this tradition is ancestral to the Tlingit, Haida and Athabascan speaking peoples.

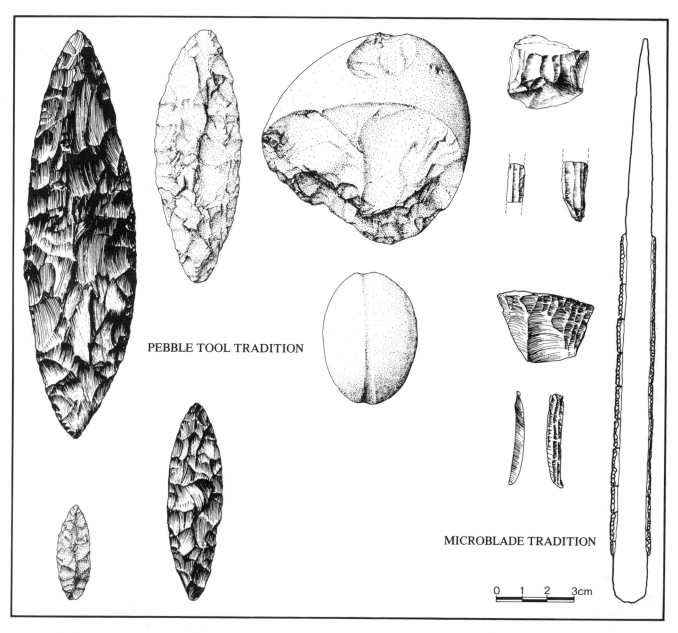

Fig. 1:3. PEBBLE TOOL TRADITION: Bifacial points and knives and pebble chopper from the lower levels of the Milliken and Namu sites, and grooved bolas or sinker from Namu . MICROBLADE TRADITION: Microcores and microblades from Namu (upper) and Lawn Point (lower). The drawing (at right) of the wooden point with blades inset along the edge illustrates one way microblades were probably used, although such points have not yet been found on the Northwest Coast.

The preceding summaries indicate that knowledge of the cultures of the Early Period is rather meagre and almost entirely limited to tool technology and subsistence pursuits. What of the better things in life? There certainly was a belief system, but either we haven't yet found much evidence of it, or it was not yet being expressed in art forms or other tangible objects. Red ochre suggests body painting, and the few animal teeth pendants may well have been charms with associated spirit power. It is not until the Middle Period that more definite expressions of the belief system are found.

By the close of the Early Period about 5500 years ago, the cultures of the peoples of these early traditions were already becoming less distinct, and more and more alike. Part of this phenomenon was the result of post-glacial environmental responses which saw the coastal habitat becoming more similar throughout, part the result of population growth, and part the result of interaction through trade and diffusion of ideas and technologies. The grooved bolas or net sinkers in both early traditions on the Columbia, and a single stemmed point in the early component at Glenrose may be examples of this phenomena, as well as the microblades at Namu. By the Middle Period the early cultural traditions are no longer recognizable on the basis of the same artifactual criteria used to define them originally, and acculturation was clearly one of the mechanisms responsible for this change. Although archaeology cannot prove that acculturation was taking place, it can show that interregional exchange was occuring through the obsidian trade.

Obsidian is a naturally occurring volcanic glass highly valued for its cutting qualities. It only occurs naturally in a limited number of locations in the pacific Northwest. Peoples remote from obsidian sources had to receive it by trade or by trips to the quarries. The widespread distributions of some types indicates trade as the most probable distributive mechanism. There are four main source areas for obsidian in the pacific Northwest, and many more flows within these source areas: Mount Edziza near the Stikine in northwestern British Columbia; the Rainbow and Ilgachuz Mountains including Anahim Peak high in the coast range near the divide between the Fraser and Bella Coola drainages; a source near the northeastern end of Vancouver Island or the adjacent mainland whose exact location is unknown, but may be the Tsable River; and a great many sources in interior Oregon east of the Cascades. Obsidian from each source has a slightly different chemical composition called a "fingerprint". Obsidian artifacts found in archaeological sites can be fingerprinted using a technique called X-ray fluorescence, and the resulting fingerprint matched with with fingerprints of obsidian from the quarries. The map in Figure 1:4 illustrates the widespread trade in obsidian in the period 4000 to 6000 years ago, the time of transition between the Early and Middle Period. Obsidian from eastern Oregon reached not only Puget Sound, the Gulf Islands, and the Fraser delta, but is found as far north as Namu on the central coast of British Columbia. Obsidian from Anahim Peak reached the Fraser to the east, and the coast to the west. Obsidian from Mt. Edziza went as far north as the headwaters of the Yukon, west to Ground Hog Bay in Alaska, and south to Burke channel in British Columbia. If we had more archaeological knowledge of sites of this time period, the obsidian trade would, I am sure, prove to be even more extensive. The available evidence does demonstrate trade over wide areas and with trade undoubtedly went other ideas.

The Early Period is the most important period in Northwest Coast prehistory as it is probably the time when the ancestors of most of the ethnographic Indian populations reached the coastal regions. The natural events of the Early Period were overwhelming in their consequences for human settlement. The whole episode of glacial retreat which opened up new migration routes and new places to live, the shifting land and sea levels, and the changed ecology seem to have stabilized about 5500 years ago. There were also volcanic eruptions of which the most significant was that of Mt. Mazama. About 6700 years ago this volcano in southern Oregon erupted and spewed volcanic ash at least as far north as the Fraser Canyon where it overlies cultural remains of the Early Period. Some sea level changes continued to occur in younger periods also, but their magnitude was considerably less, and the effect on human settlement, greatly reduced. About 5500 years ago there occurred a worldwide change in sea levels. This change affects the archaeological record of coastal areas and roughly coincides with a change in technology of coastal cultures. How much the two are interrelated remains to be determined, but the date does provide a convenient boundary between Early and Middle periods.

Middle Period 5500 to 1500 Years Ago

In the Middle Period evidence for cultures which are more easily recognizable as ancestral to those of the ethnographic period starts to accumulate. Culture patterns based on wealth and craft specialization are evident, and indications of inter-regional exchange of ideas and innovations are clearly there. Changes from the Early Period are probably not the result of the arrival of new peoples on the coast, but instead the product of more extensive collections of materials partly because of better preservation of remains, partly because of great numbers of people who would leave larger quantities of archaeological refuse behind, and partly because of socio-culture factors such as population growth, food surpluses, inter-regional trade and the continued diffusion of ideas and technologies from both Asia and America. Most of our present knowledge comes from the second half of this period (3500-1500 years ago), and the generalizations presented here are best supported by data from that period.

Similarities in wealth, prosperity and luxury goods indicative of a stable food supply, leisure time and a social system involving status and wealth are found throughout the coast, although some regional divergence in types and styles of tools can be recognized. By 2500 years ago knowledge of the normally perishable items of technology which have survived by waterlogging are known: fish nets, plaited and twined baskets, bentwood fish hooks, wooden bowls and wooden splitting wedges. Regional centres of cultural elaboration which shared many of the same characteristics came into being; the best known are the LOWER FRASER and GULF OF GEORGIA, the WEST COAST of Vancouver Island, the PRINCE RUPERT HARBOUR area and the CENTRAL COAST of British Columbia, but there is evidence for habitation and some cultural build-up in all coastal regions. Less is known about Puget Sound, the Pacific coasts of Washington and Oregon and the Alaska Panhandle. Human occupation continued from the Early Period at Five Mile Rapids on the Columbia River near The Dalles, but types and styles of tools suggest greater

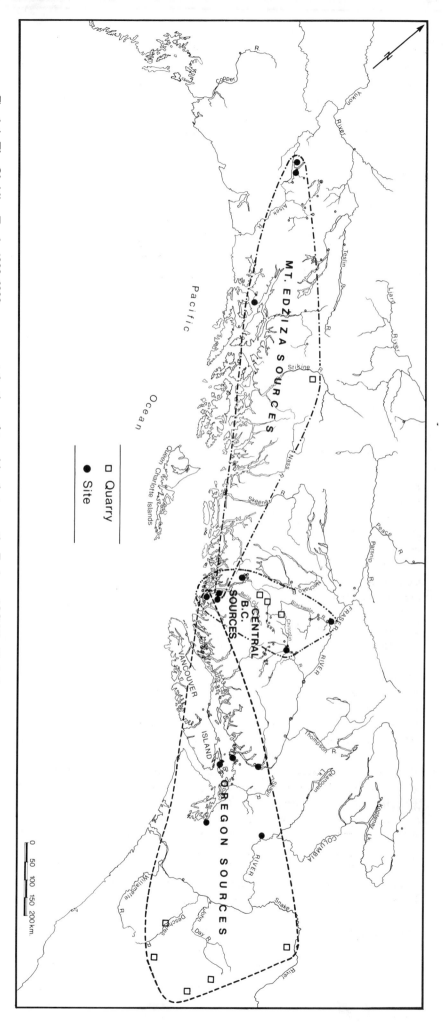

Fig. 1:4. The Obsidian Trade 4000-6000 years ago at the time of transition between the Early and Middle Periods.

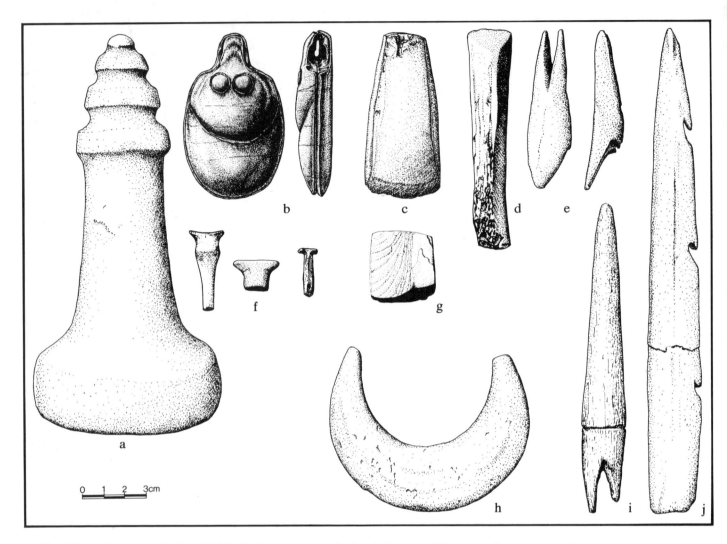

Fig. 1:5. Artifacts typical of the Middle Period, *a* hand maul of pecked stone; *b* lignite pendant; *c* stone adze or chisel blade; *d* bone chisel; *e* one-piece socketed harpoon head; *f* labrets (lip ornaments) of shell and stone; *g* chisel blade of mussel shell; *h* gorget of scallop shell; *i* harpoon fore-shaft; *j* barbed bone points; *k* chipped stone knives; *l* ground slate points; *m* bone point; *o* chipped stone points. For Middle Period harpoon heads, see Figure 1:6.

affinity with interior Plateau cultures at this time. Although the quality of data varies from region to region there is enough evidence to indicate the major culture patterns of the ethnographic period were taking shape in the main centres. These patterns are: emphasis on marine fauna, particularly salmon for subsistence; extensive wood-working for houses, canoes, tools and utensils including bark for clothing; ceremonialism and ceremonial art; and emphasis on status and wealth. The archaeological clues to the major culture patterns of the Middle period consist both of the specific locations of archaeological sites along the extended coastal shoreline and up the rivers, and the particular kinds of artifacts, features and faunal remains recovered through systematic excavation.

Large shell middens are common along the coast and along the banks of the larger rivers, although not all sites contain shellfish remains. Most site locations indicate

skill with watercraft, and a marine or riverine food supply which is probably a carry-over from the Early Period. Fishnets have been found only at Musqueam on the lower Fraser, and bentwood fish hooks only at the Hoko River where there is exceptional preservation of normally perishable material (Croes 1976). Small bone barbs which are also parts of fish hooks are common in the Nootkan and Kwakiutl areas, but seem only weakly represented in the Gulf of Georgia and Lower Fraser where netting may have been the more typical method of obtaining fish. Sea hunting is indicated in most areas by the presence of various types of harpoon heads, and the spear thrower was probably in use throughout the area. Small bone hooks which were part of the spear thrower are known from both the Gulf of Georgia and the Central Coast regions, and one wooden spear thrower from a waterlogged site at the mouth of the Skagit River may belong in this

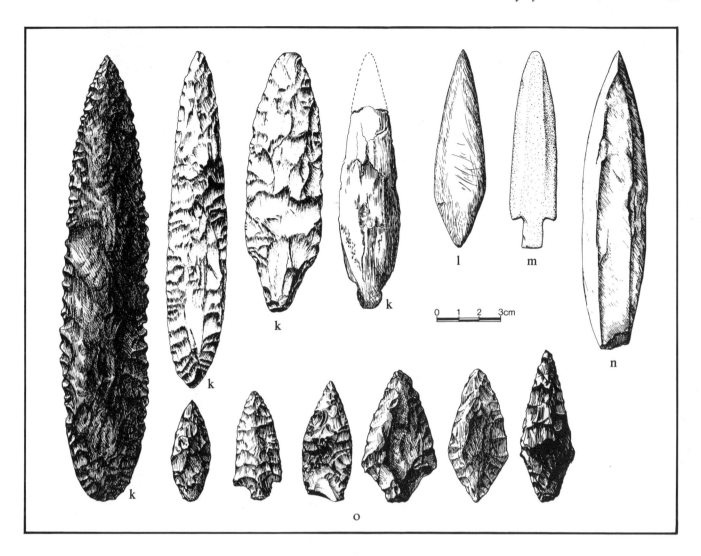

period. The actual remains of fish and sea mammals are plentiful in sites, and there is some evidence suggesting increasing use of fish during the course of the Middle Period. Wooden arrow shafts have been recovered from waterlogged deposits in the Prince Rupert Harbour area and were probably armed with small wedge-based bone points. Chipped stone points of sizes more appropriate for spear than arrows are found in many regions, and are probably indicators of hunting land mammals. The bones of elk, deer, bear and other contemporary land fauna occur in most sites as do bones of many smaller mammals. Land hunting was certainly present in all regions, and important except possibly on the West Coast of Vancouver Island. Specialized tools for transforming wood into houses, dugout canoes, tools and utensils become increasingly common during the course of the Middle Period. The crude pebble tools of the Early Period gradually give way to beautifully made chisel and adze blades beginning about 3500 years ago. The simple hammerstone was supplemented by the pecked and polished hand maul toward the end of the Middle Period. The cedar bark

industry so important to the ethnographic peoples is indicated earliest by a shredder of whalebone at the bottom of Zone II deposits at Yuquot dated about 3000 years ago (Dewhirst 1980:339). Stone bark shredders occur in Middle Period deposits in the Prince Rupert Harbour region (MacDonald 1970). Good examples of houses are still lacking, but large post holes have been found at Marpole on the Fraser Delta, and structural features suggestive of a house are known from the Central Coast during this period. Basketry containers are known from several sites, and a small figurine from Locarno Beach is wearing a conical hat similar in shape to basketry specimens of historic times.

Ceremonialism is indicated by an increasing number of art objects found in Middle Period components. Many of these objects are described in detail in the chapters which follow, and are clues to the belief systems basic to ceremonial phenomena. Several related belief systems were present on the Northwest Coast in ethnographic times; all were based on a belief in spirits. The first salmon ceremony in which the first salmon of the season

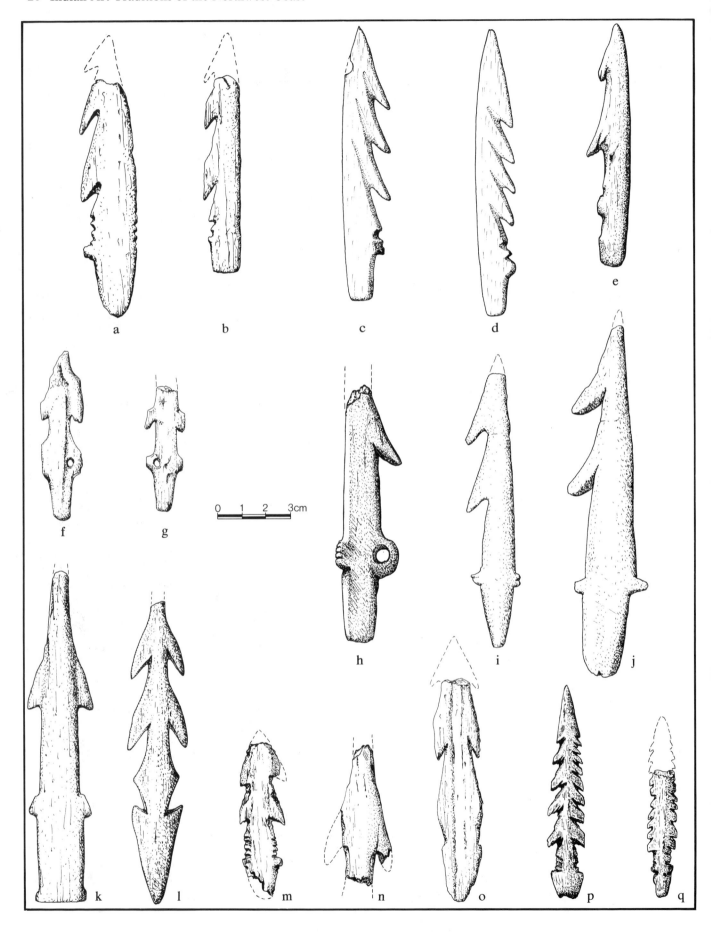

a   b   c   d   e   f   g   h   i   j   k   l   m   n   o   p   q

0 1 2 3cm

is honoured is a widespread and very old practice related to first fruit ceremonies all over the world. Archaeological evidence for this system would be impossible to come by, although it has been suggested that some of the rock art at the mouths of salmon streams is related to this practice. Guardian Spirit power, found principally in the Salish area of the coast, is another belief system. Artifacts ranging from simple tooth pendants to various tools bearing bio-morphic motifs could conceivably represent spirit power of their owners and be related to efficiency in the tasks they were designed to accomplish.

Shamanism is another system related to Guardian Spirits, but differs in that shamanic spirits enabled their possessor to cure the sick, and a shaman usually obtained multiple spirits. Pendants and small incised "worms" found in Middle Period sites may be part of shamanic paraphernalia, as may be tubular pipes for smoking and seated human figurine bowls for grinding tobacco. Some petroglyphs could be the results of shamanic or other spirit quests, but dating them to the Middle Period is not yet possible.

Wealth and status were interrelated aspects of ethnographic Northwest Coast culture. Wealthy men were the leaders and wealth as well as high rank were required to lead. Wealth was ostentatiously displayed as a sign of rank and one of the mechanisms for this display was the potlatch; another was the art system which portrayed hereditary family perogatives and rights to certain crest symbols. This system likely rose in prehistoric times in response to food surpluses and the need to concentrate the surplus in the hands of a leader so that it could be redistributed to a wider population. From there it became extended to incorporeal property, and both concentrating the surplus and giving it away became mutually reinforcing aspects of leadership. No one has ever dug up a prehistoric potlatch, nor is it conceivable that anyone would ever be able to do so, so it is not possible to determine whether the above process took place during the Middle Period. However, there are some evidences for wealth and status differentiation at this time: some burials at Namu, Prince Rupert Harbour and Marpole have different amounts of grave goods which may be

Fig. 1:6. Styles of Middle Period harpoon heads. *a, b, f, g, o,* Prince Rupert harbour sites; *c, d, e, l* Namu site on central B.C. coast; *e, h, i, j, k, m, n, p, q,* sites in the Gulf and San Juan Islands.

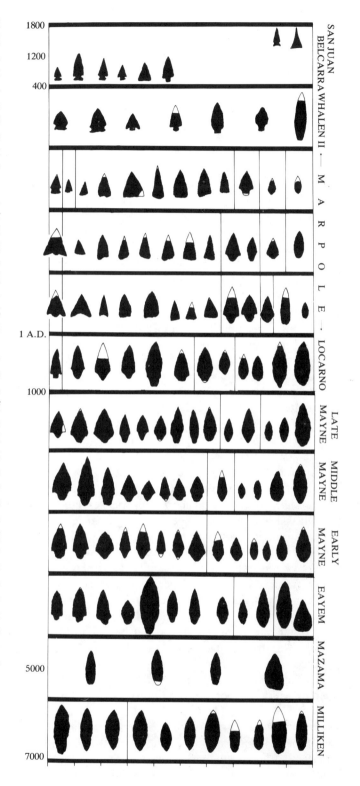

Fig. 1:7. The chipped stone point sequence for the lower Fraser region and Gulf Islands based on data from the following sites: Milliken (Milliken, Mazama, Eayem phases); Helen Point (Mayne, Locarno, and Marpole phases); Whalen (Whalen II phase); Belcarra (Belcarra phase); Cattle Point (San Juan phase). Data from other sites where the Locarno Beach phase is better represented indicate a higher percentage of narrow stemmed points than shown by this sample. Leaf-shaped and single shoulder points (or knives) typify the Early period. Contracting stem points appear at the beginning of the Middle Period (3500 B.C.) and small side-notched points toward the beginning of the Late Period (500 A.D.)

indicative of differences in rank, but in view of the perishable nature of many grave objects this interpretation is far from secure; artificial head flattening appears in Marpole at this time and may be an indicator of high rank; labrets occur throughout the coast in the Middle Period and were probably high status items; wealth in the forms of small disc beads laboriously ground from stone or shell is found in the major centres at this time; beautifully flaked stone knives similar (but not as large) to those displayed as wealth objects by historic California Indians are found; and the presence of a sophisticated art style which in itself suggests full time artisans and commissioned art. Crests are suggested by various animal motifs carved on spoons and bowls of this period. There is no reason to believe that the concentration of wealth extended beyond the familial (lineage or extended family) level, or there would be evidence of the rise of a ruling class of either a religious or secular nature. No palaces and no temples appear in the archaeological record, only the remains of a hunting-fishing-gathering society adapting to a settled existence and abundant food supply. There is some evidence for warfare in the Middle Period. A number of the skeletons from Prince Rupert Harbour show parry fractures of the bones, a type of injury attributed to hand to hand combat. Some evidence of the taking of heads as war trophies as was practised historically has been found in the Middle Period but no fortified sites can be demonstrated to date this early.

Although trade, rather clearly indicated by obsidian distributions and probably also present in other scarce commodities such as eulachon oil, was serving to level cultural differences and keep development apace from region to region, some differences are apparent. Some of these differences are rooted in divergent culture history of the various regions, and others in the variant ecology. The Nootkan region comprising the west coast of Vancouver Island and the mouth of the Strait of Juan de Fuca is distinctive in the absence of chipped stone points and other bifaces in the Middle Period. This situation is in sharp contrast to the Salish Area of the Gulf of Georgia and Lower Fraser where these types of artifacts are very abundant. The Central and Northern Coasts probably belong with the Nootkan area in this respect, as although chipped stone is not absent there, it is certainly rare. Bone points for projectile heads, and small bone barbs for fish hooks are typical of the Central and Northern coasts. Differences in basic technology may be indicated with nets as the common fishing method in the Gulf of Georgia, and hook and line in the other regions to the west and north.

Another indicator of regionalism is the clustering of different styles of harpoon heads in the different regions *(Fig 1:6)*. Male harpoon heads, which fit into a socket in the harpoon foreshaft, are found in all three major regions, but on the Northern Coast they typically have a

hole for line attachment; on both Kwakiutl and Nootkan portions of the Central Coast they typically have a line shoulder; and on the Lower Fraser and Gulf of Georgia the typical harpoon head has line guards. These differences may be purely stylistic, at least there is no evidence that any type is more effective than the others.

Also present in some Middle Period cultural assemblages are artifacts suggesting intra-areal acculturation, and others indicating long range diffusion or other types of contact with distant regions in Asia and America. In the Early Period chipped stone points which were stemmed were typical only of the Lind Coulee Tradition, but in the Middle Period stemmed points are found throughout Puget Sound and the gulf of Georgia and north as far as Namu on the Central Coast. The idea of hafting points by stemming seems to have been spreading northward. Conversely, microblade technology which was typical of northern coastal regions in the Early Period, is commonly found in Middle Period sites in regions to the south. Heavy hexagonal gound slate points, lip plugs and the technique of stone sawing to make adze blades are found earlier in north coastal Asia and Lake Baikal, and in southern Alaska and suggest diffusion from that source. Tobacco pipes for smoking which make their appearance in the late Middle period as far north as the lower Fraser, indicate diffusion from American sources. The division between the Middle and Late Periods is partly arbitrary, and partly based on the time of changes in culture taking place on the lower Fraser and Gulf of Georgia by 500 A.D.

The Late Period 1500 Years Ago to Contact

The ethnographies and histories are by far a better guide to the Indian cultures of the Late Period than is the archaeology, even though much of the ethnographic data concerning aboriginal patterns of culture was not obtained until the end of the 19th and beginning of the 20th century. In both Northern and Central coastal regions, the present information strongly indicates cultural continuity and continued growth of the regional traditions which came into existence earlier in the latter half of the Middle Period. On the Gulf of Georgia and Lower Fraser the situation regarding cultural continuity is not as clearcut. There is a lack of continuity of deposits within sites of the late Middle Period and Late Period which has never been satisfactorily explained. No single site shows the entire sequence and there are changes in the culture content which require explanation.

At the end of the Middle Period there existed on the southern end of Vancouver Island, in the Gulf and San Juan Islands and on the lower Fraser a culture called Marpole which dates between 400 B.C. and 400 A.D. (Burley 1980). Chipped stone tools, particularly triangular unnotched points; woodworking tools including adzes and chisels with blades of nephrite, pecked hand mauls, antler wedges and bone chisels and gouges; elaborate art work in bone and antler and a particular style of unilaterally barbed harpoon head were typical of this culture. At the end of the Late Period there existed within the same region formerly occupied by the Marpole culture, a people collectively known as the Coast Salish. The archaeological expression of their culture is quite different from that of the earlier Marpole culture, and the problem is one of determining what took place during the period separating them. Various ideas have been expressed ranging from replacement of the Marpole population invading Salish speakers, to changes in the way of life which led to the development of the one from the other. Most data favour the latter explanation.

Coast Salish culture can be traced back archaeologically to at least A.D. 1200. Two known winter village sites have been sampled, Old Man House at Squamish in Puget Sound (Snyder 1956), and Stselax on the Fraser Delta (Borden 1970). A number of other sites more likely represent seasonal fishing stations. Throughout all sites the emphasis (with the exception of antler for wedges) is on *bone* for the manufacture of artifacts: unilaterally barbed points for arrows and duck spears; small pointed bone barbs for use on composite fish hooks; awls of various sorts; blanket pins; and bird bone tubes. Small, composite socketed, harpoon heads for salmon and larger ones for sea mammals are common as well. Flanged spool-shaped hand mauls, small triangular slate points, thin ground slate knives, and sawn and polished nephrite adze blades are the typical stone artifacts of the period *(Fig 1:8)*. Gone are the heavy ground slate points and numerous chipped stone tools of earlier periods. Gone also are the labrets and the well made stone vessels. Chipped stone became very rare, and when found it is mostly in the form of small, side-notched arrow points, a trait typical of Plateau cultures in the east. These points seem to be most common in sites along Puget Sound and the southern end of the Strait of Georgia between 400 and 1200 A.D., and possibly later.

On both sides of the mouth of the Strait of Juan de Fuca, and along most of the west coast of Vancouver Island are the Nootkan speaking peoples. Their late prehistory is known from excavations at three localities, Ozette on the Washington coast, Yuquot at Friendly Cove and Hesquiat midway up the west coast of Vancouver Island. The Yuquot site (Dewhirst 1980) exhibits a continuity of culture throughout the Late Period and for several thousand years back into the Middle Period. The emphasis throughout is on bone tools associated with fishing and sea mammal hunting. Whaling is added to the cultural inventory in the Late Period as is the small, socketed composite harpoon head for the salmon harpoons. Ozette material described in a later chapter indicates the complex art and ceremonialism of the late prehistoric period. Ozette was an entire village covered by a mud slide shortly before European contact. There are both the usual kinds of archaeological deposits at Ozette where only stone and bone tools are found, and entire houses in which complete wood and fibre artifacts have been preserved by the all encompassing mud. McKenzie's (1974) analysis of the artifacts from the non-waterlogged deposits indicates their close comparability to assemblages from other Late Period sites on both the Southern and Central coastal regions: hundreds of small bone points of many sizes and types which served as barbs for salmon, cod and halibut hooks, and as arming tips for composite harpoon heads.

Further south, on the Oregon Coast (Newman 1959) plank houses with inventories of small bone points, antler wedges, bone chisels, small composite socketed harpoon heads and small triangular chipped stone points indicate a culture much like that on the coast of Washington and British Columbia. At the very southern end of the Northwest Coast at Trinidad Bay (Heizer and Mills 1952) artifact inventories merge with those of California; this region retained some types which went out of use in the Middle Period of the Gulf of Georgia—large elk antler harpoon heads, and large chipped stone ceremonial blades.

The Central Coast of British Columbia provided abundant evidence of Late Period occupation. At Port Hardy Chapman (1982) has unearthed a component typified by the complex of small bone points similar to those of the southern coast. Small composite socketed harpoon heads, and triangular ground slate points are also indicative of the Late Period. Mitchell (1981) has investigated Southern Kwakiutl prehistory and the results of his work indicate a picture very much like that at Port Hardy: artifacts of bone associated with fishing and woodworking, but little in the way of ceremonial or non-utilitarian objects. Farther north on the Central Coast, excavations yielding Late Period components have been undertaken at a considerable number of sites. Sites at Kwatna and Namu (Carlson 1972; 1979; Hester and Nelson 1978; Hobler 1982) have yielded the greatest amount of information. There is abundant evidence for plank houses, ceremonial art, beaters for preparing cedar bark for weaving, spinning with spindle and whorl and a variety of pecked and ground stone implements in addition to the complement of bone fishing equipment parts also found in the Late Period elsewhere on the coast *(Fig. 1:8)*. At Kwatna, evidence of a large rectangular house with a central depression and sub-floor cache pit dates to A.D. 1280.

At Axeti at Kwatna an inter-tidal site produced wooden and basketry artifacts: twined basketry hats, twilled and plaited cedar bark baskets and mats, rope and twine, U-shaped bentwood fish hooks, wooden spoons, composite fish hooks with wooden shanks and bone barbs and bentwood box fragments. These items date toward the end of the prehistoric period, but there is every reason to believe that the technological traditions of which they

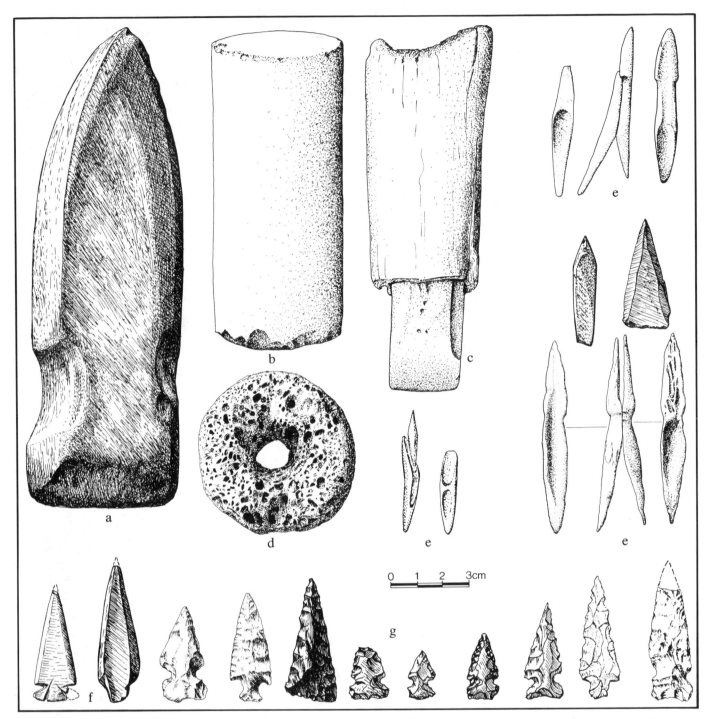

Fig. 1:8. Artifacts typical of the Late Period. *a* grooved splitting adze; *b* cylindrical hand maul; *c* antler socket with nephrite adze blade; *d* perforated stone; *e* various types of bone or antler composite, socketed, harpoon heads; *f* small ground slate points; *g* small side-notched or corner-notched chipped stone points; *h* bone spindle whorl; *i* ring and pin game; *j* bone arrow and leister points; *k* bone harpoon heads; *l* small bone fish hook barbs and points; *m* bone beater for cedar bark.

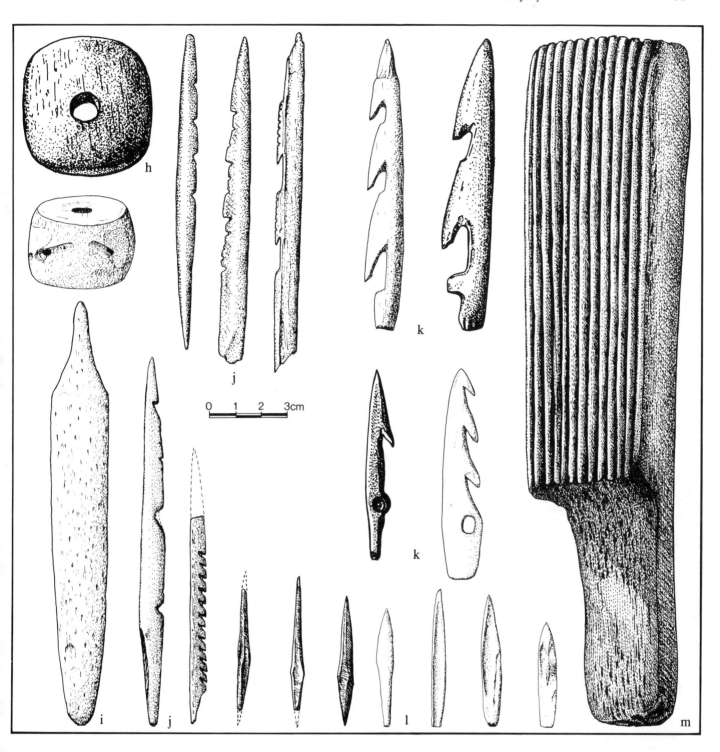

0 1 2 3cm

h
j
k
k
i
j
l
m

are a part go far back in time. Wood working is not only attested to by the actual wooden objects, but hundreds of chisel and adze blades and fragments.

Abundant evidence for fishing occurs in all habitation sites of the Late Period. Numerous stone-walled fish traps found throughout the Bella Bella region likely date to the present period of sea level covering the last 3000 years (Pomeroy 1976).

There is some archaeological information for the Northern Coastal regions of the Tsimshian, Haida and Tlingit in the Late Period. MacDonald (1968) in discussing Prince Rupert notes "There are almost 50 sizeable shell middens in the harbour that show continuous occupation for more than 4,000 years. . . . about half of these are large winter villages." In Alaska at Ground Hog Bay Ackerman (1968) describes an artifact assemblage from a plank house village dating in part to 345 years ago: blades for splitting and planing adzes, harpoon heads with a hole for line attachment, beads of jet and amber, socketed toggle harpoon heads, bear tooth pendants, carved stone bowls and lamps and bone points. Fredericka de Laguna's (1960) work in late Tlingit sites shows much of the same artifact inventory, as does Fladmark's and Severs' work in the Queen Charlottes. The entire complex of heavy pecked stone tools: blades for splitting and planing adzes, stirrup mauls and maul heads grooved for hafting are highly distinctive of the Late Period of the Northern Coast, as are harpoon heads with line holes. The heavy pecked stone tool complex has similarities with Asiatic forms (LeRoi-Gourhan 1946). The North Coast can be characterized as a region of continued cultural growth and elaboration during the Late Period. Archaeological work has not yet proceeded to the point where cultures of the Tlingit, Haida and Tsimshian can be differentiated from each other. Shared technological and social traditions seem to have extended throughout the region.

There were at least two natural events which took place during the Late Period and affected human occupation on the North Coast. Tlingit traditions (Swanton 1909:337) describe the destruction of a village by an advancing glacier; de Laguna (1958:2) gives further evidence of late glaciation. On the Nass an eruption of lava which must have taken place in very late prehistory is still vividly described in oral tradition. Nishga informants have told me of the burning of the villages, and the search for the river forced from its channel by the flowing lava. Such events caused some population displacement during the Late Period, but did not significantly alter the way of life over large regions. The most significant event of the Late Period was the arrival of Europeans: the Russians in 1741, the Spaniards in 1774 and the English in 1778. With these intrusions the prehistoric era ended and history began.

The first major effect of European contact was increased cultural elaboration through the fur trade as the Indian peoples became enmeshed into an expanding world economy, and luxury goods grew in abundance. The long term effects were, however, of social disorganization and cultural decline as disease wiped out some entire peoples, and greatly reduced others in numbers, as missionization worked at destroying the belief systems which fostered art and ceremony, and colonization resulted in loss of control over natural resources. It is only recently that the descendants of those peoples who survived this period are increasing in number.

The culture of the Northwest Coast retained up into the period of European contact the subsistence base and associated classes of implements which are known earliest in the late Paleolithic and Mesolithic cultures of the old World. Fishing, supplemented by shellfish gathering and by sea and land mammal hunting, became the subsistence pattern which persisted long after food production through plant and animal domestication had overtaken major parts of both the Old and New World. The harpoon and the bow and arrow were widely used, and among the northern Tlingit even the spear thrower survived into the historic period. Containers of wood, basketry and bark remained the norm as in most other cultures of the northern boreal forests.

The Late Period merges almost imperceptibly with the ethnohistoric cultures. Small notched projectile points usually identified with the introduction of the bow and arrow reached southern and central coastal regions, diffusing from the interior to the east. Cultural continuity throughout the Late Period is indicated for the Central and Northern Coasts, and probably for the Salish region.

The art examined in the following chapters should be looked at in the context of the prehistory outlined in this chapter. The emphasis has been on technology and subsistence as items relevant to these cultural sub-systems constitute the overwhelming mass of discernable archaeological data. The art described in the following chapters, though limited in quantity, provides more insights into belief systems and other aspects of culture available from no other body of data. These chapters begin not with the earliest art found, but with the ethnographic art, where context and meaning are known, which can then be used to help understand the prehistoric art of the later chapters.

CHAPTER 2

Form in Northwest Coast Art

BILL HOLM

My subject is form in Northwest Coast Indian art, and of course it is much too big a subject to deal with at all adequately in one paper. Without form there is no Northwest Coast Indian art. Its form, the two and three dimensional shapes and their characteristics, their relationship to one another, their relationship to the whole composition, and the final composition itself, enable us to recognize Northwest Coast art as an entity. The Northwest Coast is a long coast with many sub-styles, and the art extends over a long time period; there are many variations and it is difficult to discuss them all at one time. Some of these statements I shall make are not fully thought out. I know I don't have all the answers yet.

The Northwest Coast is an area known for its three dimensional, sculptural art, and yet the conceptions of form which underlie the Northwest Coast art tradition and link the sub-styles together are basically two dimensional. From what I have seen up until now, the concept of dividing flat space with incised lines or shapes seems common to all the early styles. The resulting compositions may be geometric, straight line designs, or curvilinear; they may be representational, or not. Somewhere along the line of development the incised lines and spaces came to be seen, or perceived, as a negative part of the relationship.

What I mean by the positive-negative relationship is that the recessed areas in these essentially two dimensional works can be seen as background, and the intervening, by contrast raised areas, as positive forms. If the incisions are deep and/or wide, and especially if the design is applied to a curved surface, the result then becomes effectively sculptural. In the end, I think, all the truly

sculptural styles of the Northwest Coast can be seen to be at least partially derived from a two dimensional space division through a continual process of refining positive-negative form. Early silhouette figures with incised features and detail are perhaps the immediate forerunners of fully sculptural work on the Northwest Coast. At the same time that the two dimensional art tradition was developing, I propose that it diverged into a number of different styles, each retaining some of the basic conceptual features, such as the raised positive-recessed negative concept, and some formal features such as crescent and T-shaped reliefs (or cuneiform reliefs as Suttles prefers to call them), the so-called Northwest Coast eye of varying forms, and skeletal representations, especially ribs and joint marks. None of these features is altogether unique to the Northwest Coast. You will find examples of each one of them in many parts of the world, but, refined and in combination, they make up the elements of a pan-coastal art tradition.

The transformation of such a straightforward two dimensional style into the sophisticated northern form-line system must have required the catalyst of painting. I see the techniques and versatility of a painting style, perhaps initially derived from the incised negative-raised positive concept, in its own turn refining relief carving as it began to conform to the painting formline. Figure 2:1 illustrates a bone comb from Prince Rupert harbour on the northern coast. It must have been from that period of refinement. It can almost be analyzed in terms of early nineteenth century massive formline design. At the same time, it shares features with the historic Halkomelem style of the southern British Columbia coast. The positive-negative relationships we see here are the basics of the

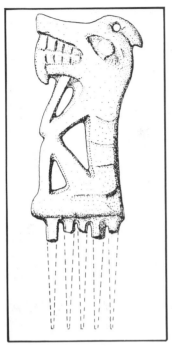

Fig. 2:1. Bone comb with wolf image from the Garden Island site in Prince Rupert harbour dating to ca. 800-900 A.D.

Fig. 2:2. Beaver bowl with continuous, massive formline design.

formline system. I like to refer to this relationship as the "donut theory." Maybe I should recite the poem from which the theory got its name:

As you travel on through life, friend
No matter what your goal
Keep your eye upon the donut
And not upon the hole

If you remember that, you have a key to Northwest Coast Indian art. It's very important! The comb is an amazing piece, to take us back that far with the concepts that were later involved in the development of the formline system.

The importance of the donut theory, or any more scholarly term that one can give it, wasn't always recognized by students of Northwest Coast Indian art. There is a classic example of the failure of a person who really did understand a great deal of it and gave us the basis for our later understanding—the failure to recognize the primacy of the formline in a typical northern design—Franz Boas' description of this nineteenth century bent-corner bowl *(Fig. 2:2)* in *Primitive Art* is that "it represents a beaver, the face indicated by disconnected eyes, mouth and ears." The primary formline here which really delineates those parts is however absolutely continuous in the traditional way. There is not a disconnected eye, mouth and ear.

Another good example of the native artist's conception of the figure—ground relationship is in this appliqued shirt *(Fig. 2:3)* in the Burke Museum. It was collected in the

1890's from the Haidas. The dark patterns on the red figure of an eagle could be and often have been mistaken for positive decorative elements, artfully but somewhat arbitrarily spread over the design. However, if we look at the detail *(Fig. 2:4)*, we can see what the artist's real intent was, in these pencil lines still remaining, outlining the primary formline of the body and tail. The body and tail were then partially defined by cutting away the negative (tertiary and ground) areas. So the primacy of the formline in this northern art is really universal there.

I'd like now to look at some objects from the different parts of the coast, starting at the Columbia River and moving northward, to see how the artist handled this form that I've been describing.

These carved bone or antler fragments *(Fig. 2:5)* are from the Dalles region on the Columbia and they're perhaps as much Plateau as Coast. But the design concepts involved are closely related to those of the lower Columbia and the Washington coast. There's a strong geometric tradition here, just how old I don't know. These pieces may be as much as 500 years old. They're good examples of the incising technique I mentioned and illustrate the idea of developing a positive linear design by cutting out grooves and triangles. In these small fragments the resulting positive, zig-zag, forms can be easily seen. But in this bowl *(Fig. 2:6)* of mountain sheep horn, also from the Columbia River, it would be possible to read the incised triangles as the positive elements. I believe, however, that they should be perceived as negative, and

Fig. 2:3. Appliqued shirt, Haida, ca. 1890.

Fig. 2:4. Detail of Figure 2:3.

Fig. 2:5. Bone or antler carvings from Columbia River near the Dalles, Oregon.

Fig. 2:6. Mountain sheep horn bowl from the lower Columbia River region.

the pierced triangles at the top reinforce that idea. The bowl bears a typical lower Columbia rendition of a human figure: symmetrical, frontal, very geometric, carved on the bottom and flanked by the usual rows of zig-zags. This piece is typical Columbia River style, with the round head, elliptical eyes, three-step facial structure and small mouth. But how really different is he from some simple, flat, bone figure or even some petroglyph from far up the

Fig. 2:7. Antler figure from the Columbia River.

Fig. 2:8. Horn spoon from the lower Columbia River region.

coast? He has the large head, static frontal pose, crescent ribs and some of the other features that we see in other places. Now if you cut away the surrounding material, as in this antler figure *(Fig. 2:7)*, then you're a long way toward sculpture. The basic organization of the figure is just as in the flat design on the bowl. There's more modeling in the limbs and in the kilt, but basically the figure, although carved in the round, is a deeply carved flat design. Stone was handled in pretty much the same way in the lower Columbia area, that is, by recessing the spaces and lines around the features, allowing them to stand out, in accordance with the donut theory.

Utilitarian objects can be sculptural even if they're not decorated. This one *(Fig. 2:8)* is decorated, but a plain spoon can be a sculptural form, and such forms relate to the rest of the system. This elegant spoon of sheep horn is sculpture, and it has the usual rows of zig-zags and a wonderful little animal on the handle in full three dimensional carving. The structure of this face on a straight-adze handle of elk antler *(Fig. 2:9)*, flat with the forehead plane separated from the plane of the cheek and eyes by a sharply cut underbrow, with the nose coming down narrow from the plane of the forehead, and the small flat mouth on the chin plane, is typical for the whole southern coast. It is such a natural way to represent a face in its simplest terms, that the fact that it was so universal isn't surprising at all. The face is really fine, along with the elegance of the horns with their wonderful repeated curves, which are echoed in the circles; recessed, raised and bordered. It's really a fantastic piece, one of the finest, from the lower Columbia River region.

Moving up to Salish Puget Sound, we see another variation on the flat, ovoid face with the long nose extending down from the sharply cut brow. The modeling on the face of this spirit canoe figure *(Fig. 2:10)* is almost entirely negative. In fact, the simple line outline of the brow and nose is just a step away from this kind of modeling, where the space around the groove is cut away to leave the raised nose and the projecting brow. It's very close to the simple outline form. The entire figure is three dimensional, deep and rounded, but the emphasis of the design is frontal and flat.

This comb *(Fig. 2:11)* from the Halkomelem area is an excellent example of the British Columbia Coast Salish elaboration of the two dimensional design system which also gave rise to the northern formline system. Even more surely than in the case of the Columbia River lines and triangles, here the incised crescents, the triangles, the T or cunieform shapes and ovoids, must be seen as ground. There's no way that these Salish pieces can be watered down northern designs. The concept of the placement of these reliefs is too sure and too knowledgeable, too perfect. In fact, the most certain point of breakdown in copying northern formline designs without understanding is in the improper use of these reliefs. So this is not a watered down or backwater copy of the northern formline.

This adze *(Fig. 2:12)* is a small puzzle without any documentation, but it has to come from the general Georgia Strait—Juan de Fuca Strait area. It's a beautiful piece with its flaring handle, fine sculptured face, narrow nose, eyes on the cheek plane, flat small mouth. These are attributes of Salish style. Those great, bold, T-shaped

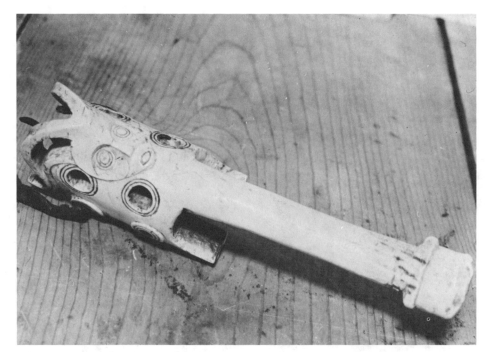

Fig. 2:9. Antler adze handle from the lower Columbia River region.

Fig. 2:10. Head of spirit canoe figure, Puget Sound Salish.

reliefs have to be thought of in terms of their relationship to the projecting, positive forms. Their very sensitive placement was certainly designed to define positive shapes. Those shapes which they define are, of course, real "Northwest Coast" forms.

One could continue by illustrating some further Salish pieces which are really sculptural with full rounded forms and yet with the basic structure of the face, the handling of the detail, in that frontal Salish style. Then to confuse the picture, there are the prehistoric seated human bowl figures, which in the structure of the body and handling of the details fit right into this old Salish system. But the faces of many of them, with their deeply rounded sculptural form, heavy, arched eyebrows over eyes on a full orb, distinct eyelid lines, flaring nostrils, modeled cheek structure and projecting mouth with full lips, are unlike other Salish carved objects. I don't know just where they fit in.

The handle on a bone club *(Fig. 2:13)* is very Nootkan, yet one can see its close relationship to the Salish system of incised areas, defining the raised positive areas. The face is a good example of how a slight bit of modeling can change this really lineal style into a sculptural form. Now it is interesting to see the similarity of this late nineteenth century Nootkan, humanoid mask *(Fig. 2:14)* to the bone carving on the club. The general feeling is almost exactly alike, and structurally they are alike. Here is a truly three dimensional carving but it retains the features of an essentially flat object. In fact the two sides of this mask are basically flat with only slight modeling on the cheek and nostrils and a long, sloping underbrow

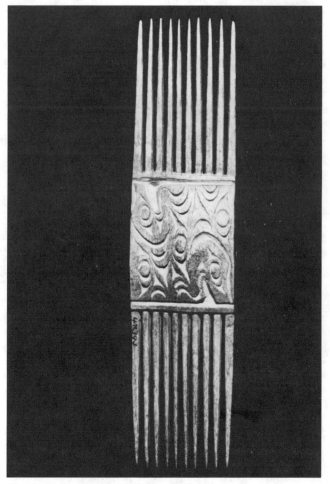

Fig. 2:11. Comb, Strait of Georgia Salish.

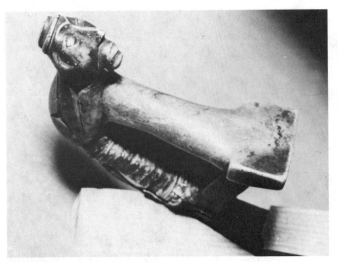

Fig. 2:12. Adze, Georgia Strait-Juan de Fuca Strait region.

Fig. 2:14. Nootka humanoid mask.

Fig. 2:13. Handle of Nootka bone club.

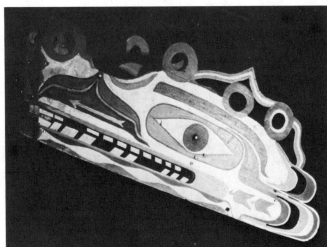

Fig. 2:15. Nootka Winter Dance headdress.

plane over the large eyes on the cheek plane. The latter is a Nootkan sculptural characteristic, somewhat different from the usual way of handling it in the Salish area. Many similar examples could be illustrated.

Even more striking in its resemblance to flat art is this constructed headdress *(Fig. 2:15)*, a typical Winter Dance headdress from the Nootka, with its completely flat surface and painted design. The formline painting on the surface may have been influenced by the Northern system, but conceptually it is also related to the old Nootkan design principles.

One of the most impressive figures in Kwakiutl mythology is the Tsonoqua and this mask *(Fig. 2:16)* is among the most impressive representations of the Tsonoqua. Here is a creature with its own special characteristics so that the tribal characteristics of form are submerged. Its bony face with bulging forehead, hollowed cheeks, deep set eyes, strong arched nose and lips pushed out, all

Fig. 2:16. Tsonoqua mask, Kwakiutl.

Fig. 2:17. Kwakiutl humanoid mask.

Fig. 2:18. Bella Coola humanoid mask.

characterize this creature, as do the black graphite surface, shaggy hair, beard and eyebrows. This one might be the epitome of Kwakiutl dramatic sculpture.

Not fearsome here, but plenty dramatic, is this Kwakiutl humanoid mask *(Fig. 2:17)*, and in it we see the most typical characteristics of Kwakiutl sculpture: bold carving, based on a deep half cyclinder. The planes of the face are deeply modelled and defined, with the eye on a bold orb set in a deep socket. The forecheek plane is sharply cut back allowing a strong mouth projection with broad modelled lips. The nose is prominent with rounded, flaring nostrils. Kwakiutl sculpture is often painted as boldly as it is carved, with contrasting details of black, red and green, often on a white ground. It's easy to talk about Kwakiutl carving as being bold and dramatic, but it really can be specifically described in terms of form. However it would take more space than we have here.

Probably the most easily identified tribal style is that of the Bella Coola *(Fig. 2:18)*, yet it shares some basic formal concepts with Kwakiutl work. It is bold and direct; typically there is a relatively small, sharply defined, truncated cone for the orb of the eye. The underbrow plane and the upper cheek plane come together, with the side of the nose forming a sharp angle with the orb. There is a convex swelling of the cheek at the outer

Fig. 2:19. Bella Coola sun mask.

Fig. 2:20. Mask owned by George Catlin.

Fig. 2:21. Bella Bella humanoid mask.

corner of the eye socket which is typical almost to the point of being a primary recognition feature: I call it the Bella Coola bulge. It is a very typical feature, although sometimes absent. Unlike on a typical Kwakiutl mask, the eyelid line often is not carved at all, and eyebrows are heavy, often bent sharply over the temple. The lips on Bella Coola humanoid masks are unique and distinctive. They are more naturalistic than those of any other style as a type. In fact, with all of its boldness and fantastic elaboration, Bella Coola humanoid sculpture is based clearly on human anatomy.

The Bella Coola sun mask *(Fig. 2:19)* exhibits typical blue, vermillion and black painting on a natural wood ground. The painted areas on Bella Coola masks generally take the form of broad "U"-like figures separated by reliefs of either natural wood or vermilion, which must be seen and read as the negative spaces we find in positive form just as in the Halkomelem flat art and the Northern formline system. The complex Bella Coola pantheon no less than the imaginative use of sculptural form gives the Bella Coola artist tremendous variety of possibilities.

The mask in Figure 2:20 was once owned by George Catlin, the early nineteenth century American painter. It is an early piece. It may have come from the Bella Bella country, an area that is particularly hard to pin down

stylistically because the region of the Northern Kwakiutl speaking peoples is bounded by the strong stylistic areas of the Haida, Tsimshian and Bella Coola, and there is considerable merging of the art traditions. Styles seem to take two major directions, one represented by this mask *(Fig. 2:21)* in which the sculptural planes are bold and distinct, and suggest a northern influenced Bella Coola—Kwakiutl approach, and the other a more naturalistic style very different to distinguish from Haida or Tsimshian work. One of the problems is that we try to lump too much of an area under one name, Bella Bella. There seem to be features of Bella Bella sculpture which are distinctive enough to be isolated but they are not as strongly recognizable as the others. A flattened orb with a narrow and sometimes sharply cut rim in the eye socket is distinctive, for example.

This beautiful settee *(Fig. 2:22)* in the Berlin Museum is a very important link in the attribution chain. Adrian Jacobsen had it made for him by the best carver in the village of Bella Bella in the early 1880's. Although the name of the maker was not given in Jacobsen's published account I still have hopes that he may have recorded it somewhere. In any case we do know its date and its provenience, and it is also important because of the combination of very distinctive flat and sculptural work.

Fig. 2:22. Bella Bella settee.

The carved thunderbird face is in a recognizable Bella Bella style and the formline detail matches exactly with that on a large group of boxes and chests which we believe originated in Bella Bella, although many of them were collected on other parts of the coast. I believe that there was a native box "factory" at Bella Bella in the nineteenth century.

This northern mask *(Fig. 2:23)*, which is catalogued as Bella Bella, was described in Swanton's *Contributions to the Ethnology of the Haida.* It could be seen as either Bella Bella or Haida. An interesting sidelight on the painting is in Swanton's comment that it is "another representation of cumulous clouds, the clouds being indicated by the white, triangular marks." Anyone who is familiar with the donut theory will recognize the mistake of this interpretation.

Wingert expressed the character of Tsimshian mask sculpture very well when he wrote, "There is also a strong expression of fleshy forms and tightly drawn surface skin over these bony structures." The effect of the large orb pressing against the eyelid is really beautifully expressed here in this frontlet from the Skeena River *(Fig. 2:24)*. Some of the specific formal details characteristic of Tsimshian sculpture are the pyramidal cheeks, the wide, rounded orb and the eyelids without defining painted or carved rim.

Fig. 2:23. Bella Bella humanoid mask.

Fig. 2:24. Tsimshian frontlet.

Fig. 2:25. Tsimshian humanoid mask.

A profile of a typical Tsimshian mask *(Fig. 2:25)* shows the aquiline nose, smoothly rounded forehead and foreward thrust of the chin, which is relatively short vertically. The three cheek planes converging on a common point are also characteristically Tsimshian. This feature is very pronounced here, in fact this mask could be used as a type illustration.

Totem pole sculpture of the Tsimshian follows the same principles, modified by the monumental scale and the restrictions imposed by the log. Tsimshian poles tend to retain the cylindrical form of the original material. The aquiline profile, short chin and smoothly stretched orb and cheek resemble those same features of masks, but the nostrils are widened and the lips drawn back around the pole cylinder. These features are shown in their most exaggerated form here *(Fig. 2:26)*. The orbs are turned downward which is a northern characteristic also. The deeply cut socket below and the shallowly cut socket above is a northern concept which contrasts with the southern custom of depicting the eye on a more or less flat cheek plane with an outward slanting or sharply cut underbrow plane very much unlike this. The surmised two-dimensional ancestry of Tsimshian carving shows best in totem pole figures where the relatively cylindrical surface is relieved with modeling around the eyes, nose and mouth.

Many Haida masks are very naturalistic, portrait-like.

Fig. 2:26. Tsimshian totem pole.

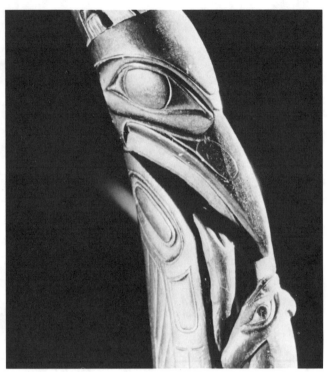

Fig. 2:27. Haida horn spoon.

The more realistic representation a piece of sculpture is, the more difficult it is to see tribal stylistic characteristics. But another aspect of Haida sculpture is much more easily recognized by the custom of placing clearly two dimensional figures on cylindrical or other broadly curving surfaces. Spoon handles are good examples of this aspect of Haida work, and this tiny raven *(Fig. 2:27)* on an elegant mountain goat horn spoon handle is really two dimensional; it is almost pure formline in all its details, and yet the result is totally sculptural. In reference to such objects as spoon handles, totem poles, etc., I would propose a development along the following lines: that a direct, representational, two dimensional, incised ancestor led, on the one hand, through the influence of painting to the sophisticated formline system, and on the other hand to a simple naturalistic sculpture, and finally to convergence of the two lines with formlines overlaying and modifying the sculptural forms. Another way of seeing it would be the two lines, sculptural and flat, developing together rather than coming together at a later time. It could work either way, but I think they did both develop from the flat system.

Another Haida piece is this fine grease dish *(Fig. 2:28)*, combining a conventional bowl shape with head, wings and tail developed in formline detail. This is another beautiful example of the figure-ground relationship (the donut again) in northern formline art. You can never see the design by looking at the holes; you must see the positive, continuous formlines around those holes. We

see here one of the most intellectualized, logical design systems in the history of art.

Single artists stamp the system with their own individuality and artists of a village or an area influence one another in the development of village or area styles. For example, nineteenth century poles at the southern Queen Charlotte village on Anthony Island are recognizably different from the less two dimensionally organized, interlocked and elaborated poles of Skidegate, in the central part of the Queen Charlottes, and they in turn can be differentiated from the northern Queen Charlotte poles of Masset with their rounded contours, separately defined figures and somewhat more dynamic arrangement of limbs and supplemental figures. Other formal differences of detail can be seen and isolated.

The bear's head on a Tlingit grease dish *(Fig. 2:29)* illustrates the tribal sculptural characteristics. The lips in a continuous flat band are typical. Although the piece was collected in the nineteenth century, it may well have been a century old at that time.

This crest mask *(Fig. 2:30)* from the northern Tlingit area probably goes back to the early nineteenth century if not before. It is one of the most perfect examples of the style of sculpture which utilizes rounded contours, with hard edged details derived from formline conventions. The subtleties of the form in the carving cannot be appreciated from the photograph, and need some careful contemplation to be fully appreciated even with the mask in hand. It is a real Tlingit masterpiece. The ears are

Fig. 2:28. Haida grease dish.

Fig. 2:29. Tlingit grease dish.

Fig. 2:30. Tlingit bear mask.

almost identical to those of the famous Tlingit twin stone masks.

The preceding paragraphs are really only an introduction to form in Northwest Coast Indian art. The following are the main points raised: The "donut theory" of positive-negative relationships, the influence of painting on the development of the sculptural system, the tendency to submerge tribal stylistic characteristics whenever specific beings are represented, the primacy of incising in the progression to both the painted formline system and to sculpture with subsequent formal interaction between the two, and the descriptions of some of the regional stylistic characteristics.

CHAPTER 3

The World is as Sharp as a Knife: Meaning in Northern Northwest Coast Art

WILSON DUFF

The understanding of the iconographic meaning of northern Northwest Coast art has lagged far behind the descriptive analysis of its form. I suggest that we are still very far indeed from a full understanding of its deeper levels of meaning. "Meaning" may be defined simply as the answers to two questions: "what things is it about?" and "what is it saying about them?" In other words, what are the subjects and what are the predicates? As for the "deeper" meanings, the question is: "what else, by analogy, is it also about?" What other topics and relationships does it also symbolize? Meaning is not just interpretation of the subject, identification of the creature that is "represented." We are frequently able to take that first step. However, in Panofsky's (1939) terms, to do only that is to fail to penetrate beyond the pre-iconographic to the iconographic and iconological levels of meaning. It also fails to perceive the latent structural symbolism. "What does it mean?" is a much broader question than "what does it represent?" Existing studies of the art contribute to the understanding of other aspects of its significance. A knowledge of its cultural context is necessary to understand the process of its production and its significance in action (Gunther 1966). Analyses of its form (Haeberlin 1918, Wingert 1951, Holm and Reid 1975) contribute immeasurably to its aesthetic appreciation. Holm's (1965) descriptive analysis of the elements and rules of composition of the two dimensional art has been a giant step toward the understanding of its deeper meanings, but to describe its form is not yet fully to explain its meaning.

Existing interpretations of the meanings of the iconography provide partial answers. The first of the usual explanations is that the images represent totemic crests, which metaphorically differentiate social groups. A second explanation is that they represent spirit creatures or characters and episodes from the mythology. Art, that is to say, is a servant of the social and religious systems, and has its existence in order to make these tangible and visible. A third explanation, that art may be pure decoration or formal design for its own sake, speaks more in the language of form than of meaning. It is not my claim that any of these explanations are wrong. I only want to show that they fail to provide complete answers to questions of meaning raised by the art itself.

Examples will be shown of images whose meanings are not sufficiently explained by the currently available interpretations. I want to suggest an additional way of looking at this art. It is my hypothesis that further agendas were also at work in it, such that it was coming to express more powerful symbols and therefore deeper and more general meanings. In addition, it was becoming an autonomous, non-verbal medium for thinking in images. Without relinquishing its other functions it was also invoking deeper symbols, and was becoming a primary language of thought in the medium of images. It was a system of imaging in which the deeper meanings were coming to receive as much conscious attention as the shallower ones.

Images. A number of concepts will be introduced. "Image" is the term I use for the principal segment of iconography. An image is typically a more complex unit than a single-figure depiction, showing an act or relationship as well as a subject. Having both a subject and a predicate it is a system which has structure. It is therefore a statement of meaning. Images have two aspects: content and structure. The iconographic content consists of "symbols." The inner structures may be called "armatures." Images are therefore structures consisting of symbols set upon armatures. Each image is unique, but regular rules presumably exist in the use of symbols and the kinds of armatures.

Symbols. Symbols in art are those pictorial figures which reveal what it is about, identify its subject. The subjects may be things or acts. They may be depicted literally or metaphorically. In this art, they may literally depict the crests and mythic creatures of the social and religious systems. But also, or instead, they may metaphorically have reference to more general and abstract powers, or to that primary source of deep symbolism, the human body-self. For the art is also about being human; ultimately, about those aspects of being human which are most sacred and therefore most repressed and tabooed. Sexual parts and sexual acts are almost never depicted literally, but frequently receive metaphorical representation. Human faces, eyes and whole figures are not subject to visual taboos, and may be used to express figuratively the tabooed parts and acts. "Beaks" and "mouths" carry great symbolic weight in this art.

Armatures. Armatures are the structural relationships between symbols. They are the ways of making visual equations. They are the predicates of statements in which symbols are the subjects. They are the inner structure of images. Examples will be shown of armatures which use bilateral symmetry, reciprocal or part-whole relationships, a trinity arrangement, a facial beak-mouth relationship.

Paradigms. Paradigms are the forms in which specific problems get worked out in the art. Each paradigm is related to an artifact type (e.g., spoon paradigms, house-post paradigms) and its meaning has a relationship to a meaning of the artifact. The image, that is to say, is "about" the artifact. Paradigms are repeated solutions to the same problems. The problems are hidden agendas, known to the artists and having to do with the deeper meanings of the art.

Boas (1955:12) once said that it is esential to bear in mind the two-fold source of artistic effect, the one based on form alone, and the other on ideas associated with form otherwise the theory of art will be one-sided. I think that what Boas meant by "idea associated with form" is what I mean by "meaning." Today thanks to Holm we are in a position where we can describe with great detail and great sensitivity the form of Northwest Coast art. We can describe the ovoids, and the primary, secondary and tertiary formline structure in a vocabulary he designed for us. However to describe the form is not to explain the meaning. It seems to me that the description of Northwest Coast art has suffered from the dangers Boas forecasted and has become a little bit one-sided, because we can say a lot about form but not very much about meaning. The explanation of the meaning of the art has lagged very much behind the description of

Fig. 3:1. Tsimshian crest carving representing a frog.

Fig. 3:2. Horn spoon showing sexual symbolism. At one end is a phallus, and at the other a large-mouthed creature, possibly a seal.

where we seem to have three episodes from the raven mythology of the northern coast, probably the Haida. The figure in the centre, for example, seems to be Raven who has become voraciously hungry, and wanting to eat the bait off the halibut fisherman's hook turns himself into a halibut, gets himself caught, and then when he is cooked he comes out of the halibut again. So some of the images of Northwest Coast art plainly depict episodes from myths, and also some of the images of Northwest Coast art depict spirit figures. They show us what the spirits look like (otherwise how would we know?), and these are all correct interpretations as far as I am concerned; the trouble is that they don't seem to be sufficient for my purposes.

Now they are not sufficient for two reasons. One is that they don't seem to allow us to tie this great art style in with any of the general theories of art in the world. There is no tie, for example, with the theories of George Devereau, or with the theories of Panofsky on meaning in art. The direction along the road that we have taken doesn't seem to get us that far. Furthermore the explanations that we currently have don't seem to do justice to what we feel are the masterpieces of Northwest Coast art.

Now in Figure 3:3 is another crest helmet, which I take to be Tsimshian, and we can say that the animal figure is a bear. But what are those hands doing there? This figure is a bear with five human hands and the hands are very prominent; they are not explained in a story, as far as we know, or on the crest. I have to tell you one thing about the hands; the one at the back has no thumb. That hat has five hands, one of which has no thumb. It seems to me there is an additional agenda going on there which we don't understand, and it seems to me that when we are describing the ethnological masterpieces of Northwest Coast art the things we know intuitively are very important. We have great difficulty in talking about their meaning, and I always refer back to the kind of spectacle which has to do with the Chilkat blanket *(Fig. 3:4)*. Under each illustration of a Chilkat blanket design in Emmons' (1907) monograph there is an interpretation by Emmons which says that it depicts a particular thing, perhaps a whale diving. Then there is another interpretation by Boas who steps in as editor and says "No, it represents a bear sitting up on his haunches." Sometimes there is even a third interpretation by Swanton, giving a third thing that it might depict. Now it doesn't seem to have occurred to anybody at that time that there may have been different agendas at work, that maybe these designs were dancing to a different tune as well as just trying to represent creatures.

This box illustrated in Figure 3:5 is the "final exam" on northern Northwest Coast art. This is a very famous box, and when we get to the point of being able to say, "What is going on in that design," we will really understand the

the form. Now since I really don't know what meaning is, I think I will let you figure it out from my paper as we go along. I'll leave it with Boas' "idea associated with form."

We do have existing interpretations of meaning of Northwest Coast art, and these take us a long way along the road to understanding it. For example, the Tsimshian crest in Figure 3:1, we can all, having studied Boas, recognize the figure as a frog. This frog figure is a crest referring to a particular social group, and really all that needs to be said about it is that this image of Northwest Coast art represents a crest. In addition quite frequently the images of Northwest Coast art plainly represent episodes from myths as on this spoon (not illustrated)

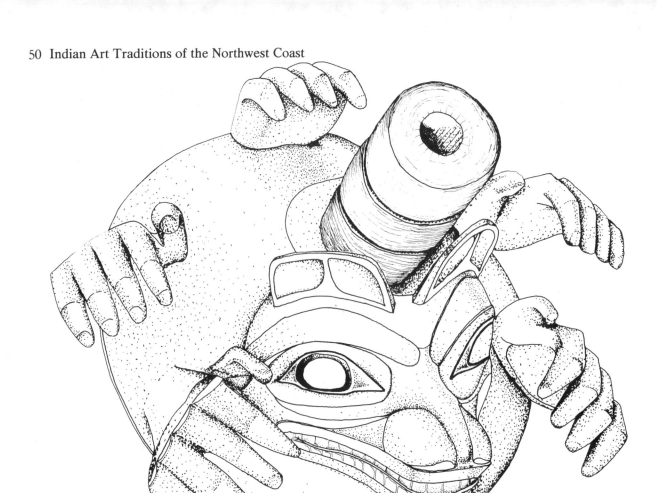

Fig. 3:3. Tsimshian crest helmet with bear face and five hands. Why does the hand at the back have no thumb?

Fig. 3:4. Chilkat blanket. Different authors give different interpretations of these designs. How many agendas were at work?

Fig. 3:5. The "final exam" on northern Northwest Coast art. Design from a wooden box identified by Charlie Edenshaw as four episodes of Raven, the culture hero. We do not understand this design.

meaning in Northwest Coast art. The box is in the American Museum of Natural History, and was collected by Emmons way back in the early 80's at Chilkat. Boas studied it, and actually brought pictures of it to show to Charlie Edenshaw, who said it represents four episodes of raven, the culture hero. Boas didn't believe him and didn't report it for thirty years afterwards. We have all been intrigued with this box; it's a favorite of Bill Reid, who has copied it in many forms, but we don't know what to say about the design. It doesn't seem to represent a crest, it doesn't seem to represent a myth, and it doesn't seem to represent a spirit. We bring ourselves to believe that it is just empty design, whatever that might be. Some other agenda is at work which we don't yet understand. One of the things we don't fully understand yet, either, in terms of meaning is the raven rattle.

The raven rattle *(Fig. 3:6)* is one of the most important single bundles of iconography on the northern Northwest Coast. I know that we have all been intrigued with it for a very long time. Three, four or five years ago I had one of my students, Jennifer Gould, do an M.A. thesis on the raven rattle, trying to get at its meaning. She brought to bear Panofsky's concepts of iconographic and icono-logical interpretation with some success. I think Bill Holm has had a student do an M.A. thesis which would presum-ably be on the raven rattle form. But the raven rattle is also one of the "final exams" of northern Northwest Coast art. When we get to understand it fully, we will understand meaning in Northwest Coast art.

Now, that is the problem, it seems that the greater the masterpiece in Northwest Coast art the less we can say about its meaning. What I hope to do is kind of jolt you or pique you a little bit with some new ideas (I think they are new), about ways in which we can look at this art, and suggest other agendas that may be going on in it.

Specifically what I plan to do is to try to show that there is a level of symbolism at work deeper than just crest spirit, and also to try to begin to develop a terminology that can get to the sculptural analysis of the images of the art. This is something we are just starting on.

The first thing I want to do (I have to introduce some new terms, and I am not happy with the terms; afterwards I would be happy if you people would come up with better terms) is define the essential iconographic unit. It isn't a single figure depiction. This tobacco mortar *(Fig. 3:7)*, probably Haida, is one of my examples of the unit which I am going to call the image. The image is a more complex unit than just a single figure depiction. This image depicts a beaver; it's a beaver face; it does have beaver teeth, although they are not visible in this shot; it has a beaver tail, and it has beaver hind legs. But it also has hands, and they are human hands, and the hands are on backwards, so to speak. It is a complex image which has symbolic content and the content is arranged in a set of relationships which can be called a structure. An image is a system with content and structure which is presumably subject to a structural analysis.

Here is another image *(Fig. 3:8)* on the base of a horn spoon. I don't know what it represents, but it seems to be a large bird-like creature associated with a human face; it has four-fingered hands, which are rather strange and up at the top what may be wings. I don't know what it is saying. I am calling this type of unit an image and saying that it has content, it has arrangement, it has structure and should therefore be subject to a structural analysis. I think it is probably a statement which has a subject and a predicate.

Now the second thing that I want to do is to try to get at a deeper level of symbolism which is operating in the art. It isn't a case where only one thing is going on at one

Fig. 3:6. A raven rattle: another "final exam" in northern Northwest Coast art whose meaning we do not fully comprehend.

Fig. 3:7. Tobacco mortar, probably Haida, with a beaver face and backward human hands.

time. It is operating at different levels at the same time, and one of the deeper levels that I want to get at is the sexual symbolism at work. Now the image in *Figure 3:9* is one of the very important ones in my argument; it is the Sechelt image which was one of the key images in *Images Stone B.C.* (Duff 1975). It is quite large, about twenty inches high or so, and is not from the northern Northwest Coast. It is from the southern Northwest Coast from Sechelt, north of Vancouver. One of my assumptions is that some of the roots of Northwest Coast art are in the south. I find intriguing hints in Bill Holm's presentation of this too. This image has been interpreted as a blatantly sexual symbolism at work. Now the image in Figure 3:9 is powerful male figure with, in the front, a huge phallus. It is a phallic male, but in addition it has a vulva form place down here which is a female symbol. Now I have given a great deal of thought to this punning, to this double meaning that is going on and I am convinced, although not everybody else is, that it is two things at once. It is male, phallic, and it is also a female, mother and child. It is both. Now one of the reasons I want it to be that, is that it solves one of the fundamental problems of sculpture around the world, and that is to depict the human indivi-

Fig. 3:8. Base of a spoon of mountain goat horn. Note the four fingers. What does it mean?

Fig. 3:9. The Sechelt image. This figure is male, phallic, and also female, mother and child.

duum, not the individual, but the individuum, the eternal human. The forms in which we have it in our background are usually mother and child, between mother and male child but there is some attempt to depict sculpturally either a pair or a triplet which would be, in effect, mother and father and child in the same figure and this is the solution to the problem of the individuum. It is male, mother and child at the same time. Now we don't find this in later Northwest Coast art, and one of the assumptions that I am making is that sexual symbolism was shown more literally in earlier days than it was in recent North-

west Coast art. In fact, in recent Northwest Coast art is so conspicuous by its absence that we should be suspicious. Sexual characteristics are practically absent completely from recent northern Northwest Coast art.

In Figure 3:10 a human figure on the base of a totem pole at Hazelton. It is generic human, it isn't a portrait of any kind and it has conspicuous absence of any sexual characteristics. Now I think that this generic human in northern Northwest Coast art is another solution to the problem of the individual where instead of having a figure that has sexual characteristics of all, it has sexual charac-

Fig. 3:10. Figure at base of totem pole at Hazelton. Note the conspicuous absence of sexual characteristics.

teristics of none. It is not a portrait, but it is a generic figure; it is in effect half male, half female, half child, half adult. You can see it in many forms on totem poles, and on frontlets, where it is a perfect blend, part male, part female, part child, part adult. The human individuum in the recent northern Northwest Coast solution to that problem begs the question of sex, and leaves it out completely. Now sexual symbolism is so important in the arts of the world and elsewhere that I feel that its virtual absence on the surface of Northwest Coast art permits us to suspect that we might find it in metaphorical forms below the surface.

We can go back to an earlier stratum. Fortunately, there are a few examples of things that are fifteen or twenty centuries old from the northern Northwest Coast, and I refer specifically to the stone clubs from the Hagwilget cache found up the Skeena River near Hazelton in 1898. This is one of the most remarkable archaeological finds in North America; a group of thirty-five stone batons or clubs were found cached together, and many of them are sculptured. We brought together several of them for the *Images Stone B.C.* show. On a lot of these clubs there are explicit sexual characteristics. Figure 3:11, for example, is pretty phallic on the handle end. The most remarkable of these clubs in this way is this absolutely amazing piece of stone sculpture shown in Figure 3:12. It is about fifteen inches long and is one of the so-called clubs. I don't know what else to call them, although they were obviously not functional clubs as war clubs. The power was more in the symbol or the image than in the actual utility.

The club in Figure 3:13 is a very remarkable piece of

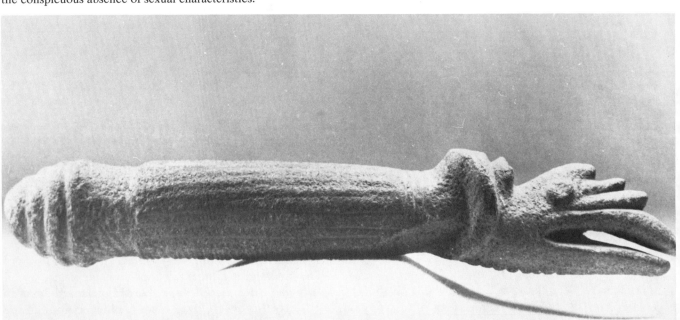

Fig. 3:11. Phallic club from the Hagwilget cache.

sculpture and still has paint on it. If the handle end is not phallic then my whole argument fails. I read one end as phallic, but now I want to hark back to the idea of the image which is a system. In a sense it is an equation and the other end of the same club is not phallic, but I take it to be the opposite. Now, I invite you when you have time, to contemplate the problem of an artist in depicting the opposite of phallic symbolism. I think it is a problem that could be said to have something to do with the donut and the hole, but I'm not quite sure. However, with the vulvic symbolism it seems it is often more necessary to resort to metaphor, and I take the opposite end of Figure 3:13 to be a mouth which doesn't have to be the mouth of any particular thing; it is just a mouth; it is a toothed mouth; it is a very elaborately toothed mouth. I take it to be a vulvic symbol. So I take this club to be a kind of an equation, an image, a very carefully worked out image, a very powerful image, which is phallic on the one end and vulvic on the other, a phallic-vulvic image. Some of the terminology is really me.

I am going to take you on a bit of an adventure here. Take this phallic-vulvic image with the phallic end up and subject it to a metaphorical transformation keeping the same underlying image, changing the scale and changing the metaphor, and you get something like this. The frontal pole, in Figure 3:14 is one of the largest on the Northwest Coast, and was in front of Chief Wheya's house at Masset. It's an image, the whole thing, and on the top is a big expandable hat which is another metaphorical way of saying it, I guess, and on the bottom is a huge mouthed creature, and basically the underlying image I take to be a phallic-vulvic woman. Now we have

Fig. 3:12. Phallic end of fifteen inch long stone club from the Hagwilget cache.

Fig. 3:13. Stone club from Hagwilget cache showing equation of phallic and vulvic ends.

Fig. 3:14. Frontal pole from house at Masset exemplifying phallic-vulvic symbolism.

Fig. 3:15. Small seal figure bowl exhibiting vulvic symbolism. Found near Yale, B.C.

Fig. 3:16. Seated human figure bowl found near Lillooet, B.C.

always suspected that there might have been something phallic in totem pole imagery. A little bit of confirmation in the idea of the phallic-vulvic image in these older Haida totem poles which have an oval door opening at the base, is given by Jimmy Deans, a Scotsman who got to the Queen Charlotte Islands before the missionaries and wasn't as inhibited as they. He did record that the oval entrance at the base of the totem pole was considered to be the female generative organ, so it is a vulvic image. I invite you to look at the bear, just above it, with the upside down human figure. We are going to come back to that.

Now, if there is phallic symbolism and images based on it, it would be male chauvinism to suggest that there isn't the opposite. Looking for vulvic symbolism, I take as my type specimen, this little ancient, archaic stone vessel *(Fig. 3:15)* from the Fraser Canyon near Yale. This is another case where the more explicit imagery is older and southern. This is a little seal figure and the vessel has that distinctive, what I call vulvic form. If this isn't a vulvic image, then my argument about vulvic imagery fails. Now, seal and vulva as a metaphor persists on the Northwest Coast, farther north, in the seal grease dishes. Many of them have as their vessel that vulvic form shape. It is another case of the persistence of an image in a different medium.

The seated human figure bowl in Figure 3:16 comes from the Fraser River near Lillooet. We don't really know its age, possibly something like fifth century. I was very interested to note Bill Holm's comment on the similarities between the style of such bowls and northern Northwest Coast style, because I see that too. I see these as North-

Fig. 3:17. Seated human figure bowl from near Lytton, B.C.

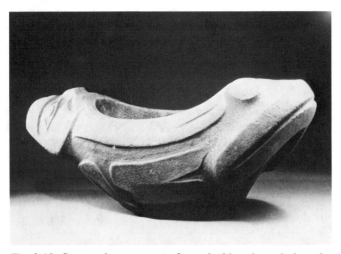

Fig. 3:18. Stone tobacco mortar from the historic period on the northern Queen Charlotte Islands.

west Coast sculpture despite the fact that they are inland and quite far south. Now how to interpret this, what do they mean? It is a human figure, and humans can be either male or female; there is nothing at all on these to suggest that they are male. They have a vessel in the belly or in the lap or between the legs or however you want to put it, and they seem to have been used for female puberty rituals. So one could suggest that it is a female figure that is represented, and that the vessel is the female vessel, and that the vessel and the figure are of the same size. In other words the part is the same size as the whole, I am going to be saying a few enigmatic things like that, and doing it purposely, because I think the language of imagery of the Northwest Coast does use some of the figures of speech of that kind, the part and the whole being the same thing. This is a rhetorical figure called synecdoche where the part represents the whole. The part and the whole are the same female figure with sexual meanings, perhaps.

Now I want to show you an example of what might be the persistence of an image through time and in a different medium. Figure 3:17 is one of the seated human figure bowls from Lytton. This bowl has a very Northwest Coast face, and down on the front of the vessel here with the head down is a creature that might be called a frog or a toad. It is a human figure bowl with a frog on the front of the vessel. Now some 1500 years later in time and 500 miles farther north in space we find Figure 3:18 on the northern Queen Charlotte Islands, which I call the Edenshaw tobacco mortar. It too is essentially, when you look at it this way, a seated human figure bowl with a creature on the front which might be considered to be the frog. This is a human; it has arms; put it down on its face, and it has a backbone and legs here, and these can be read as its arms. It is in fact a seated human figure bowl with a frog on the front. I think it is even more complex than that. I think it is a seated human figure bowl, a seal dish and a bowl with a frog on the front all at the same time.

Now what about the logic? The frog or whatever that creature is on the front has become much larger; the part has become greater than the whole. That frog or whatever that mouth creature is, is larger enough so that its mouth could swallow the entire mortar of which it is a part; the part *has* become greater than the whole.

Now in Figure 3:19 is a little wooden dish, which turns out to be a seated human figure bowl as well with a human figure with arms and hands around the rim of the vessel, a backbone and legs. It has a seated human figure bowl with the vessel as the bowl but the vessel is bigger than the whole now, and the part is greater than the whole. That progression up the coast seems to hold, and here an equation is made so that the seated human figure bowl is also a raven, so that the female part of it is in the back of the raven. The raven symbol, I read as being phallic on the front with the beak, and vulvic in the back.

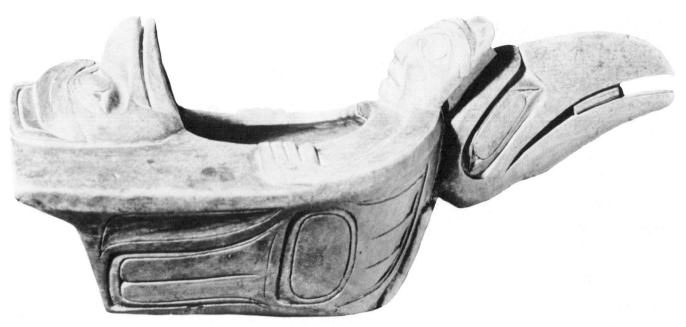

Fig. 3:19. Wooden bowl from the northern Northwest Coast showing similarities with the raven rattle.

Putting a couple of these together you can see the close similarities between that kind of bowl and the raven rattle. It seems that when you are working on the northern Northwest Coast, all roads lead to the raven rattle. The seated human figure bowl type here punned as a raven is so similar to the raven rattle that they could almost be from the hands of the same artist. If there is an equation of imagery being made here, it means that this vessel, being a vulvic symbol, is somehow related to this thing on the back of the raven rattle and I will come back to that a little bit later.

So much for phallic and vulvic symbolism. What about the symbolism of the sexual act itself? Unlike the arts of other parts of the world, the act of sexual intercourse is never depicted on the Northwest Coast, and here again is what I think the archaeologists would call a significant absence. When you never see it, it is probably evidence that it is tabooed and repressed, but we might still look for it in disguise or in metaphorical forms. The only place where sexual activity occurs explicitly in Northwest Coast art, is on Haida argillite panels showing the bear mother myth and the sexual activity that takes place between the bear husband and his *human* wife. Marius Barbeau discovered this sexual activity on the bear mother panels and described it with some surprise (Barbeau 1957). Haida myths define a great variety of sexual activity, but Barbeau characteristically finds that this sort of thing couldn't have been at home on the Northwest Coast, and he would bring it from the Orient or across the Pacific. It is another one of Barbeau's importations. There is sexual activity on these panels between the bear husband and the *human* wife, that seemed to interest the carver of these panels. The carver of many of them may

have been Charlie Edenshaw. He wanted to depict that particular episode of the myth. The one illustrated shows the interacting metaphorically as bears or as a bear and a human, and on the left side there is an interaction between the bear and the human which has a detail which is of interest to me, and that is the joining of tongues of the human creature and the bear *(Fig. 3:20)*. In the 1830's or so the Haida panel pipes developed one form where there is a great deal of activity with tongues and joining of tongues. We don't know what to say about the meaning of the panel pipes either, but here, as of the 1830's a great deal of play was joined tongues, maybe metaphoric or something. On some of the panel pipes of this kind, some of the activities (if you look at them with the eye of a dirty old man), can be seen as pretty sexual. If you will just contemplate the poses of this group of three in Figure 3:21, and forget that they are metaphorical beasties in term with the humans, you've got something that is pretty explicitly sexual going on, or at least that is the way I see it. There is sexual fun going on with the joined tongues on these 1830 panel pipes. Now where does it come from? It does hark back, I think, to an earlier source, and I think it is this source: the joined tongues that form such an important feature of the thing on the back of the raven rattle.

Now, this human reclining figure on the back of the raven rattle *(Fig. 3:6)* is one of the most daring pieces of Northwest Coast art. There is only one purpose, I think, for which a human being will assume that particular posture. Here we have a situation where a human being (sometimes this is called a man, but that is male chauvinism; it could just as well be called a woman) is in that particular posture, which is a sexual posture, but the thing

Fig. 3:20. Detail from an argillite pipe panel relating to episodes in the bear mother myth.

Fig. 3:21. Detail from Haida argillite pipe showing explicit sexual activity.

that is going on is not literal but metaphoric. This it seems to me is an act of sex which is shown half literally and half metaphorically, and in the crazy logic of Northwest Coast imagery, that fits perfectly. This, I think, is raven's original act of self-incest by which he created himself, and a very daring piece of sexual imagery. Sometimes we find it in a variant form with the frog. The joined tongue coming from the mouth of the frog, and in some ways frog's tongue and frog himself or herself or themselves seem to be associated with sex.

The roads lead to the raven rattle and some of the roads had to do with metaphorical sexual activity. I think the idea of a baton with raven beak may be a phallic male, and the thing that happens on the back of the raven rattle is perhaps vulvic female, and there is a sexual activity going on. There is I think this deeper level of sexual symbolism. Now I don't think I should have to say this, but I am going to say it, I don't think it is sex, pornographic sex or anything like that. This is cosmic sex, this is sex because this art is also dealing with the much deeper human concerns of life and death and creation.

I've talked a little bit about the problem of structural analysis of images. We have all heard of bilateral symmetry on the Northwest Coast, but this is ridiculous. An image is something that has content, but it also has

Fig. 3:22. Double images on a bilateral armature.

Fig. 3:24. Haida chest showing a double image on a bilateral armature.

Fig. 3:23. Condensed double image on a bilateral armature.

Fig. 3:25. Soul catcher, probably Tsimshian, showing the bilateral armature.

structure. I have been trying to get at ways you can get at the inner structure of images because I think that half of the meaning is in the content and half of the meaning is in the structure. That is why the subtitle of my paper is "The World is as Sharp as a Knife." This is a Haida proverb in which half the meaning is in what it says and half of the meaning is in what it is. It is an aphorism which seems to contradict itself. It is the exact counterpart of a Haida image, I think, in art.

Now, the term I have borrowed to describe the inner structure of images is armature and armature is a term that Lévi Strauss (1969:199) has used for the inner structure of myths and so I have borrowed it for the inner structure of art, and I think I can see several different kinds of armatures in Northwest Coast images. One of the most common of course, on the Northwest Coast, is the bilateral armature. The two big bicycles in Figure 3:22 are described as double images on a bilateral armature. There is something that happens to images that you have to mention right away, and that is that they become condensed; they become refined down to a more tightly compact form. The bicycle in Figure 3:23 is condensed double image on a bilateral armature. So much for that armature. There are several places to find it in Northwest Coast art. One of the places I think it is most important is on these Haida chests *Fig. 3:24)* where that big creature

with the four eyes is in effect a double face. I think what we have is a double image on a bilateral armature and that, that is part of the meaning. Obviously I don't know all of the meaning but I think that is part of it. Now, bilateral armature occurs in all sorts of things. This beautiful little charm *(Fig. 3:25)* is probably Tsimshian, and is almost nothing else than a bilateral armature. It is bilaterally symmetrical, as we would say, and each end is a mouthed creature, a generic mouthed creature. The iconographic content isn't very much at all but it is expressing that relationship of bilateral symmetry. That is part of the meaning.

Now those of you who are archaeologists will perhaps understand now my excitement at discovering this little "whatzit" in Figure 3:26. This is a little stone piece, less than two inches long, from an archaeological site on the southern coast in the Gulf Islands. We don't know what to call it, so we call it a "whatzit." It is the most marvelous little piece of abstract stone sculpture that one could want to see; it also feels very nice; it's smooth; it would be a touching stone but iconographically what it is, is a pure armature. It has no iconographic content at all. It is a pure expression of relationships, a piece of sculpture reduced down to pure and simple; it is a marvelous little thing.

Now here is another thing *(Fig. 3:27)* which seems to

Fig. 3:26. Minature stone "whatzit" from the Gulf Islands which is a pure expression or relationships with no iconographic content.

Fig. 3:27. Soul catcher, probably Tsimshian, showing the Triadic armature.

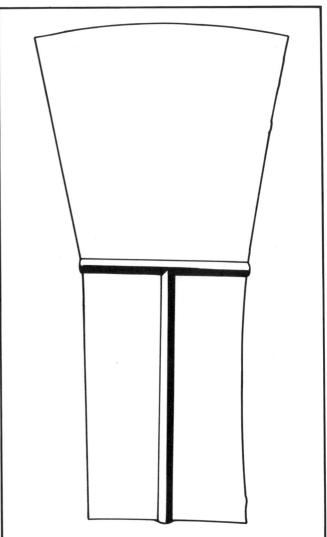

Fig. 3:28. The copper wealth object is basically an expression of relationships without iconographic content.

be on a bilateral armature, but actually it is on a slightly different armature which I call the triadic armature. This northern soul catcher is a thing which has two symmetrical mouths, one at either end. You don't really have to say what those mouths are. I don't think that in this classic form they are meant to be a bear or this or that or anything. It is just a big toothed mouth, perhaps conceptually the biggest toothed mouth you can think of. But there is a third element in the middle, a human element, and it illustrates the relationship of a triad. A triad is a pair of opposite things with a third thing which mediates them. It is one of the forms of human contemplation that is basic, and I think what the soul catcher is, is a triadic armature with very little iconographic content on it. Now a triadic armature pure and simple is the copper, which has two opposite things with a third thing that mediates them *(Fig. 3:28)*. The two bilaterally symmetrical opposite bottom pieces with the third upper thing has the same except its opposite relationship to both of them. It doesn't have, usually, or I think ideally any iconographic content at all. I think a copper should be plain, although it is also taken as a torso and a face is put on the top. I think a copper should be plain, but I think by approaching the copper from this direction we are getting at its essential meaning. It is essentially an expression of relationships.

Now there is another kind of armature which I find quite difficult to illustrate, but a drawing of hands *(Fig. 3:29)* gets at it. It is what I call a reciprocal armature. One way of putting what is going on here is that a hand is a hand's way of creating another hand. I would sooner

have had something like a chicken is an egg's way of creating another egg, where the two parts are different and have the relationship part and whole.

On the base of this Haida horn spoon *(Fig. 3:30)* is this image often called a bear eating man. This face is read as a bear and the little upside down human figure is called a man. Turn it on its side so that you can see the bear and the human figure more closely. Ignore the wings, there is something else going on there, and ignore the joined tongues, there is probably something else going on there, and see that the human figure and the bear are each other. They are parts of each other, and they are coterminus with each other, and this relationship I call the double twist. It is a part/whole relationship where the part is greater than the whole. The part is the bear and it is metaphoric, the whole is the human and it is literal, and that combination of literal/metaphoric, part/whole with the part being greater than the whole is a type of

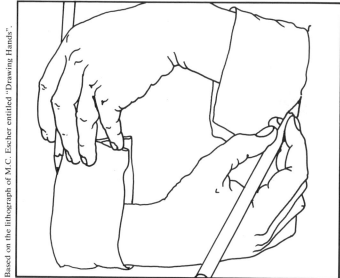

Fig. 3:29. Illustration of a reciprocal armature.

Fig. 3:30. Detail from a Haida horn spoon showing the double twist relationship.

Fig. 3:31. House post showing the bear eating man which can be interpreted as a vulvic symbol.

Fig. 3:32. Haida mortuary pole.

image you find on the Northwest Coast as that bear eating man.

On this house post *(Fig. 3:31)* we again see the bear at the base of the pole metaphorically restating the meaning of this oval entry and the little upside down human figure, a literal human figure with a metaphoric part which thereby becomes the vulvic symbol. So in addition to being a crest, if that is what the bear is, I read this bear eating man figure as a vulvic symbol on the base of the pole. You find it not only on poles, but on things like this mortuary *(Fig. 3:32)*, a Haida mortuary with the little human part almost invisible, but the whole is smaller than the part; the whole is literal; the part is metaphoric and the whole thing is a vulvic symbol. Here we have this bear vulvic symbol as a tomb, and if you think that the clang relationship in our own language between womb and tomb is accidental I think you are wrong. This is a womb/tomb in the Haida, and has a much deeper meaning than just a symbol.

Now in concluding I would like to mention just a little bit about how these things get worked out in the art. Each image is the solution of a problem; there are a series of problems and these have to do with different artifact types. Now the word we have chosen for these series of problems solved is the word paradigm. What I have here is a hammer paradigm. We talk these days about house post paradigms, mask paradigms, panel pipe paradigms and so on. I want to give you an idea by tracing the outline of the hammer or hand maul because it is really a hammer pestle, Northwest Coast paradigm, which I worked out in more detail in *Images Stone, B.C.* The basic type is this beautifully sculptured and beautifully efficient implement *(Fig. 3:33)*. There is nothing wrong with these things as tools even though they are also sculptural forms, and it seems to be many, many centuries old along the Northwest Coast. I see it as the basis of a conceptual evolution or paradigm of hammer types which proceeded from it.

Something went on with the armature of the hand hammers. Somebody turned the handle at right angles and created a thing that was the same at both ends, creating an image on a triadic armature. He made it also, at the same time a more effective or at least a comfortable implement that handles absolutely beautifully. It hugs your hand as your hand hugs it. There is nothing wrong with the thing as an artifact. It is just that it is also an image, a sculptural image on an armature. Conceptually, the next step was the stirrup maul where the two sides are the same but it encloses the hand and you have an image where in effect the grasper is grasped. Your hand that grasps the hammer is also grasped by the hammer. Then there was play on that armature, where instead of being exactly at right angles, this took on a slight slope and there was some play with the bilateral symmetry of the two sides. The fully evolved maul comes out looking

Fig. 3:33. Stone hand maul from the southern Northwest Coast.

like something that's eating itself. You will notice that as this process goes along that there is more and more care with the sculpture. They become clothed in beauty which is a characteristic of art as well. They culminate in the slope handled pestle or maul. It can be used as a pestle or a hammer; the handle is turned at 45 degrees which is half way between upright and at right angles, and I think that is part of the meaning as well. Now you don't have to see sexual imagery, you don't have to see that as an image that is phallic above and vulvic below if you don't want to, but for me now, that is part of the meaning, and it adds a great deal to the meaning of the sculpture.

Now there are other paradigms. There is a panel pipe paradigm. Panel pipes were formed that had their beginning at Skidegate slightly after 1815, and had a very quick development for two or three decades, into two forms.

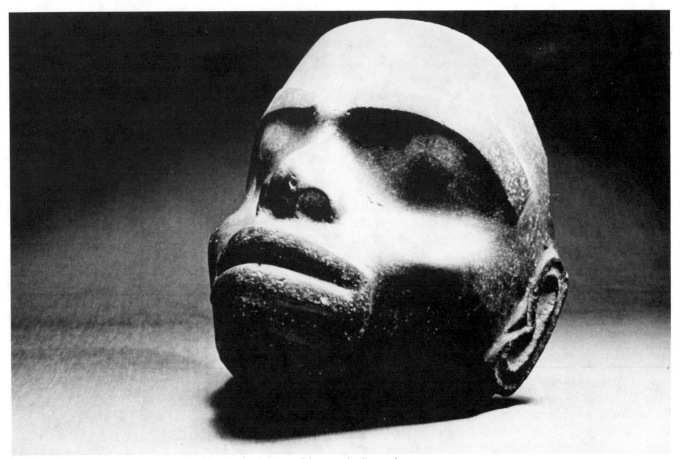

Fig. 3:34. Stone mask from the Tsimshian region. A matching mask shows the eyes open.

Spoon handles-spoon paradigms are very complex images especially at that point of the juncture between the handle and the bowl. Headdress frontlet paradigms are very, very complex pieces of iconography. One of my colleagues, Marjorie Halpern, is working on a mask paradigm.

Of all the Northwest Coast masks the one in Figure 3:34 has to be the epitome. This stone mask from the National Museum in Ottawa was the key image of *Images Stone, B.C.* It is an absolutely marvelous artifact slightly larger than life-size, a beautifully modeled, beautifully smoothed human face, a mask, these strange eyes, which being stone have never opened. It is half of one of the great, great masterpieces of Northwest Coast art because in the Musée de l'Homme is its partner with the same face, the same size except a little bit smaller in the front, and perfectly round circle eyes which being stone can never close. When we get to these masterpieces we are usually left speechless about their meaning, but the point I want to make is that the meanings are very deep, deeper than just depictions of a crest, a spirit or an episode from a myth, and they are not just decorative. In masterpieces like this there is deep meaning at all levels. There is meaning in the artifact and the artifact is part of the meaning. This is a mask which has to do with human identity, and in this case there is meaning in the material, which is of stone. The eyes of the one in the front can never open and the eyes in the one in the back can never close. There is meaning in the armature, and I think the armature of this composite image is a triadic armature, because there are two opposite things in the masks and an implied third thing, the human face of the person that would wear those masks which would mediate them both. There is some kind of meaning there. I am sure there is meaning at every level. There is meaning in the symbols which come from the body self, from the eyes which have to do with seeing and recognizing. These are deep meanings. In conclusion I would just like to say that I think that the explanation of meaning of Northwest Coast art has lagged behind the explanation of form, and that there are deeper meanings, deep symbolic meanings many of them having to do with the human body self of which some show sexual symbolism. The image as I have defined it might be taken as an image, as a unit for structural analysis subject to structural analysis, and that some of these images have a life and a prehistory of their own and great time depth. Northwest Coast images have deep meanings, deep structures and some of them, deep time depth.

CHAPTER 4

Productivity and its Constraints: A Coast Salish Case

WAYNE SUTTLES

On the Northwest Coast in historic times the area to the south of the Kwakiutl seems to have produced far less carving and painting than the area to the north. But a number of carvings of high quality - both naturalistic and stylized - produced in a part of the Coast Salish area suggest that neither technical skill nor stylistic tradition was a limiting factor. Why then did Coast Salish carvers not produce more? This is the question asked recently by Bill Reid in a discussion (Holm and Reid 1975:58-61) of an especially fine Coast Salish spindle whorl. Reid asked, in effect, when they could produce such a well designed and executed piece as this, why did the Coast Salish not produce more such pieces and more kinds of art? Bill Holm commented that the answer must lie in the whole Coast Salish area, trying to show what features of their way of life may have limited productivity, and I shall try to show what I think this analysis implies for the reconstruction of Northwest Coast culture history.

But first let me dispose of a couple of answers to Reid's question that might easily occur to anyone who has read the general and popular works on the Northwest Coast. One of these might be: The Coast Salish did not produce much good work because the whole of Northwest Coast art was a northern development that has only recently diffused southward; the peoples living south of the Wakashan were merely imitating Wakashan (Kwakiutl or Nootka) versions of northern art (cf. Drucker 1955a:162,181). But several facts argue against this view. The area in which people decorated some of their containers, canoes and houses with carvings and paintings representing human or animal forms extended southward at least as far as the Chinookans of the Lower Columbia Valley. There the earliest European visitors, in the late eighteenth and early nineteenth century, saw house fronts "painted in the form

of a human-like face with open mouth, or legs, straddling the doorway, holding up the roof" (Silverstein Ms). In 1846 Paul Kane painted the interior of a "ceremonial lodge" somewhere near Fort Vancouver, showing a house-post carved in the form of a humanoid face and a carved wooden screen topped by confronting animals (Harper 1971, pl. xxxvii). Before the great epidemic of 1830 the Chinookan area was probably more densely populated than the Wakashan area and the Chinookans were probably not in direct contact with any Wakashans, but certainly received from Nootkans, in trade through intervening Salishans, dentalia shells. They may also have received Wakashan slaves and decorated objects, both of which could have been sources of Wakashan influence. But to suppose that a population numbering in the thousands could produce no art that was not mere imitation of Wakashan art is preposterous. Also, there is a prehistoric tradition of stone sculpture on the Lower Columbia (Wingert 1952, Butler 1957) that seems to have a respectable antiquity, perhaps beginning c. A.D. 200 (Pettigrew 1976), which could more easily be the source of historic carving in wood. Moreover, some distinctive styles have been identified in the historical materials from the Coast Salish and Chinookan areas, by Wingert (1949a, 1949b) and Holm (1972), which are clearly not simplified versions of something Wakashan.

Another answer to Reid's question might be: The Coast Salish did not produce much good work because they were "johnny-come-latelies" recently emerged from the interior who had not yet had time to shed their Plateau heritage and acquire a decent foundation in Northwest Coast art from their Wakashan neighbours. Or, considering that art may be old on the Lower Columbia, we might add— from their Chinookan neighbours. But this theory of recent

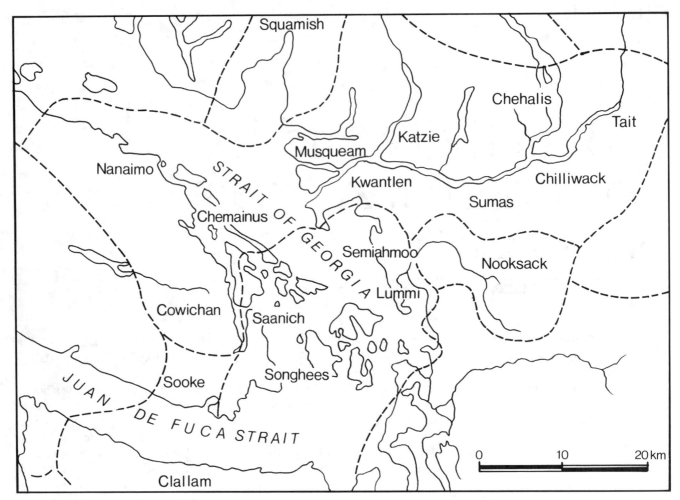

Fig. 4:1. Map showing the locations of the Central Coast Salish.

Salish emergence from the interior, which goes back to Boas, has little to support it. The supposed evidence for it from physical anthropology seems to have been an illusion; the archaeological evidence can be read either way (to support cultural replacement or cultural continuity); and the linguistic evidence is, if anything, against it, suggesting rather a homeland for Proto-Salish on the coast and an early movement into the interior. For all we know, the Salishan languages have been spoken on the coast for as long as the Wakashan languages. Without the biological, archaeological and linguistic evidence for Salish emergence from the interior, the ethnological arguments become very weak. With no proof that there was a time when the Wakashans had plank houses, sea-mammal hunting and social stratification while the Salish did not, we cannot argue that the Salish got these things from the Wakashans except by begging the question. And if we try to use such supposed borrowings as evidence of Salish emergence, we may find ourselves arguing in a circle—the Coast Salish must have borrowed these features of coast culture from the Wakashans because they came from the interior

where they could not have had them; the Coast Salish must have come out of the interior because they have these features of coast culture they borrowed from the Wakashans. This circular arrangement seems to be supported by presuppositions about Wakashan creativity and Salishan imitativeness. (I am expanding this discussion elsewhere.) Now, I am not saying that the Salish have never borrowed anything from the Wakashans or other neighbours. Borrowing in all directions has probably occurred many times. But in each case only careful study will show which direction the trait went. Art is no exception.

But before I return to art I must establish clearly *which* Coast Salish I shall be talking about and what position they occupy within the Coast Salish area. This is essential because from the literature one might also easily get the impression, on the one hand, that the whole Coast Salish area was culturally homogeneous, or on the other, that the Coast Salish of Puget Sound were somehow the most typical or true Coast Salish while those living farther north were peripheral deviants. Neither of these impressions would be correct. There were a dozen or more Coast

Salish languages spoken through a continuous area extending from Johnstone Strait in the north to the Columbia River in the south. The speakers of these languages seem to have formed a biological and social continuum, which may have extended far beyond in all directions. But within this continuum there were some pretty clear cultural differences, seen especially in the distribution of ceremonial activiites (cf. Barnett 1938, Smith 1941, Elmendorf 1960:298-305).

I am especially concerned with the speakers of two languages, *Halkomelem* and *Straits,* who occupy one segment of the Coast Salish continuum, a region extending from the Lower Fraser Valley to the Strait of Juan de Fuca *(Fig. 4:1).* These people are better known under a number of "tribal" names, each of which designates a village or group of villages sharing a dialect of one of these languages. The *Tait, Katzie, Kwantlen* and other Lower Fraser people collectively called *Stalo,* the *Musqueam* at the mouth of the Fraser, and the *Nanaimo* and *Cowichan* of Vancouver Island all spoke dialects of *Halkomelem.* The *Semiahmoo, Lummi,* and *Samish* to the south of the mouth of the Fraser along the mainland shore and the *Saanich, Songhees,* and *Sooke* of the southeastern end of Vancouver Island all spoke dialects of *Straits. Clallam,* on the southern shore of the Strait of Juan de Fuca is either a divergent dialect of *Straits* or a closely related language. The *Nooksack,* inland to the south of the Fraser, and the *Squamish,* to the north, spoke their own separate languages but culturally seem to have been somewhat closer to the speakers of *Halkomelem* and *Straits* than to their neighbours beyond. In spite of this linguistic diversity, the absence of any formal political organization, and occasional conflicts, the people of this region were linked together by continual inter-village marriage and participation in economic and social activities and the exchange of foods, goods, information and personnel. Such ties extended beyond this region, of course. But the *Halkomelem* and *Straits* people shared patterns of subsistence activities relying especially on salmon runs ascending the Fraser (see discussion in Mitchell 1971:19-29). And within the region, I believe, certain concepts and values were held and expressed more frequently than they were outside it.

It would be useful to have names without linguistic connotations for culturally distinguishable regions within the Coast Salish area. Elsewhere (Suttles 1968:58) I have used "Central Coast Salish" for the Halkomelem-Straits region. Geographically, Straits was at the very centre of the total Coast Salish area. Demographically, Straits and Halkomelem territories together seem to have been a peak, perhaps the most densely populated region on this part of the Northwest Coast. Mooney's (1928) estimates, accepted by Kroeber (1939) and not yet superseded, give it more people than the rest of the Coast Salish area combined and also more than the entire Wakashan area.

Thus "Central Coast Salish" might be justified on two grounds. I should note that in using the term I do not mean to imply that other Coast Salish were peripheral deviants nor that the people to whom I apply the term were a unit in all things. I do think we can make some generalizations about these people and we need a collective name.

Art, Power and Prestige

During the nineteenth century the Central Coast Salish carved and/or painted ritual paraphernalia of several kinds, house posts and (in some places) house fronts, grave monuments and several kinds of implements of practical use. Discovering what this art meant to the people who made it and used it is now very difficult. But perhaps we can make a start by sorting it out by its association with some native concepts. It seems to me that, while some Central Coast Salish art may have been purely decorative, much of it can be related to four sources of power and prestige—the vision, the ritual word, the ancestors, and wealth. (I believe I have considered most of the available ethnographic data—works by Boas, Hill-Tout, Jenness, Barnett, Duff and others, but inevitably I have been guided most by my own field experience, which began in 1946 and has continued now and again over the years.) I shall discuss these four sources of power and prestige first and then return to the kinds of things that were carved and painted.

The *vision* was the unique experience of the individual, the source of his or her skill at subsistence activities or crafts, and the essential basis of professional status as warrior, seeress or shaman. In theory, though not always in practice, the exact nature of the vision experience was something one ought to keep secret, perhaps until old age. The vision experience inspired a unique individual performance in the winter dance, but its nature was only hinted at by the words of the song and the movements of the dance (cf. Jacobs 1959:13 on Clackamas Chinookan, Collins 1974:145-146 on Upper Skagit, Barnett 1955:146 on Georgia Strait secrecy). Any other representation of the vision experience we might expect also to be vague, ambiguous or covert.

The *ritual word* was for some purposes more important than the vision. It too was an aid in subsistence and crafts and was the basis of a profession, that of "ritualist" (Barnett's term, Jenness says "priest"). The ritual word was the heart of the first salmon ceremony, of incantations to quell wounded bears and sea lions, and of the "cleansing rites" used at life crises and to wipe away shame. These cleansing rites included the use of masks, rattles and several illusions—one in which stuffed animals appeared to climb a pole, another in which a basket appeared to float in the air, etc. The ritual word was also associated with designs, which the ritualist painted with red ochre on those he protected or purified (see especially Jenness 1955:37-39). the rites and the designs were the property of individuals, who kept to themselves the knowlegde of the ritual words that made them efficacious, but they could be used on behalf of descendants, descent being reckoned bilaterally, of an ancestral owner.

The *ancestors*, for the Central Coast Salish (perhaps with a few exceptions), had always had human form. Some of these first humans dropped from the sky at the beginning of the world. Others seem simply to have been here. In a few myths they were created by the Transformer. Some animal species are the descendants of people, as the sturgeon in Pitt Lake came from the daughter of the first man there; some are the affines of people, as the sockeye salmon are for the *Katzie* through a marriage of another first man (see Jenness 1955:12, 18-21). But people are not the descendants of animals. In the most common kind of myth, when the Transformer came through the world and brought the Myth Age to an end, he transformed some of the First People into animals but left others, who pleased him, to become the founding ancestors of villages. Some of these founders received, from the Transformer or from other sources, the ritual words, incantations and ritual paraphernalia of the cleansing rites, which have been transmitted generation after generation to their present owners.

The value of the vision, the ritual word, and the ancestors was reflected in *wealth*. In native theory, they were responsible for one's having wealth and so having wealth demonstrated their presence and efficacy. Giving wealth, as Barnett (1938b) and others have pointed out, was a necessary step in validating claims to status, ultimately confirmed by being given wealth. Wealth for the Central Coast Salish included slaves and dentalia obtained from elsewhere but consisted mainly of items made within the area by skilled craftsmen and, more importantly, craftswomen. Probably the most important item of wealth was the blanket woven of mountain-goat and/or dog wool. These blankets had several advantages as wealth; they were made of materials of practical value and available in large but finite amounts and they were divisible and recombinable, since they could be cut up or unraveled and the material rewoven into new ones.

When I began work on this paper I did not see wealth as something I might discuss in relation to art in the same way I saw the vision, the ritual word and the ancestors. But I have come to see it this way, for reasons I shall return to later. But now let me go on to the art itself, taking up in turn each of the main classes of things that were carved and painted.

Ritual Paraphernalia

The Central Salish did not have very much in the way of decorated ritual paraphernalia associated with vision power. Shamans evidently had little or nothing of the sort. Winter ("guardian spirit") dancers of a few types had a few items. In recent years, and perhaps earlier, dancers with the type of song called "male," once sung by the professional warrior, have induced possession by shaking staffs that are often decorated with animal forms (see Stern 1934, frontispiece; Hawthorn 1967:214, fig. 250, centre). These forms may have vision-related meanings, but I have no information on this. There were also men and women, perhaps mainly among the Salish and Lummi, with the vision-empowered boards, poles and duck-shaped floats that were used more often in the Northern Puget Sound region and generally known by their Lushootseed (Puget) names, repectively sgʷədílič, tə́stəd and čáju (Suttles 1951:370-378; Jenness 1955:6164; Lushootseed orthography as in Hess, 1974). I have no information on the decoration of these items in the Central Coast Salish area, but on Puget Sound some sgʷsədílič boards were painted with designs symbolic of the songs revealed by the vision (Waterman 1924, pl. 1) and tə́stəd poles were decorated with red ochre, cedar bark and deer-hoof rattles (Hess 1974:495). While these items appeared in the winter dances, they were also occasionally used in a form of divination to find lost objects or persons, though the owners were not regarded as shamans.

In not having any portable representations of their visions, Central Coast Salish shamans differed markedly from those of two other Coast Salish regions to the south. In the centre of the Puget Sound region the best known works of art are the posts and boards used in the famous "spirit canoe" ceremony in which several shamans dramatized a trip to the Land of the Dead to recover a lost soul *(Fig. 4:2)*. This ceremony seems not to have been performed in the Central Coast Salish area and the styles of carving and painting seen on the "spirit canoe" paraphernalia do not closely resemble anything in the Central Coast Salish area. To the southwest, among the Quinault (and others?), shamans used small boards and "wands" carved with representations of their "guardian spirits," the wands with deer-hoof rattles attached (Olson 1936:148-150; Wingert 1949a, pl. 1-7). Again, nothing like these has been reported for the Central Coast Salish area.

In the Central Coast Salish regions the most important decorated objects of ritual use were the rattles and masks used to "cleanse" (z̓xʷát, in Halkomelem, Musqueam dialect, orthography mine) persons worthy of that honour. Such a rattle or mask, or perhaps the physical object together with the ritual words and acts that it was used with, is called a z̓xʷtén, literally "cleansing instrument." I shall refer to a ceremony in which the rattle, mask, etc. is used as a "cleansing rite" (Jenness 1955:71 calls them "community rituals," Barnett 1955:154 "privileged performances"). These rattles and masks are instruments empowered by the ritual word and used by the ritualist.

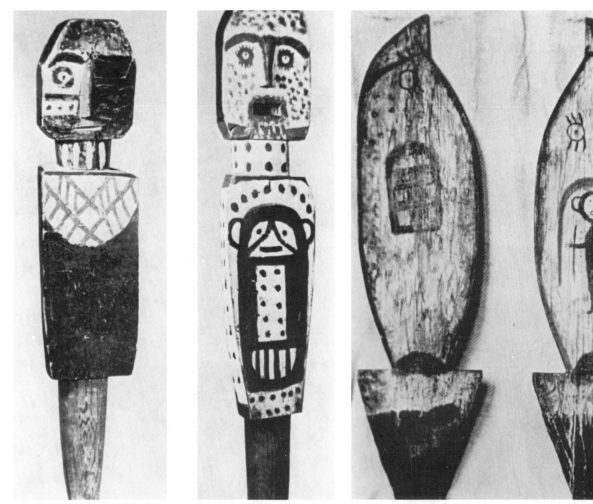

Fig. 4:2. Spirit canoe figures and boards from Puget Sound. These objects were used by shamans in a dramatized trip to the Land of the Dead to recover lost souls.

They belong to a cultural complex that is separate from, though not altogether unrelated to, visions and shamans. The use of the cleansing rites is not confined to the winter dancing season. In fact, at one time they were used most often in the potlatch, which was most often a fair-weather gathering. But recently they have appeared most often at the larger winter dances.

The Rattles (Fig. 4:3). The ritualist's rattle is called sxᵞélməxᵂcəs in Halkomelem (Musqueam dialect). This word is certainly Salish and specifically Halkomelem in form but cannot yet be wholly analyzed. It may mean simply "something round held in the hand." A number of ritualist's rattles that are known to be old are made each of a sheet of bighorn sheep horn bent over and sewn along the edges to form a bulging triangle (like the pastry called a "turnover"), provided with a wooden handle extending from the apex, and having strands of mountain-goat wool attached to the sewn sides. Both surfaces of the bulging horn usually have incised designs and the end of the wooden handle is usually carved. There are also some uncarved horn rattles and a number made in

about the same shape but of metal, said to be a modern substitute. In pre-contact times the California bighorn sheep ranged westward to the eastern edge of Central Coast Salish country (Cowan 1940:554, 558, 574) and so some coast hunters may have hunted it. But the animal is little known among the Coast Salish today and probably most of the horn was imported from the Plateau.

In recent years ritualists with rattles have appeared as participants in the "work" (the potlatch-like activities) that accompanies the winter ("guardian-spirit") dancing. Acting in pairs they usher into the big house the young people to receive names or the photographs of the dead to be honoured. The audience first hears the chanting of the ritualists, coming faintly and then gradually louder, from outside the house, and then sees them enter, walking slowly and pausing every few steps, chanting with a slow steady beat of the rattles. After the young people are named or the dead honoured, many members of the audience receive blankets or silver coins as thanks for their witnessing the event. Such "work," once part of the summer potlatch, seems to have been only recently

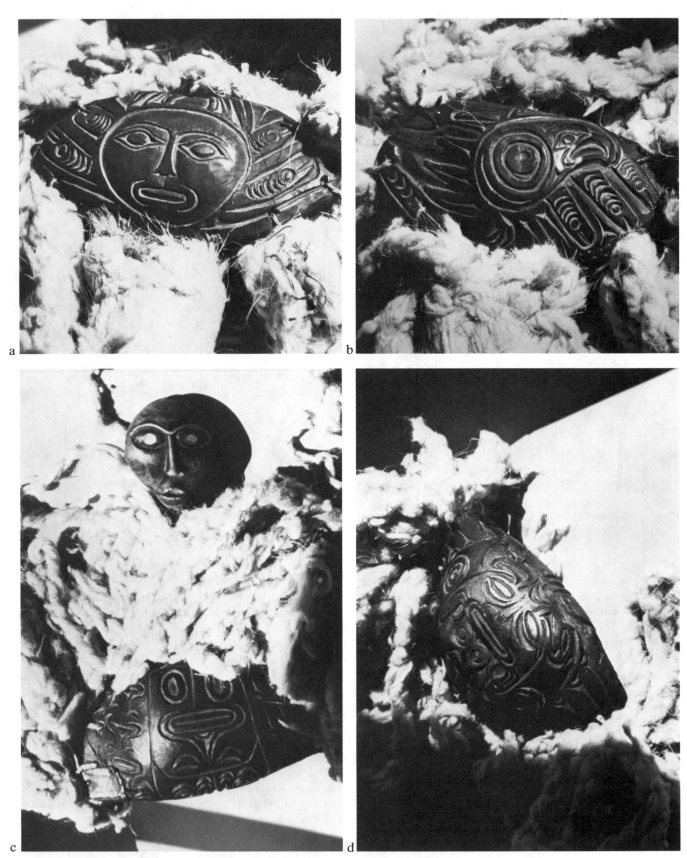

Fig. 4:3 a,b,c,d. Coast Salish ritualists' rattles made of horn and carved on both faces. Mountain goat wool is attached to the sides of the rattle.

inserted into the winter dance and is still only an optional adjunct to it (Suttles 1960b).

But at one time the ritualist's rattle had another use directly related to the winter dance. In a text dictated in Halkomelem, one of the Musqueam teachers describes her great-grandmother's work as a ritualist. That woman had four rattles, one of which she used to induce possession in a person expected to become a "new dancer." She would first simply paint designs directly on the body of the initiate, reciting the proper ritual words. But if that did not work, she would choose the rattle that had a face carved on it, put red ochre on it, and then stamp it onto the body of the initiate, at which point he would become possessed with his song. She used this method to bring out songs of one of the several categories of "spirit songs." She also used a rattle for a girl who had reached puberty. After painting the girl four mornings and four nights, she led her down to the river, recited the ritual words to the water and bathed her.

The designs *(Fig. 4:3)* carved on the sheep-horn rattles vary in complexity. But several I have seen appear similar in features of composition and style. Three I have seen have on one side a clearly defined, roundish humanoid face. On one, the face has what seems to be bunches of hair, feathers or rays radiating from it; on the other side are what appear to be fishes. The second has a face with radiating rays and fishes and on the reverse a bird with fishes. On the third, the face has fishes above it and facing birds enclosing it, while on the reverse another pair of birds face each other to enclose a space in which the features of another face appear. As recurrent elements of style there are circles, concentric circles, crescents and elongated wedges that I have been tempted to call "cuneiforms." Bill Holm has suggested to me, and I am convinced he is right, that the crescent and cuneiforms are "holes in the donuts" between formlines. Holm's analysis of the northern two-dimensional style seems to work for this style too, yet this style generally lacks the ovoids that are such a prominent feature of the northern style.

(A rattle of unknown provenience shown in the Art of the North show in 1973—see Collins et al. 1973:262, *Fig. 341*—is clearly the same kind of rattle in form and style, though the design is somewhat more complex than any known Central Coast Salish rattle that I have seen and it seems to contain an ovoid.)

I do not know what these designs represent, nor do I expect to find anyone who does. Forty years ago Diamond Jenness (1955:37-39) learned that ritualists painted the faces of those they worked on, every ritualist having "his own hereditary set of designs that varied with different functions," such as healing the ghost-struck and recovering lost "vitalities" as well as performing puberty rites for both sexes. Jenness worked, in 1936, with Old Pierre of Katzie, perhaps the most famous shaman in the Central Coast Salish region. To Pierre, all power came from "Him

Who Dwells Above" and the ritual words, which Jenness identifies as "prayers," were initially addressed to this deity, though they have come to have power of their own. The rattles too, according to Pierre, came from the deity, who gave one with a different design to each of several village founders. However, "No one now knows the meanings of the patterns."

Are the designs on the rattles related to the designs painted with red ochre by ritualists on their patients? It seems reasonable to suppose so, in view of Pierre's attributing them to the same source and the use by one ritualist of her rattle as a stamp. Were the designs the ritualist drew on their patients the formlines or the crescents and cuneiforms—the donuts or the holes? If the unincised surface of the horn transmitted the paint, the ritualists must have been drawing formlines. Holm (1965: 92-93) has compared the flow of movement that produced the Northern formlines with the flow of movement of the Northern dance. Did the ritual painting of esoteric designs among the Central Coast Salish provide a link here between dancing and carving?

What about the recurring face on the rattles? Is it "He Who Dwells Above?" Probably not. That name is Jenness's translation of cícəł siʔém̓, a phrase that appears to be a loan-translation of the Chinook Jargon sáx̣ali táyi "chief above," perhaps better "Lord Above," used by the missionaries as the term for "God." Similar loan-translations can be found in several other languages along the coast. A "Lord Above" does not play any role in other origin myths collected in the Central Coast Salish or neighbouring regions. So it appears to me that the "Lord Above" is a post-contact concept and that Old Pierre's theology is a synthesis that post-dates the rattles (cf. Suttles 1957:377-381). But there are at least three other possibilities. First, the face on the rattle may be the face of the Daylight (swéyəl in Musqueam, skʷéyəl or skʷéčəl in some other dialects of Halkomelem and Northern Straits, skʷáčəy in Clallam), seen as something of very great power to which—or to whom—people who knew the ritual words addressed them as spells—or prayers; I have the impression that to some the Daylight was simply a very powerful impersonal force, while to others it may have been a deity-like entity. Second, the face may be that of x̣é·ls, The Transformer of the mythology of the region and the source, according to some myths (e.g., Stern 1934:107), of ritual words. Third, the rattle may have been used in the first-salmon ceremony, and so the face and the fish on the rattle may represent an ancestor and the species he made a compact with, a compact to be maintained through the ceremony. But this is sheer conjecture. The face on the rattle may represent no particular person or being at all. Perhaps a human face simply symbolizes consciousness and purpose, which are, at least, attributes of the ritualist that should be reassuring to the patient.

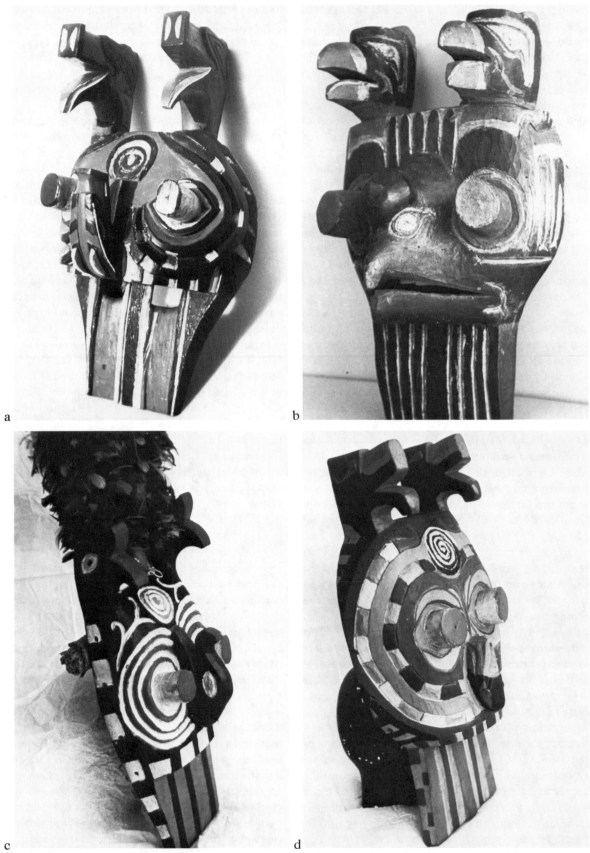

Fig. 4:4. Sxwayxwey Masks. *a* Snake sxwayxwey from Musqueam. *b* Raven sxwayxwey from Cowichan. *c, d* Masks from Squamish.

The distribution of the ritualist's rattle is not altogether clear. Its centre seems to be the Halkomelem area but some ritualists among the Northern Straits people to the south and among the Squamish and perhaps others to the north also used rattles. The decorated rattles that I know of are from the Halkomelem and Vancouver Island Straits area.

The Masks (Figs. 4:4, 4:5). The mask used in one of the cleansing rites is known in the literature under a variety of representations of the native name, which seems uniform throughout the Central Coast Salish region and which I record as sx̌ʷáyx̌ʷəy and will spell "sxwayxwey." The name appears to be Salish but I can give no etymology for it. I know nothing to justify identifying it with "whirlwind" as did Emmons (Notes in the Provincial Archives and Catalog of the American Museum of Natural History) nor with "earthquake" as Boas (1897:497) did for its Kwakiutl counterpart. Recently Levi-Strauss (1975: 1–39) has followed an earlier suggestion by Codere (1948:7) that there is a relationship between this name and the word used on Puget Sound for "potlatch," but this is highly unlikely.

The name refers, I believe, to the whole character portrayed by the dancer in his costume rather than to the mask itself, which exists in several named varieties. As it appears in a performance, the mask is worn high on the head, surrounded by plumes and a bib-like collar. The dancer's whole "outfit" includes a cape worn over the back of his head and shoulders, lines of large white feathers wrapped around his middle, leggings of downy swan-skin and deer-hoof rattles at his ankles. In his right hand the sxwayxwey dancer carries a rattle made of perforated scallop shells strung on a wooden hoop or pair of hoops.

The mask itself is carved of wood. Most now in existence may be of red cedar but at an earlier time they may have been made of maple. Most are painted with three colours—black or blue, red and white. Masks used in the Halkomelem area, with a few exceptions, conform to a standard pattern (Squamish and Lummi carvers have produced some different types, to which I shall return later.) The mask consists of a fairly round face, the most conspicuous features of which are a pair of projecting cylinders representing the eyes, or more precisely the eyeballs or irises, since the lids appear in low relief around the bases of these stalks, which look like the eyes of a crab or snail. Rising from the top of the head is a pair of horn-like projections carved in the form of animal or bird heads. (I use "animal" in the sense of a creature with a snout rather than a beak; "animals" may include reptiles and amphibians as well as mammals.) With the possible exception of one type, the face seems to lack a mandible, the straight lower margin of the face appearing as a maxilla. Projecting downward from the face is a long, broad, flat, grooved surface that appears to be a tongue.

Perforations at the root of this tongue, under the maxilla, allow the dancer to look out. The "nose" of the face and the area surrounding the eyes vary with the type of mask.

List of types of sxwayxwey given by Jenness (1955:72, 91), Barnett (1955:158), Emmons (n.d.), and my own informants add up to some thirteen names: Thunder, Raven, Sawbill, Snake, Two-headed Snake, Beaver, Spring Salmon, Owl, Ghost, Buzzard, Eagle, Bear and Clown. The actual number of types may be somewhat less, since "Owl" and "Ghost" may be the same, as may "Bear" and "Clown." Some of these named types are identifiable with masks in museum collections; some are not. I will not try to present all of the data here. I will describe briefly only the most clearly identifiable types.

One type (*Fig. 4:5d*) was identified at Musqueam, by Mr. and Mrs. Andrew Charles from photographs, as "Sawbill-Face" (x̌ʷá·q̓ʷəs, from x̌ʷá·q̓ʷ "sawbill, merganser, fish duck," -əs "-face"). This name appears in every other list that I have. On the masks so identified, a fully carved head of a merganser forms the "nose" of the mask as a whole, while the rest of the bird may be shown in low relief, the wings and feet appearing around the eyes of the mask and the tail on the forehead. There are variations: on several Sawbill-Faces the "horns" are birds, but on one so identified they are animals; and while on several the body of the merganser is shown in a clear though stylized fashion, as just described, in one mask the body of the bird is much less clearly indicated.

In the type the Charleses identified as "Snake-Face" (*Fig. 4:4c*) (xʷʔə́łqəyəs, from ʔə́łqəy "snake"), an animal head facing upward forms the nose of the mask. In some examples, two feet extend upward from the head toward the eyes of the mask. In all, ridges I take to be the snake's body extend from the head in an arc up and around either side of the face of the mask. A spiral or set of concentric circles appears on the forehead of the mask. The horns are animal heads.

In a type identified as "Ghost-Face" (*Fig. 4:5b*) (pəlqʷə-ẑáyəs, from spəlqʷízeʔ "ghost, corpse, screech owl") the nose of the mask is neither an animal nor a bird head but a simple triangular projection with an inverted V incised in the flat end, which looks (to me, anyway) like the nasal aperture of a skull. If the identification with a skull is correct, the lines on either side of the nose may represent the malars and the few simple incised lines above the eyes may represent the sutures. In two masks but not in a third, the upper jaw seems to be painted with teeth.

Photographs of two masks with similar triangular noses were identified as Ghost masks by the Charleses but one was identified as a Beaver by Emmons. The latter identification may be correct, since they have nostrils cut in a different form and they have pairs of wide incisors projecting downward from their upper jaws.

On a mask Emmons identified as a Raven (*Fig. 4:4b*),

Fig. 4:5. a Raven mask from Nanaimo. *b* Ghost mask from Musqueam. *c* Mask showing plumes and ruff. *d* Sawbill mask from Katzie.

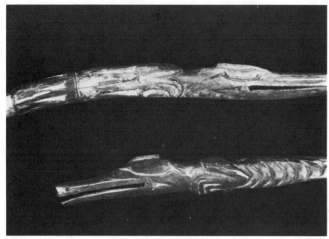
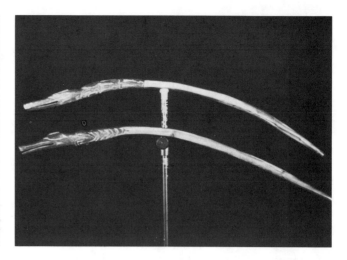

Fig. 4:6. Wands used with the sxwayxwey mask.

the nose is the bird's head, facing downward, with its mouth extending nearly across the width of the mask. If we focus our attention on the Raven's mouth, it may appear that it is also the mouth of the mask itself. But the Raven's eyes are not identical with the eyes of the whole mask and so I am inclined to think that the Raven's mouth is still the upper jaw of the whole mask. On this type of mask, the Raven's mouth is cut all the way through the wood, providing a slit the dancer may see through, which suggests that this mask was worn a bit lower on the face than the others.

In style, most of these masks share two organizational principles with the art of the more northerly Northwest Coast peoples: the bird or animal (the snake, anyway) is spread out and wrapped around the space available to it; and, a part of one creature may be simultaneously a part of another, as when the head of the sawbill is also the nose of the mask (a relationship Laura Greenberg and Bill Holm have called "visual punning"). Also, elements of the northern style are present; we can certainly see formlines created by the cutting away of the "holes in the donuts (cf. Ch. 2 by Holm). But just as in the ritualist's rattles, the incised elements are cuneiforms, crescents, circles and arcs; rarely, if ever, ovoids.

When the sxwayxwey mask is worn, various things are attached to it. In the top of the mask there are holes into which are thrust large feathers (Golden Eagle tail feathers?) or Chinese feather dusters. (Photographs dating back to the turn of the century show that the latter have been in use at least that long.) Behind the top of the mask is attached a roll of rushes into which are thrust a number of flexible stalks, earlier sea-lion whiskers but now usually (I believe) wood and wire, tipped with tufts of white down. The bib-like affair that surrounds the rest of the mask consists of a fan of feathers cut evenly at the perimeter and covered with patterned or embroidered cloth. A mask in the American Museum has a carved wooden attachment projecting from either side, perhaps

originally to hold up the "bib." The British Columbia Provincial Museum has a pair of slender "wands" *(Fig. 4:6)* said to have been attached to a sxwayxwey mask; the end of each is carved in the form of an animal and very much in the style that appears on the ritualist's rattles and, as we shall see, on the spindle whorls. I shall come back to the identity of these animals later.

The sxwayxwey, like the ritualist's rattle, is a cleansing instrument. And like the rattle, it was formerly used in the summer potlatch but has recently been used in the "work" accompanying the winter dance and for the same purposes. An even number of sxwayxwey dancers, usually four or six, dance around the person, persons or photograph for which they have been hired. The owner of a mask may dance with it himself or may engage someone else to wear it. Men only dance with sxwayxwey masks, in contrast to the winter dance (the "guardian-spirit" dance), in which both sexes participate equally. However, women are hired to sing as the dancers perform. A sxwayxwey dancer moves with high, short steps, raising the right arm with the right foot and the left with the left ("like a pacer"). The style of dancing does not resemble those of the winter dancers. At one time, it is said, the different types of masks were used with appropriate movements. I have also been told that at one time the masks were much heavier and hard to breathe through so that the dancers engaged in a kind of endurance contest. Two kinds of songs are associated with the sxwayxwey. In the past, at any rate, on the morning of the day of the potlatch when the sxwayxwey was to be used, at dawn the owner beat a box drum and sang an incantation (széləm) that announced the event and, I believe, empowered the sxwayxwey with the ritual word. Later, as the sxwayxwey danced, the chorus of women sang a "song for a person" (stələméyəł), which is either an inherited song or one composed for the occasion in order to wipe away an insult.

The box drum used for the sxwayxwey was another

piece of decorated ritual paraphernalia. A Lummi man who saw one used at a Quamichan (Cowichan) potlatch said that it had animals on the front of it but he could not make out what they were. The Field Museum's box drum from Cowichan that has four little human figures on it (Wingert 1949, pl. 44) may have been used for the sxwayxwey.

Two generations ago a Musqueam man, and perhaps no one else, owned the q^{w}í niye (probably "hairy thing") identified as a "clown." This character appeared with the sxwayxwey dancers, wearing a somewhat different type of mask and a costume of cured bearskin. The "clown" chased the sxwayxwey, poking at their eyes with a stick, and threatened the women in the audience. The owner of the "clown" is said to have lost the costume and so abandoned the practice. Old photographs (e.g., Barnett 1955, p.XIX) show it as having less projecting eyes than the sxwayxwey, proper and a single "horn" on the head. (Barnett 1955:178-179 discusses the clown. See also Stern, 1934:57-59, but note my later comment on Stern's work.) This figure of the "clown," with its dark fur and audience-oriented behaviour, contrasts sharply with the figure of the sxwayxwey, with its white feathers and down and behaviour oriented toward the subject of its purifying power.

What does the sxwayxwey really represent? I do not really know. The myths that account for its origin usually identify it as a mask and costume worn by a human being or human-like being. There is no evidence that I can see that it represents a "spirit" (there is no equivalent of "spirit" in Halkomelem) or some non-human species of bird or animal (cf. Suttles 1972 on "natural" vs "supernatural" in relation to the "sasquatch"). Perhaps the question is misguided. Feathers are themselves a ritual substance, like red ochre and hogfennel seeds. Central Coast Salish ritualists scatter feathers as they purify dance floors. The purification would not be effected, I believe, without the ritual words used by and known only to the ritualist, but the feathers evidently help make them efficacious. Perhaps the sxwayxwey is not more than an elaborate use of the magical powers of feathers and patterns, which increase the efficacy of the ritual word. If so, it need not represent anything. It is just what it is called, a "cleansing instrument."

The sxwayxwey has a much wider distribution than the ritualist's rattle, but it too may have been spreading, on the coast at least, from the Halkomelem area. It has been used northward as far as the Kwakiutl and southward as far as the immediately adjacent Saanich and Lummi. But the conclusion that it originated in the Halkomelem area or more specifically among the Lower Fraser people, reached by Barnett (1955:167, 178-179), Duff (1952:123-126), and Levi-Strauss (1975:1-44ff), is based largely on judgements about the historicity of myths and traditions of who got the sxwayxwey from whom (especially in Duff's

case) or on a structuralist theory of myth applied to insufficient data (as in Levi-Strauss's cases). I see serious problems here but cannot go into them at this time. The sxwayxwey may indeed be old in the Upper Stalo area. But I do not believe that myths and traditions prove it. Some ethnographic evidence seems to support it. Inland neighbours of the Upper Stalo used carvings of the sxwayxwey as grave markers; this is reported for the Nooksack by Fetzer (n.d.) and for the Lower Lillooet by Teit (1906:272-273). Teit also reports (253-254) that both the Lower and Upper Lillooet used various kinds of masks. But most important is the archaeological evidence. Among materials taken from a prehistoric site at Chase, in the middle of Shuswap country, Sanger (1968) discovered pieces of scallop shells used as rattles and a broken mask that looks like a sxwayxwey. A scallop-shell rattle was also discovered in the Lochnore-Nesikep locality (Sanger 1970:94, 101). In both places there was other evidence of trade with the coast. This does suggest that the szwayxwey was in use on the Lower Fraser in prehistoric times.

Another object that must be mentioned in this context of art relevant to the ritual word is the stone bowl. Wilson Duff, in his thorough treatment of these bowls (Duff 1956), has summarized the scant ethnographic evidence that they were used by ritualists in historic times. I have nothing at this time to add to what Duff has said. Still other objects that we may be able to consider in this context when more is known about them are the paraphernalia of the Nootka-style secret society that has flourished at the western end of Straits country. Whatever members think, non-members have seen it as a kind of cleansing ritual. Finally, among decorated ritual objects we should include painted drums. These used to be less common than unpainted drums, but are fairly often seen today at big dances. I have no information on the meaning of the designs.

The Central Coast Salish house was a long, shed-roofed structure consisting of a sheath of huge planks over a frame of posts and beams. The posts were often decorated and in rare cases so were the beams. Also, early European observers saw decorated house fronts on the Lower Fraser. In 1808 Simon Fraser saw one in what may have been a Kwantlen village. The 640-foot long house he visited had, in "the chief's" section, a post with an oval opening serving as a door, above which on the outside "are carved a human figure as large as life, with other figures in imitation of beasts and birds" (Masson 1889-90:197). Fifty years later, in 1858, Charles Wilson saw decorated houses in the same area. He wrote (1865: 287-288):

The buildings at Langley and Chilikweyuk are the only ones on which there is any attempt at ornament, the former being adorned with some curious pictographs, in which a bird something like a crow figures conspicuously; the latter with some grotesque carvings, apparently representing tortoises, large snakes, and some animal of the crocodile type.

In his journal (1970:37) he mentions not being able to copy the "pictographs on the lodges because of the rain," so we can assume they were on the outside. In the same year (1858) James Madison Alden visited the same area and produced a series of watercolours of the country, several of which show native houses with large circular designs on their fronts, but at too great a distance to give any details (see Stenzel 1975, plates 37, C-21, and 40). Alden also produced a watercolour of the village at Nanaimo (pl C-24), which does not show any external decoration. Probably features of structure and use worked against the decoration of house fronts. The heavy wall planks were held horizontally, overlapping, between pairs of upright poles. The planks covering a section of a house might be owned by the family occupying it. They were easily removed so that they could be laid across a pair of canoes as a "raft," taken to cover a frame at a summer fishing site, or taken to another village by a family changing residence. It seems likely that houses with decorated fronts would be only those whose owners would not have to remove the planks seasonally or could be assured of getting them back in the right order. Perhaps there was less moving of planks on the Lower Fraser than elsewhere in the area, where decorated house fronts have not been reported. Paul Kane in 1847 sketched two carved house entrance posts he must have seen at or near Victoria (Harper 1971:260, *Fig. 195*) but shows no decorated house fronts in his scenes of villages (e.g., p.254).

The posts that stood inside the house, holding the beams and constituting part of the frame, were often decorated. In the Northern Straits area, it seems, they were decorated with representations of vision powers. One that survives (*Fig. 4:7*) (at the Whatcom Museum of History and Art in Bellingham) is as stark as a Puget Sound shaman's figure. It belonged to Chowitsut, who was the wealthiest Lummi in the early 1850s, and it is an incised pair of concentric circles linked with two smaller circles. In the 1940s my oldest Lummi teacher identified this design as representing one of Chowitsut's wealth powers—"sun carrying two valises of expensive things." Other posts with carvings representing visions stood in Victoria and Boas tells us (1891:564) that the Songhees owner kept them covered except during festivals because he did "not like to be constantly reminded of these his superhuman friends and helpers."

In the Halkomelem area, it seems, house posts were carved to represent ancestors and ancestral heritages related to the ritual word. A post at Musqueam (*Fig. 4:8*) represented the famous warrior named qeyəplénəxᵂ ("Capilano"). Another Musqueam post represents c̓simlénəxᵂ (*Fig. 4:8 right*), a descendant of the man who bore that name, according to Old Pierre, at the beginning of the present world, who became the founding ancestor

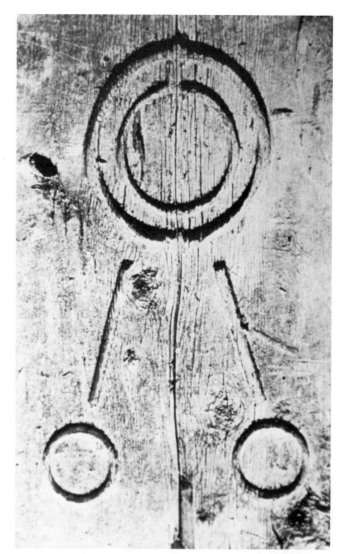

Fig. 4:7. Carving on house post of Chowitsut at Lummi. These figures symbolize the sun carrying his two valises of valuables.

of a Musqueam village, and received a ritualist's rattle, a sxwayxwey mask, and the empowering incantations from the Lord Above. On this post the bearer of this famous name is seen quelling a bear by shaking the rattle and chanting the incantation (cf. Barnett 1955:54). The post honours both the ancestor and the heritage.

A house post that once stood in a Nanaimo village (now in the Field Museum and illustrated in Wingert 1949, Pl.40) portrays a sxwayxwey dancer and thus illustrates that a house post can represent a cleansing rite alone.

A cleansing rite is probably also the source of a number of animals that appear on house posts (and also grave monuments) in museum collections, several from the Cowichan village of Quamichan but others from Musqueam, Saanich and Songhees. On some posts there are only animals; on one set of posts there are six to a post

Fig. 4:8. left. Housepost at Musqueam depicting "Capilano".

Fig. 4:8. right. Housepost at Musqueam depicting Csimlenax.

Fig. 4:9. House interior at the Cowichan village of Quamichan showing posts with mustelids.

(*Fig. 4:9*). On other posts the animals appear on the fronts of large human figures, two or four to a post; on still others a large human figure holds a small animal (*Fig. 4:10*). Recent informants have identified these animals as some kind of mustelid (member of the weasel family)— minks, otters or fishers. Early collectors recorded a name for them as "scowmidgeon" or "sqa-mit-chen" (Wingert 1949:39; Barbeau 1950-51), which must represent the Halkomelem šxʷə́məcən, "fisher," an animal that does not live on Vancouver Island (Cowan and Guiguet 1965: 308). I have been told of cleansing rites using several kinds of stuffed animals. But the most detailed information was given to Jenness (1955:72-73) by Old Pierre on the use of stuffed fishers. In this rite they cleansed a dead youth by climbing up a pole set up to represent him or cleansed a pubescent girl by climbing up and down her body. Thus the posts show the animals only and those that show them climbing on a human figure may both commemorate a cleansing rite. The posts that show a human being holding a single animal may have some other significance.

At Musqueam there were once posts that are much harder to interpret. In 1963 I showed photographs of

Fig. 4:10. Exterior houseposts at Quamichan. The weasel-like animals on these posts are associated with curing ceremonies.

them to older people at Musqueam but could learn nothing about them. These are posts that were collected at Musqueam in 1898 by Harlan I. Smith for the American Museum (*Fig. 4:11*). According to a note in the museum's catalogue, three stood in the house of "Kaplänux, the old chief." The people I talked with thought this most likely; that would have been Capilano the Second, the son of the First, who was the famous warrior portrayed by the post mentioned earlier. A catalogue note that may refer to post 16/4652 reads:

> Top row of circles they say represents stars, then moon, sun, then row of stars. The sun with moon it in. Below represents ancestors who taught them of sun, moon, and stars—a carved woman.

Perhaps somewhere a Smith journal note will tell more. Two other posts (*Fig. 4:12*) (16/7947 and 16/7948) that evidently came from the same house portray, among other things, two-headed creatures that are probably the s⁷i·łqəy or s⁷ínəłqəy, the two-headed serpent, which is as important in Coast Salish traditions as its Kwakiutl counterpart is in theirs. It is a very important source of vision power for a shaman. But it also appears in a Musqueam legend

Fig. 4:11. Houseposts collected in 1898 at Musqueam.

Fig. 4:12. Houseposts from Musqueam dating to 1898. The lower post has since disappeared.

that accounts for the winding stream that ran through the village and the growth of rushes that gives the village its name and symbolizes the capacity of the Musqueam to multiply again after a catastrophe. The being holding the two-headed serpent (on 16/7948) may be thunder, also an important figure in Coast Salish tradition and a source of shamanistic power. But in view of the absence of representations of shaman's visions generally in the Halkomelem area, it seems more likely that these represent something else.

Another post that Smith photographed at Musqueam with the previous three seems to have disappeared, perhaps through someone's censorship (*Fig. 4:12*). It was a striking piece of sculpture that, informants agree, must have represented a man being attacked anally by a giant "lizard." In Central Coast Salish belief, this "lizard" (to judge from one description, probably really a salamander, the Pacific newt), if stepped over in the woods, will follow you home, creep into your bed and attack you in this fashion, ultimately destroying you from within. But why should this kind attack be portrayed, with a giant "lizard" as the attacker, on a house post? Did this post belong to a shaman or ritualist who could remove the intrusive amphibian? Or did it belong to someone who could direct one to attack an enemy? And did the owner have this post covered except on festive occasions?

At the time of first contact with Europeans, the Central Coast Salish disposed of the dead in wooden coffins and in canoes set up in graveyards. In some places, at least, the coffins were decorated with carvings and in some places carved figures were set up as monuments. As Duff (1952:51) points out, in 1808 Simon Fraser saw "tombs" carved with "figures of birds and beasts" near Yale, where the Halkomelem and Thompsom met. In 1847 Kane sketched a single human figure standing beside a group of graves at Port Angeles in Clallam country (Harper 1971:251, Fig.179). In 1854 Alden sketched a group of grave posts near Victoria. The sketch (Stenzel 1975:33, Pl.9) shows five human figures, two of which each hold a pair of animals and look very much like the house posts that seem to show purifying mustelids, while another is holding what looks like a cedar-bark hoop. (What appear to be the identical grave posts are shown in a watercolour, Pl.23, but the location is given as Departure Bay.)

Photographs taken by Harlan I. Smith in the late 1920's at Saanich and at Musqueam show grave carvings of animals and men holding animals. A carving (*Fig. 4:13*) that stood at Patricia Bay is described as a "grave figure of a man holding a scowmidgeon" (National Museum Neg. No. 72,843, caption on back of print). If this is the sxʷə́məcən used as in Old Pierre's description, the carving must represent a man being cleansed by having a stuffed fisher climb up his body. A grave box at Musequeam had four animals on its front and is probably the one men-

Fig. 4:13. Coast Salish grave monuments. *a* Carved board at Musqueam showing sturgeon. *b* Monument at Patricia Bay showing man with a scowmidgeon. *c* Carved grave box at Musqueam showing fishers (scowmidgeon).

tioned by Jenness (1954:73); according to Old Pierre, the ancestor of a village that merged with the Musqueam was given a fisher cleansing rite by the Transformer, but

> The last priest [ritualist], having no descendant to whom he might impart his knowledge, hired a skilled wood-carver to make him a coffin showing on one face four fishers in full relief. This coffin is now in the National Museum of Canada.

Above the slab with the animals, on this coffin, is a board decorated with concentric circles and cuneiforms, while below it is a longer board carved with a head at each end, forefeet and a scaly body; both boards are done in the style that appears on rattles and spindle whorls.

Another grave at Musqueam had on the upper part of its face a large board *(Fig. 13)* carved in low relief with a pair of sturgeons flanked by two larger creatures with snouts and ears, short legs, fish-like tails and dorsal fins and what seem to be fish-like backbones. I was told at Musqueam that the grave of a famous sturgeon fisherman had a sturgeon on it; this may be it. But I do not know what the flanking creatures might be.

Could some grave carvings represent visions? A few statements in the literature suggest it. Jenness (ms, p.66) says that the National Museum has "a carved wooden coffin depicting a man's guardian spirit flanked by two wolves," the coffin of a famous Saanich warrior who died early in the nineteenth century. But I have no indication of what the "guardian spirit" (vision) looks like. Hill-Tout, writing on the Chilliwack (1902:364-365) says

> On the exterior of the coffin were painted the family crests or totems, called *salúlia* (collective of *súlia*) = 'the dream objects'. Among these figured the bear, goat, and beaver. Human effigies roughly carved in wood were also sometimes placed nearby, similar to those found among the N'tlaka'pamuQ [Thompson].

When Hill-Tout writes "family crest" he is usually referring to the sxwayxwey or some comparable possession but the native term he gives is "vision", which is puzzling' but in general it is hard to disentangle Hill-Tout's ethnographic data from his theorizing about "totemism." Writing on the Chehalis of the Harrison River (his "StEélis"), Hill-Tout says informants told him that grave boxes were "never decorated with paintings or carvings of the *súlia* of the owner." But he supposes this to be because they had only recently adopted the practice of putting the dead in boxes or slab shelters.

As noted above, the Nooksack and the Lower (Douglas) Lillooet both set up grave monuments carved to represent the sxwayxwey. One of Fetzer's informants at Nooksack, a woman originally from Matsqui on the Fraser, said that "high-born" families had "totem-poles" called

Fig. 4:14. Twelve Coast Salish spindle whorls. *f* Katzie *i* Sardis *j* Chemainus *k* Becher Bay.

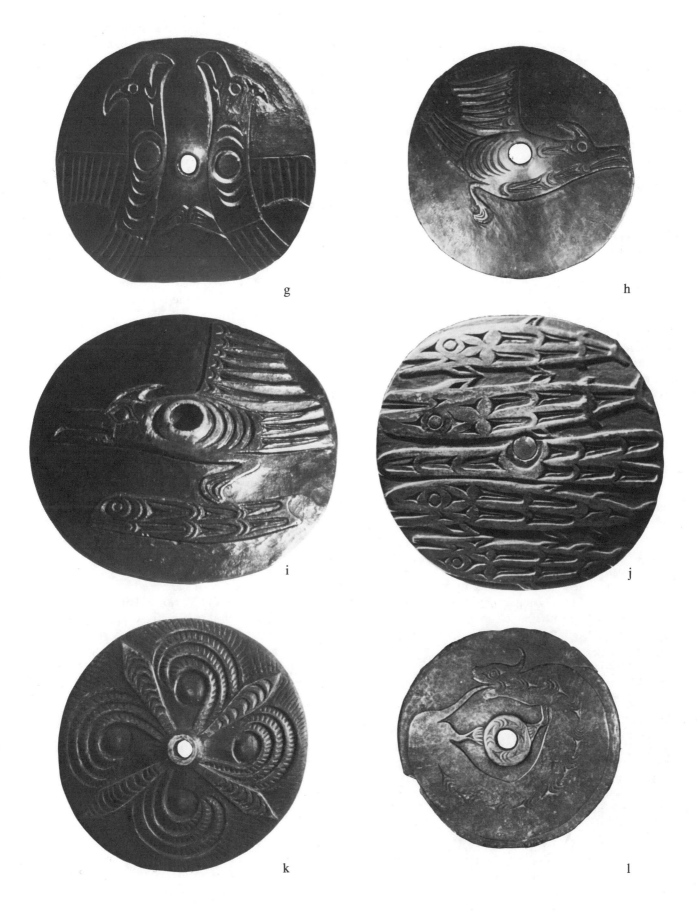

g

h

i

j

k

l

"sx̌ʷáyx̌ʷoi" (and described as sxwayxwey-like) set up at their graves, while other families had "totem-poles" with other things—"sometimes animals were used, especially those that are scarce (among these šx̌ʷomóc̓al, 'like otter but walks in the woods')." This animal would be the fisher. The informant did not mention any purifying function for either the sxwayxwey or the animals. But she told a myth accounting for the origin of the Matsqui "totem," presumably the sxwayxwey, unlike any other I know of: the people of a certain house swept it out with hemlock boughs; after many years a great pile of debris had accumulated away from the house, and the "totem" emerged out of this pile of sweepings. A purifier out of impurities? A cleanser to reward the cleanly?

The tools, weapons, canoes, etc. made by men and used by men seem to have been usually undecorated or decorated sparingly, e.g., an adze handle might bear just the suggestion of an animal form. Perhaps this was because of the association of skill and success with vision power and the dangers inherent in revealing or calling up the source of that power.

Household equipment of wood, such as boxes, buckets, dishes and spoons, things that were used by both sexes, were also usually undecorated. (The Museum of the American Indian has three decorated dishes, but one is said to have been used at a wedding; perhaps none is an ordinary household utensil.)

In contrast, implements made by men but used by women, such as mat creasers, spindle whorls, swords for beating wool, the posts of weaving frames ("looms"), etc. were often,though not always, decorated with carving and/or painting. These decorations included both geometric patterns and representations of birds, animals and people. (The women themselves, of course, produced geometric patterns on blankets, mats and baskets.) I have looked at one time or another at seventy or eighty spindle whorls. Some are wholly undecorated. A good many *(Fig. 4:14)* are decorated with simple curvilinear designs, either painted or incised in the surface that faces the spinner as she spins. And a number are decorated with incised representations of bird and/or animal figures or human figures with subordinate birds and/or animals. The design may be radially symmetrical or it may consist of a pair or quartet of creatures pursuing each other around the circle, a single animal chasing its tail or a single figure crossing the circle, facing either right or left. The direction of the spinning seems not to be relevant. In both composition and design elements these spindle whorl designs resemble the incised designs on the cleansing rattles. And as we have seen this is a style that also appears on some sxwayxwey masks and grave monuments.

How can we interpret this disparity in the decoration of implements? Why should men, or some men, be more interested in, or more willing to, decorate women's implements than their own? And why should they use what appears to be the most structured style on one particular article, the spindle whorl? Are the designs on the spindle whorls purely decorative, do they symbolize the power of the vision, or do they symbolize the power of the ritual word?

My guess is that the answers lie in the use to which these implements were put, producing that other, essential source of power and prestige—wealth. It seems unlikely that the designs are purely decorative, though the circular form of the whorl may have challenged the artist. It also seems unlikely that they represent vision power, though it is possible that the production of wealth gave the artist the courage to portray something he might not dare reveal elsewhere. Moreover, since he is not doing the spinning, he might portray his "superhuman friends and helpers" (Boas on p.184) without being constantly reminded of them. Could he create something relating to the spinner's vision power? As long as she is spinning it would be an invisible presence for her, reminding her only when she stopped and so driving her on. But I doubt this. The style on the spindle whorls is associated, on the rattles and on the masks and perhaps too on the grave monuments, with the power of the ritual word as used in purification. Ritual words may have played a part in the spinning and weaving processes, for example, the spinner may have recited them to the wool or to the spindle, but I have no information on this. There may, however, be a more direct association between spinning and purification. Mountain-goat wool, one of the substances spun though not the only one, seems to be itself associated with purification; it appears on the ritualist's rattle and on costumes worn by persons undergoing crisis rites, for example, the "new dancer" at the winter dance. It is white, like the feathers and down of the sxwayxwey. And it is the stuff of blankets, which are given out when the purifying rattles and masks are used.

(Laura Greenberg and Marjorie Halpin have suggested to me that a structuralist analysis would show a parallel between the rattle and the spindle whorl: both are involved in transformations, the rattle in the transforming of human beings from one state into another, the spindle whorl in the transforming of wool into wealth.)

Constraints on Productivity

Let me return to the question I started with. Why did the Central Coast Salish produce some great works of art yet neither the range of kinds of things nor the quantities of things produced farther north? Were there constraints at work here restricting and channelling productivity? It seems to me that there were. Clearly there were limits on the representation of visions ("guardian spirits"). In native theory, everyone (or every male perhaps) ought to "train" and have a vision. But it was dangerous to reveal too much about it. If you talked about it, you could "spoil" it; it might leave you or even make you sick or it could be taken away from you by an enemy shaman. Yet eventually you wanted others to know that you "had something." Probably all of us who have worked in the area have heard hints and half-revelations about what people "have." Possession by a song at the winter dance is, of course, evidence that you "have something" and the words of the song and movements of the dance may hint at what it is. But it must be tempting to hint in other ways, though dangerous to go too far.

Sources vary on the strength of the prohibition. Barnett (1955:146), referring to the whole of Georgia Strait from the Saanich and Musqueam northward, says flatly that visions were not concretely represented in carvings on house posts, etc., though they were portrayed in the song and dance. But this contradicts what Boas says for the Songhees and Hill-Tout for the Chilliwack. It is my impression, from both my own field work and this survey of the art of the area, that all are right. There were very likely differences within the region, perhaps especially between the Halkomelem and Straits areas, not of an absolute sort but statistical differences—in the frequency with which visions were concretely portrayed.

Farther south, in the Puget Sound region, visions were more commonly portrayed but still, I think, with constraints. The Puget Sound shaman's guardian-spirit figure used in the spirit-canoe ceremony, that seemingly crude stick of wood, was perhaps deliberately made stark and empty because it only hints at the secret, invisible, unique power of the shaman it belonged to. Probably asking the man who made it, "Why don't you produce the kind of explicit forms the Kwakiutl made?," would be like asking a Protestant who has just set up a rugged cross, "Why don't you decorate your church with all those nice plaster images the Catholics use?" The ideological difference is not really analogous but it may be as great.

The dangers that lie in portraying a vision too clearly may have affected artistic expression generally unless it was clearly identifiable with some other source of power. It may be that men refrained from decorating tools and weapons in order not to suggest even falsely the source of their vision powers. Or if they did decorate things they may have done so vaguely and ambiguously so that they could hint vaguely and ambiguously about what they had.

With art related to the power of the ritual word, the constraints must be different. The viewers of a rattle or mask know that its efficacy depends not on the private experience of a vision but the private knowledge of ritual words that have inherent power. That power cannot be diminished by concrete representation. You can lose it only through revealing (or forgetting) those carefully guarded words. Yet you may want to suggest their power or that you are the possessor of esoteric knowledge. The style that appears on the rattles and in the masks may be a useful medium for expressing this. (I am following a suggestion that Wilson Duff has made about the Northern art in supposing that it may imply esoteric knowledge.)

In the portrayal of ancestors there may have been a still different kind of constraint—fear of ridicule. When the man carved the house post at Musqueam portraying the ancestor confronting the bear, a Musqueam friend told me recently, he introduced something into the carving that was a covert insult to the subject. Whether this is true or not I do not know. Nor is the truth important for my argument. Covert insults were certainly a part of native life. When the sxwayxwey is dancing, an old Lummi friend told me years ago, if the dancer shifts his scallop-shell rattle even for a moment to his left hand it signals to the spectators who have received the proper "advice" that the person for whom they are dancing has some lower-class ancestry. In the old days, I suppose, a man thinking of having a carving made of an ancestor must have had to consider whether he had the wealth or influence to protect that carving from slurs. Probably no one was permanently safe from such slurs. In native society, leadership was specific to an activity; there were no all-purpose leaders and no great concentrations of authority. Perhaps few men could live without fear of ridicule.

I have tried to show how the people of one region had different forms of art related to different concepts and limited by different constraints. It appears to me that within the region there were local differences in the degree to which each of these concepts might be expressed, depending on the strength of fears about the harmful consequences of concrete representation versus desires for the useful consequences. These constraints are such that they may have varied in intensity through time and so may account for variations through time in kind and amount of artistic output. We need not, therefore, interpret qualitative or quantitative changes in prehistoric art as evidence of cataclysmic culture change or population replacement. They may have been the result of shifts in importance, back and forth, between the power of the vision and the power of the ritual word or shifts in the concentration of wealth and authority.

I am grateful for comments and suggestions from a number of people, including Harry Hawthorn, Marjorie Halpin, Pamela Amoss, Jay Miller, Darleen Fitzpatrick, Erna Gunther, Bill Holm (with whom I have discussed Salish art at length on several occasions), Randy Bouchard, Doe Kennedy and others, and for help with photographs from the National Museums of Canada, Lynn Maranda and the Vancouver Centennia Museum, Audrey Hawthorn, Madeline Bronsdon and Carol McLaren at the University of British Columbia, Peter Macnair and Allan Hoover at the Provincial Museum, Barbara Lane and most especially Doe Kennedy of the British Columbia Indian Language Project. I have also had much help from the Audio-Visual people at Portland State University.

CHAPTER 5

Styles of Coastal Rock Art

DORIS LUNDY

There are over six hundred rock art sites presently known along the Northwest Coast from southeastern Alaska through British Columbia to the Lower Columbia River and into Northern California. It is only in recent years that researchers have begun to comprehensively record these rock carvings and paintings and until this task is completed it is somewhat premature to attempt analysis. However, it is already quite clear that there is both tremendous variety and also a curious repetition in the rock art of this culture area. Recent research has isolated at least six major stylistic groups in Northwest Coast rock art, although there are, no doubt, others still to be recognized and examined and even these main categories need refining and redefining. The six styles are:

1 The Basic Conventionalized Style
2 The Classic (or Traditional) Conventionalized Style
3 The Columbia River Conventionalized Style
4 The Abstract Curvilinear Style
5 The Abstract Rectilinear Style
6 The Naturalistic Style

The terminology used in naming these styles is based upon that devised by Campbell Grant in 1967. He noted that all rock art could be stylistically classified into one of the three following categories:

1 Naturalistic
2 Conventionalized
3 Abstract

He interprets "naturalistic" to mean work done in a realistic or natural manner, while he interprets "conventionalized" to mean recognizable subjects rendered in a conventionalized or non-realistic manner. Finally, he interprets "abstract" as having little or no reference to the appearance of objects in nature.

The Basic Conventionalized Rock Art Style

A great majority of coastal rock art designs appear to bear obvious similarities to the traditional Northwest Coast art forms yet are different enough to warrant their being classified as stylistically separate. These designs differ in that they are simpler and less detailed than the classic designs and do not contain such traits as the fully developed Northwest Coast eye, or use of ovoids or formlines. Frederica de Laguna (1960:73) put it this way:

> That the interpretation of rock pictures by the natives is so often vague may perhaps be explained by the fact that the techniques of rock painting and carving are much cruder than those employed in ordinary wood painting and carving, so that the styles of the pictographs and petroglyphs, while related to those of traditional Northwest Coast art, are yet different.

Petroglyphs and pictographs like this, because they contain certain basics of the classic Northwest Coast art style, are here considered to form a Basic Conventionalized rock art style. This is a curvilinear style which makes considerable use of circles and smoothly curved connecting lines. Typical designs found in this category include circle faces, eyes, some coppers which retain the typical "copper" shape and contain internal decoration and anthropomorphic and zoomorphic figures having simple internal detail usually involving the ribs or backbone. The rib lines of these figures may be curved, straight, or composed of undulating parallel lines. The

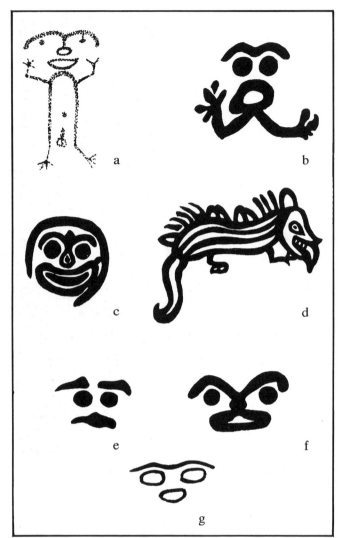

Fig. 5:1. Basic Conventionalized Rock Art Style. Design *a* is a pictograph from the central British Columbia coast. It is not drawn to scale. Design *b* is a petroglyph from the Prince Rupert area. The actual carving is about fifty centimeters in height. Design *c* is a petroglyph from the Bella Colla Valley and is not drawn to scale. Design *d* is a petroglyph from Vancouver Island drawn to a scale of one-half inch to one foot. Designs *e* through *g* are petroglyphs of the northern Northwest Coast. They are not to scale.

backbone is usually a simple straight line. Anthropomorphic and zoomorphic heads are almost always of exaggerated proportions and the less detailed bodies may be depicted in either a squatting or straight-legged position. This style appears to be the one most commonly encountered along the coast especially where petroglyphs are concerned, and its intrinsic relationship to the classic art cannot be overstressed. At a great many sites especially of the northern coast, it is really simplified classic style. At a few sites of the southern coast, notably in the Nootka linguistic region it is so simplified as to become almost a parody.

Any style spread over such a great distance as the Northwest Coast is bound to develop substyles and local characteristics confined to specific parts of the coast. A few of the more outstanding substyles are briefly discussed although there are many others.

Open Trunk-line Substyle

At some petroglyph sites there are depictions of anthropomorphic figures having open-trunk bodies. That is, the outlines of the neck and torso continue, without meeting, to form the lines of the legs. These leg lines terminate in three to five toed feet and they may be either straight or upraised in the "squatting" position. Arm and hand lines branch off at appropriate places although there are no shoulders and while no backbone or ribs are depicted the sex sign is indicated in all but three instances. This form of the basic style appears to be confined to that region of the coast between Bella Bella and southwestern Vancouver Island. Figure 5:1a illustrates an example of this type.

No Body Substyle

Another somewhat unusual method in anthropomorphic designs involves the depiction of arm lines which are attached directly or nearly so to head lines without the benefit of either shoulders or, in most cases, necks. They may join on to the lines of the mouth if the face is non-outlined, or into the "chin" line of the lower jaw. Usually, the faces involved are circle faces. This is no local design trait; it is to be found from the territory of the Tsimshian through that of Bella Coola and Kwakitul and into that of the Coast Salish. It is likely that this method of depiction is connected to the widespread preference already noted which results in exaggerated heads and de-emphasized bodies. Figure 5:1b illustrates an example of this type.

Straight or Undulating Interior Lines Substyle

One striking characteristic of some petroglyph sites of Southern Vancouver Island is the presence of parallel horizontal undulating lines decorating the bodies of nearly all of the zoomorphs. Internal decoration is common in both Classic and Basic styles but it is usually placed vertically in the body or radiates out from a central backbone. Figure 5:1d illustrates an example of this type.

Outlined and Non-outlined Circle Faces Substyle

These simple faces are one of the most commonly encountered designs of the Northwest Coast rock art. They vary from simple pairs of matched pit or circle eyes to groups of three pits or circles forming two eyes and a mouth. More elaborate faces are sometimes created with the addition of an outline, ears, a nose and forms of head

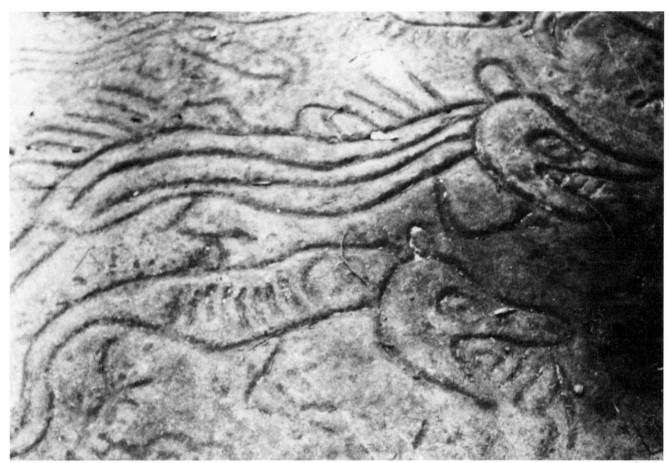

Fig. 5:2. Basic Conventionalized Rock Art. Style. The simple, skeletal structure of these zoomorphs from southern Vancouver Island is typical of designs in this style.

decoration. These face designs occur all along the North-west Coast, but are most commonly encountered in the north. Figure 5:1c, e, f, g, illustrate examples of this type.

The Basic style is well distributed all along the coast. It also spreads inland along the major river systems. It occurs up to the Nass River at least as far as Canyon City and up the Skeena to Kispiox. It is found along the deeply indented inlets of the Bella Coola region and on up the Bella Coola Valley, and is known on the Fraser River at least as far inland as the Lytton-Lillooet region. This inland spreading up the rivers can be clearly seen along the Columbia as well, where the Basic style has been noted on deeply carved riverside boulders in the Portland area and upstream past the Dalles where the Northwest Coast cultural influences are generally held to weaken. This spread of coastal artistic traits along major navigable rivers is only to be expected since these waterways were communication routes of the past; routes which served to distribute cultural traits and ideas within and outside of cultural boundaries.

The Basic Rock Art Style of the Northwest Coast appears to be related in part to the stone sculpture complexes of the Fraser River, Gulf of Georgia and Columbia River systems. Duff (1956:144; 1975:49, 112) has illustrated several pieces of sculpture which contain traits also found in Basic rock art carvings and paintings. He has commented that the stone sculpture complex hints of the classic art style known from northern wood carvings and he suggests that the stone sculpture complex of the Lower Fraser and Gulf of Georgia may have been an ancestral art form:

> The stone sculpture complex is best regarded as an early Northwest Coast art form. In style it seems closely related to the wood sculpture of the Kwakiutl and northern tribes, or, more exactly, to the basic Wakashan style which underlies the classic Northwest Coast style of these tribes. It shows less resemblance to recent Salish wood sculpture, which suggests that the latter must represent a decline or change since the climax period of the stone sculpture. It is possible that many of the basic features of the Northwest Coast style were worked out first on the soapstone carvings and then transferred to wood, so that in this sense the stone sculpture complex may be an ancestral Northwest Coast art form (1956:114).

The rock art designs in the Basic Style also fit in with this conclusion in that they hint of the classic art and may have preceded it. They may perhaps be considered to be another form of the stone sculpture complex, co-existing with it, at least in the southern part of the Northwest Coast. However, the wide coherent spread of the rock art designs of the Basic style also suggests that this style is a part of an even earlier stratum that loaned to or shared with the stone sculpture complex such traits as circled eyes and faces, ribbed anthropomorphic and zoomorphic figures with large heads and so on. These older traits would persist along with the stone sculpture and later traditional or classic art forms.

On the Columbia River too, a case can be made for relating the local stone sculpture there to the Basic Rock Art Style, since it is similar to art pieces from Butler's (1957:164) Middle Period of Lower Columbia prehistory (6500 years ago to around A.D. 500). The sculpture of this period contained massive zoomorphic and anthropomorphic pieces with prominent circle eyes, ribs and other such features.

It is likely that the Basic Northwest Coast rock art style is an early style at least on the Columbia and Fraser Rivers and perhaps by inference along much of the rest of the coast. There are several reasons for suggesting this possibility:

1. The Basic Style has a wide geographical distribution, along the Northwest Coast and into parts of Siberia. Such a distribution suggests a respectable time span. A few zoomorphic rock carvings of Vancouver Island are similar to an excavated piece from Prince Rupert Harbour (GbTo 23:850) dated to around A.D. 800. (*Fig. 6:13a* this volume.)

2. The Basic Style seems to belong "hand-in-hand" with the Coast Abstract Curvilinear Style (discussed later) especially the pit and groove designs. This particular style also occurs from Siberia through the coast and well into the heart of the North American continent in the Great Basin and Southwestern cultural areas in particular. Campbell Grant (1967) and other researchers regard the pit and groove designs of the Great Basin as being one of the oldest rock art complexes in North America.

3. The Basic Style is remarkably coherent wherever it occurs. Some designs of Siberia are strikingly similar to others from British Columbia. Okladnikov (1971: 113, 114, etc.) illustrates numerous examples of mask-like circle faces and other curvilinear designs which compare closely with examples from the Coast and which are dated to the Siberian Neolithic.

4. The Basic Style contains similarities to pieces that form part of the old stone sculpture complex isolated by Duff (1956) and which he feels to be an early art complex of the coast, ancestral perhaps to the classic

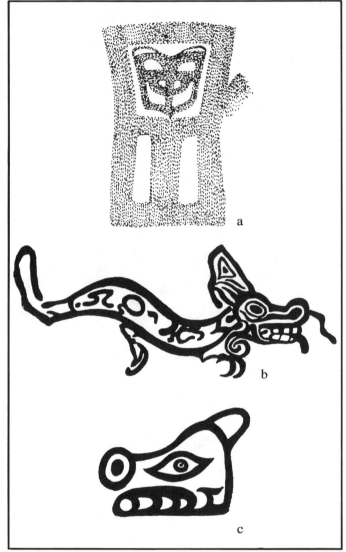

Fig. 5:3. Classic Conventionalized Rock Art Style. Design *a* a pictograph from the Fisher Channel area is not drawn to scale. Design *b* a petroglyph from southern Vancouver Island is not to scale. Design *c* a petroglyph from southeastern Alaska is not to scale.

wood art of the northern coast.

5. The Basic Style is also quite similar to pieces of Columbia River stone sculpture which, according to Butler (1957:161-165) are dated to the Middle Riverine Period of habitation near the Dalles about 6500 years ago to around A.D. 500. (The Columbia River style into which category some other rock art can be placed, appears to belong to a much later period.)

6. Finally, if the unique Columbia River art style (discussed below) did evolve from a mixing of coastal and interior styles as some researchers believe (Strong, Schenck and Steward 1930:143) then it is logical to

Fig. 5:4. Classic Conventionalized Rock Art Style. This pictograph overlooking a trade route of the Lower Skeena River was painted in the 1880's by the Tsimpsian artist Lequate. The portrait is of Chief Legaik and was commissioned by the chief to symbolize his control over the territory. The pictograph contains several traits identified with traditional Northwest Coast art.

assume that the coastal partner in this merging be the Basic Style since it is to be found along the Columbia while the only other coastal style that is suitable (the classic) does not. It is then also logical to assume that the Basic Style be initially present before becoming so modified to form the Columbia River Style.

All of this is not to say that all rock art designs of the Basic Style are automatically older than those of any other style, but that they are depicted in a style which may be an early form and which did spread over a great distance and which may have persisted for a long time on the Northwest Coast.

Classic Conventionalized Rock Art Style

This style is essentially the same as historic Northwest Coast art as known from wood and argillite carvings and from paintings. This is a highly conventionalized style,

making great use of curvilinear lines, usually formlines which taper into ovoids. The subjects, usually anthropomorphic or zoomorphic are depicted with much decorative, inner detail including circles to mark joints, or vertebrae and other "fillers." The heads are broad and exaggerated in size. The distinctive, realistic Northwest Coast eye form may be present. Anthropomorphic figures are commonly shown in a "squatting" position with knees and elbows bent.

The Classic rock art style is more commonly encountered among petroglyphs of the northern coast where it is associated with display or crest signs on rocks to mark territorial boundaries or to indicate the owner's rights to certain resources or privileges. Designs in the Classic style occur as far south, although rarely, as the Nanaimo and Squamish-Musqueam territories of the Coast Salish linguistic area. Figure 5:3 illustrates examples of the Classic rock art style.

Fig. 5:5. Columbia River Conventionalized Rock Art Style, Design *a* of the face of Tsagaglalal is a petroglyph from the Long Narrows region of the Columbia River. Scale is one-half inch to one foot. Design *b* a painted petroglyph of the same face is also from along the Columbia River but is not to scale.

Columbia River Conventionalized Rock Art Style

The Columbia River art style is found only along the Lower Columbia River from the area of the Long Narrows to that of Portland. It is characterized by the following features: the "grinning" anthropomorphic face, often heart-shaped, with eyebrows well defined and continuing

together to form the nose line. Eyes are almond-shaped and represented by two concentric lines. A curved cheek line is frequently added. The mouth is of exaggerated proportions, crescent shaped and is usually depicted as open, revealing teeth and a protuding tongue. The river style often contains a single large tooth in the lower jaw which, with the heavily circled eyes gives the appearance of an old person's face. Headdresses if present are elaborate with zigzag or straight parallel lines for decoration and often a "comb" added. The body is less detailed than the head, but ribs are always prominent. The coastal portion is represented by conventionalized appearance, the large head, prominent circled eyes and skeletal body, while the plateau portion seems to be represented by the use of the zigzag or straight or angular lines. (The zigzag while not unknown in coastal art is comparatively rare.) Strong, Schenck and Steward in 1930 interpreted the style as a unique blending of the art from down river with a more geometric art from upstream. It is generally agreed that the down river or coastal influences predominated. There are several examples of rock art sites containing designs of this stylistic category. Butler in 1957 placed all such designs into his Late Period which he dated from between A.D. 500 to about 1850.[1] During this period the carving of stone and antler reached a peak. Examples of this art in the form of cremation carvings of bone and stone have been recovered from excavations. One design commonly encountered was the grinning face of an old woman "Tsagaglalal," known as "she who watches." This design occurs in rock art as both a petroglyph and a combination site in the Long Narrows area. Another common design trait is the skeletal human figure which prompted one researcher (Strong 1945) to suggest that it indicated the presence of a comparatively recent death or ghost cult. However, this does not seem to be the case since such ribbed figures appear to be a very old, widespread stylistic trait beginning with the Basic Rock Art Style and becoming transferred on the Columbia River to the more recent Columbia River Rock Art Style. Figure 5:5 illustrates two examples of this style, and Figure 5:6 is a photograph of Tsagaglalal.

Abstract Curvilinear Rock Art Style

Designs of this category appear to co-exist along with those of the conventionalized forms, in particular, the Basic Rock Art style. The Abstract Curvilinear Style is widely but sparsely distributed along the coast and appears to link up with the pit and groove designs and style of the American Great Basin and Southwestern cultural

---

[1]Pettigrew (1975:5) has refined this period as falling between A.D. 500 and 1250.

Fig. 5:6. Tsagaglalal. Columbia River Conventionalized Rock Art Style. This painted petroglyph from the Dalles area of the Columbia River resembles traditional Northwest Coast art with its tapering, curving lines. The use of concentric eye lines and single-toothed mouth are local design traits.

areas. Many designs of this style are simple symbols, others are complex and interconnected—all are based upon the circle and curved line. Figures 5:7 and 5:8 illustrate examples of this style.

Abstract Rectilinear Rock Art Style

This style is most commonly encountered in pictographs of the central and southern British Columbia coast. Designs are abstract, based upon the straight rather than curved line and include many geometric symbols such as crosses, forked lines, rayed circles and so on. Figure 5:9 illustrates examples of this style.

Naturalistic Rock Art Style

This style contains depictions of animals, humans and objects rendered in a natural or at least easily recognizable manner. This is not a common style and it appears most often along the southern parts of the coast in particular among petroglyphs of the Dalles-Deschutes region. Designs are usually small, simple humans or animals solidly painted or abraded — with no inner or decorative detail. Often designs appear to be clustered into scenes and action is frequently indicated. Horsemen are a common design — suggesting that the style continued late or else was never very old. Figures 5:10, 11 illustrate examples of this style.

In subject, techniques of manufacture, and over-all appearance the Abstract Rectilinear and the Naturalistic

Fig. 5:7. Abstract Curvilinear Rock Art Style. Design *a* is a petroglyph from the Columbia River. Design *b,* also a Columbia River carving.

Fig. 5:8. Abstract Curvilinear Rock Art Style. These "pits" and "cups" and simple abstract designs based upon the circle occur all along the Northwest Coast as well as in all neighbouring culture areas. This site is located in southeast Alaska.

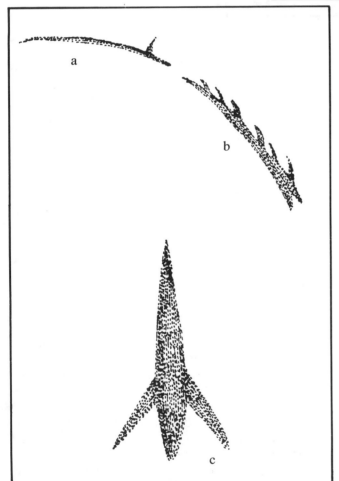

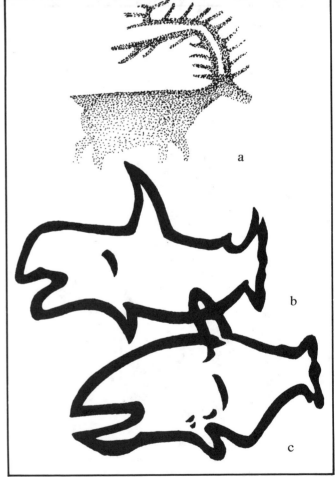

Fig.5:9. Abstract Rectilinear Rock Art Style. Designs *a* and *b* are pictographs from the Jervis Inlet area. They are not drawn to scale. Design *c* is a pictograph from the Fraser Valley. The actual painting is about thirty cm in height.

Fig. 5:10. Naturalistic Rock Art Style. Design *a* is a pictograph from the Columbia River. It is not drawn to scale. Designs *b* and *c* are petroglyphs from the western coast of Vancouver Island drawn to a scale of one inch to one foot.

Fig. 5:11. Naturalistic Rock Art Style. This pictograph of an elk from the Lower Columbia River is easily identified as to subject by the simple design and distinct antlers.

art styles resemble closely the rock art of the Interior plateaus of British Columbia, Washington and Oregon. Just as the conventionalized coastal art styles advanced into interior territories along rivers and inlets so these styles seem to intrude upon the predominantly conventionalized and curvilinear artistic regions of the coast.

Border areas are apparent. In many coastal sites styles of both coast and interior lie side by side. Such border areas include the Bella Coola Valley, Lillooet-Lytton region and Dalles-Deshutes region. Often a single design may combine both coastal and interior stylistic traits.

The southern British Columbia coast — where rock art sites have been fairly well recorded over the years — present a distribution pattern which is stylistically interesting. On Vancouver Island petroglyphs in Basic Style predominate — far outnumbering the few examples of Classic and other styles. However on the opposing mainland pictographs are far more numerous and they are in Basic, Abstract, Rectilinear and Naturalistic styles. It is almost as though the spread of later interior rock art styles onto the predominately conventionalized curvilinear coast was begun and not completed before rock paintings and carvings were no longer made on the Northwest Coast.

CHAPTER 6

Prehistoric Art of the Northern Northwest Coast

GEORGE MacDONALD

In the past decade a major critical reassessment of the artistic heritage of the world by anthropologists and art historians has resulted in a major new status for arts of the Northwest Coast. Events affecting this reassessment have been occurring across a broad range of activities, ranging from stylistic analysis of ethnographic Northwest Coast art (Holm 1965) to archaeological activity which has yielded a surprising time depth for the styles of the coast. Major museum exhibitions, international travelling shows, the entrée to fine art galleries, the major renovations of museum exhibits and the dramatic surge of evaluations of historic art pieces have all provided inspiration to native artists in the revival of traditional art forms resulting in new directions for the styles of the area. This reevaluation is most clearly stated in the now famous words of Claude Lévi-Strauss at the opening of the Masterworks of Canadian Indian and Eskimo Art Show in Paris in 1967:

I consider that the culture of the Northwest Coast Indians produced an art on a par with that of Greece or Egypt. *(Time Magazine)*

Lévi-Strauss elaborated this view to an international audience in his 1975 work on Northwest Coast art and mythology, *La Voie Des Masques.*

Although the enhanced status of Northwest Coast art affects all of the tribes on the coast, it is particularly the tribes of the northern coast, the Haida, Tsimshian and Tlingit, who produced the classic expressions of the Northwest Coast art tradition. This assessment is confirmed in exhibitions, museum and gallery displays, and is very evident in the world art market. Interest in archaeology and prehistoric sites on the coast has also been enhanced by this development, but it is painfully evident in reviewing the archaeological evidence from the northern Northwest Coast that much more work needs to be done before we can comment realistically on the problems of origin and development of the art of that area. Nevertheless, some major trends may be outlined and dated.

The following summary is based primarily on the archaeological information available from Prince Rupert Harbour and a few sites excavated on the Skeena River. Brief comparisons are also made to the limited material from the Queen Charlotte Islands. Despite the fact that roughly twenty thousand artifacts have been recovered from the Prince Rupert Harbour, scarcely more than 100 throw any light on stylistic development. Most of these artifacts are no more than fragments. Efforts to synthesize the situation on the Queen Charlotte Islands present even greater difficulties. The important work of Fladmark (1970a, 1970b) on the early lithic sites provides no examples of artistry since organic remains, including bone, are missing from the sites. Similarly the reported work of Fladmark (1973) and Gessler and Gessler (1974) on later Haida archaeology are too close to contact to provide insights into development of artistic traditions over a long span of time. The report on excavations at Blue Jackets Creek by Severs (1974) covering the period from 5000 to 2000 B.P., is indeed relevant, but is only preliminary.

The principal information presented here comes from nine excavated sites in the Prince Rupert Harbour, namely:

GbTo 23	Garden Island site
GbTo 18	Dodge Island site
GbTo 31	Boardwalk site
GbTo 30	Parizeau Point site

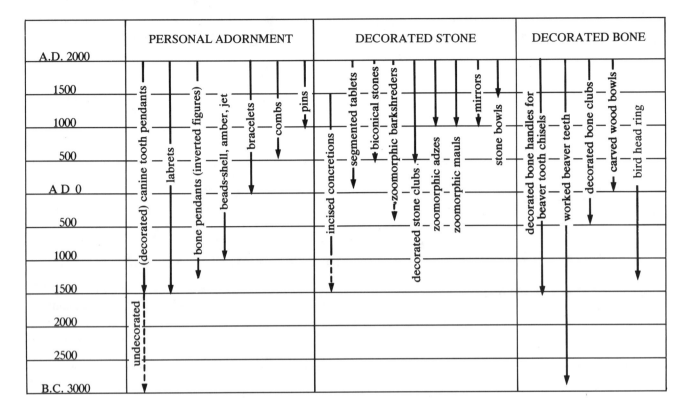

Fig. 6:1. Temporal occurrence of selected art objects from the Tsimshian area.

GcTo 1   'Knu site
GbTn 1   Grassy Bay Site
GbTo 33   Lachane site
GbTo 36   Baldwin site
GbTo 34   Kitandach site

Another major problem is the lack of radiocarbon dates from all sites which would allow precise dating of the artifacts in question. Many sites, for example GbTo 18 and GbTo 34, have only basal dates, and others such as GcTo 1 and GbTo 30 have no dates at all. The best dated site is GbTo 31, with twenty-four dates, ranging throughout the 4500 years the site was occupied. Unfortunately, only a few dozen fragments of art works came from this site. A review of the decorated artifacts in terms of earliest occurrences will provide a general picture of the data base available *(Fig. 6:1)*. The earliest remains from the Prince Rupert Harbour are almost 5000 years old. The following basal dates for four sites have been determined for the fifth millenium before present:

GbTo 34 4965 ± 95 years B.P.
GbTo 18 4790 ± 100 years B.P.
GbTo 33 4630 ± 105 years B.P.
GbTo 31 4230 ± 220 years B.P.

Between 3000 B.C. and 1500 B.C. there is evidence of personal decoration in the form of perforated canine teeth of various species, mostly of sea otter, but also bear, seal and sea lions. While the presence or absence of these items in graves may indicate status differentiation between individuals, they contribute little of significance for the delineation of artistic traditions. It is worth noting, however, that the key features of North Coast culture in other terms are clearly evident during this period. The economic pattern is established for the exploitation of fish runs in the rivers, and the extensive use of intertidal resources, along with land and sea mammal hunting. Although population density is not as large as in later periods, the settlement pattern is well established and most of the same sites continue to be occupied until the contact period in the Prince Rupert Harbour.

What is significant in terms of art is that the cultural pattern appears to be coalescing during this initial period. Symbolic modes of graphic expression have not emerged. Certainly to judge from available archaeological evidence, a distinctive coastal style did not begin to crystalize until about 1500 B.C. We can only infer that the accumulation of historical and mythological traditions by the corporate lineages of northern coast villages was approaching the threshold where graphic symbols of corporate identity became meaningful. Implicit here is the assumption that graphic symbolism expressed in art works, requires a base of shared cognitive modes, belief systems, etc., which must develop to a certain point, perhaps over several millenia, before it can be meaningfully expressed in art works. After 1500 B.C. it is possible to describe artistic development in terms of 500 year periods.

1500 B.C. – 1000 B.C.

About 1500 B.C. the first decorated tools appear, represented in the archaeological record by a decorated antler for a beaver tooth carving chisel. This would imply that finely finished carvings were probably being made, although none have survived. In terms of decorative personal effects a few canine tooth pendants have incised motifs and the first labrets appear. By 1000 B.C. siltstone concretions modified with incised ribs, joint marks, vertebral columns and other features indicate the first evidence for an animal style of art emphasizing skeletal parts. This style subsequently produces the emphasis on certain parts of animals in repetitive patterns that become very important later on. A number of beach finds of incised concretions probably relate to this period though they have not been reported from the Queen Charlotte Islands.

Between 1500 and 1000 B.C., curiously shaped bone pendants are first noted which occur with increasing frequency, and in a greater variety of forms (in later levels). The basic form is a flat bone pendant with two parts: a blade-like lower zone and an upper zone perforated at the top for suspension with knob-like appendages on either side. Although simple in appearance, the subsequent elaboration and frequency within datable contexts makes this one of the most interesting of decorative forms from the entire sequence. The single occurrence of a peculiar carved bone object is worth noting for this period 1500-1000 B.C. It is a fragment of an openwork carving which I believe bears a strong similarity to the openwork bone birds' heads from the Fraser Delta (as illustrated in Stewart, 1973:143).

1000 B.C.-500 B.C.

By 500 B.C. numerous other types of personal decoration occur in graves at the Boardwalk site. These include shell disc beads (which also occur in the burials at Blue Jackets Creek on the Queen Charlotte Islands), and beads of amber, dentalium and jet. Copper ornaments from this series of graves (Area A) include bracelets, earrings and tubes of sheet copper wrapped around a wooden core. There is some evidence that these copper tubes were found in direct association with a large basalt dagger and three different types of clubs. Decorated clubs of bone make a dramatic appearance at this time. They include one made from a jaw of a killer whale and one of whale rib which is strangely reminiscent of the ethnographic Nootka whalebone clubs.

The earliest direct evidence for the elaborate stone clubs in the Prince Rupert Harbour, which Duff (1963) called "the Skeena River club style," does not occur until about A.D. 1. Since only a single dated example has been found, I anticipate future finds should date back to about 500 B.C. Severs (pers. comm. 1976) reports a stone club in this style from Blue Jackets Creek between A.D. 1 and 500 B.C. At present A.D. 1 marks the beginning of a tradition of much more elaborate pecked and ground stone artifacts in the Prince Rupert area to which is added over the succeeding millenium and a half, all of the other elaborate pecked and ground forms.

The suggestions that stone clubs should eventually be found at 500 B.C. is reinforced by the occurrence around that time of skulls with depression fractures which match closely the knob-like butts of the stone clubs (Cybulski n.d.). Presumably the clubs were used in two ways: by delivering a blow with the blade, and by using the knob of the butt in a dagger-like fashion. A high incidence of forearm fractures (Cybulski n.d.), beginning at this time appear to relate to attempts to protect the head with the forearm which took the blow. There is further evidence at 500 B.C. of trophy-head collecting and the use of sections of human skulls as amulets. The emphasis on weaponry noted at this time coincides with the brief appearance of status grave goods that may relate to increased differentiation of rank. The development of ranked social status may also explain the concentration of materials imported over considerable distances, such as copper, obsidian, jet, amber and dentalium that may also indicate expanding trade relationships. A moderate degree of hostility is suggested by burial remains at this time, but this requires much further investigation. In any event, there is some evidence of marked intra-village, and possibly intra-tribe, hostility which carries with it an elaboration of decorative elements and weaponry.

500 B.C.-A.D. 1

In the interval between 500 B.C. and the time of Christ, ribbed and segmented stone forms occur in Prince Rupert and at Blue Jackets Creek that have no apparent function. They are usually of sandstone or slate and are generally small (under 10 cm.). I have called them amulets for want of a better term. Their main characteristic is the segments into which they are divided by sawing or incising. They are usually tabular in shape, divided by a longitudinal line (or lines) into zones that are further segmented at right angles into multiple bars or rings.

By A.D. 1 new types of decorated objects are clearly present in the deposits. A most interesting new form of personal decoration is the bent bone bracelet with elaborate engraved designs. Although minor examples of engraving on bone occur earlier, bracelets provide a relatively frequent class that are amenable to more systematic analysis of motifs. The motifs are entirely geometric and bear close resemblance to Tlingit bracelets noted in ethnographic collections. Engraved bands occur elsewhere on the coast and in the Fraser River area and are frequently called brow bands, presumably based on ethno-graphic parallels from that region. Severs (1974) reports two caribou metapodials with elaborate geometric decoration from Blue Jackets Creek at a much earlier estimated date of between 1000 and 500 B.C.

Several new categories of pecked and ground stone forms which are characteristic of the North Coast are clearly present in the Prince Rupert area by the time of Christ. Bark shredders with occasional zoomorphic designs and the enigmatic biconical stones appear. Drucker (1943:57) suggested that the later forms may have been used as plank smoothers with rope handles looped around the knob-like ends. The purpose of smoothing planks is thought to be in order to prepare them for painted decoration.

A.D. 1-A.D. 500

Between A.D. 1 and A.D. 500 there is evidence in the Prince Rupert area of a wide variety of wooden objects which were preserved due to the chance occurrence of an extensive waterlogged deposit at the Lachane site. This site was salvaged by a National Museum of Man team in 1973 (Inglis 1974). Occurring in the deposit were wooden boxes, bowls, weapon shafts, wedges, adze and chisel handles, basketry, canoe paddles, etc., that were mostly undecorated but which clearly established a technology in perishable organic material such as wood and bark, that is little different from ethnographic times. Considerable basketry was recovered from the deposit, some with simple decorative weaving but will not be discussed in this paper (Croes n.d.). Of particular interest, however, is a carved wooden handle, with two square peg attachments, which was possibly the handle of a bowl lid.

A.D. 500-A.D. 1000

There are no new art forms or decorated objects appearing at the A.D. 500 level in any sites, although all the previous forms continue through this period. About A.D. 800 the first combs appear which bear the earliest combination of stylistic features that can be considered as classic Northwest Coast style.

At A.D. 1000 another major occurrence of new forms is noted. In the category of personal decoration are bone pins with animal or human head finials. Zoomorphic labrets, though rare, make their appearance about A.D. 1100. Only three such labrets are known from the Prince Rupert Harbour and only one is from a datable context. All three have bird head decorations.

About A.D. 1000 a style of zoomorphic decoration applied to mauls and adzes is clearly present, although plain mauls and adzes occur a few centuries earlier. The zoomorphic forms are large-eyed, large-mouth creatures which cannot be identified as to species but seem to suggest frogs, wolves, birds and possibly fish. Although the earliest dated stone bowl fragment does not occur until circa A.D. 1500, the style of zoomorphic decoration on a number of undated finds relates to the same zoomorphic style that appears on mauls and adzes about A.D. 1000.

A final type that occurs at this period is the slate mirror. Only two are from archaeological context, and one of these is a surface find. There are, however, numerous examples in ethnographic collections. They are all humanoid in form, with a head and body zone and highly abstract legs and arms.

A.D. 1000 - Contact

The period from A.D. 1000 to contact is relatively devoid of new forms in the archaeological deposits. It appears that by A.D. 1000 all of the major elements of northwest coast art were in place, at least to judge from the preserved remains. No doubt changes were taking place in art styles applied to carved and painted wood, but of these there is no archaeological evidence.

The above statement on prehistoric art from the North Coast is concerned simply with first occurrences of objects relevant to questions of style, motifs and iconography, as well as to some of the questions of their broader chronological and cultural context. Once again I would stress that the small sample sizes for many forms, often only one or two examples, means that the date for first occurrences must be considered as minimal. For example, much eroded antler combs with traces of decoration have been found in a context on the Queen Charlotte Islands which date more than a thousand years earlier than do combs from the Prince Rupert area (Severs: pers. comm. 1977). The elaborateness of style integration even in the earliest finds, slate mirrors, for example, would suggest further that the use of decoration will eventually be found to be much earlier. The interpretation of dates from levels associated with the objects under consideration has also been handled in a conservative fashion. It should also be remembered that many interesting developments in various forms take place after their initial occurrence. Each category will be considered as a sub-tradition, and the variations through time associated with each will be examined. Since most pieces have not been published previously, it is necessary to include some description.

The description and analysis of decorated artifacts which follows is presented on the basis of the relative frequency and importance of the various items to the question of style definition and dating. They are mostly from the sites in the Prince Rupert Harbour, and are drawn from approximately 20,000 artifacts recovered by National Museum of Man projects between 1966 and 1973. As such the remains are then representative of Tsimshian culture in particular. Decorated bone will be examined first, since it represents the earliest decorated remains and is relatively abundant. It is also relevant to the problem of social status in the early cultures of the

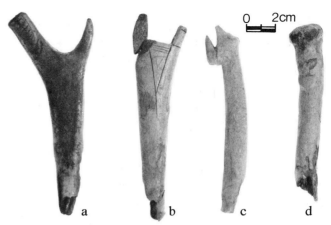

Fig. 6:2. Antler handles.

northern coast. Various classes of decorated stone artifacts occur generally later in time, with new forms introduced within the last few millennia, and these will be described next. Finally, wood objects and rock art will be briefly described as special categories.

Decorated Bone and Antler

Antler Chisels

Five antler handles recovered from the excavations in the Prince Rupert area are decorated. Four are described below. The earliest example *(Fig. 6:2d)* dates circa 1500 B.C. It is a slightly modified deer antler with a roughly carved human face. The next example *(Fig. 6:2c)* circa A.D. 1, is also of deer antler but much more extensively modified. The decoration consists of an animal head, which to judge by the short muzzle, small ears and powerful jaw, is a bear. Indications of ribs are carved along the grip of the chisel. The third example *(Fig 6:2b)* is from a yet undated matrix and is decorated in an abstract design with linear incisions. Two projecting tangs at the end provide a socket for the index finger. The fourth specimen retains the antler tangs to form the finger grip *(Fig. 6:2a)* On the widest tang an eye and large toothed mouth is incised.

All examples have a deeply incised bed to provide a firm haft for the beaver tooth bit. The lateral grinding on some beaver teeth, supplemented by ethnographic information (Barbeau n.d.) suggest that beaver teeth were often hafted in tandem or even multiples to form a wider chisel edge. The importance of these chisels is that they provide proof of extensive wood carving (mostly now perished) as well as for the fact that their hafts are always decorated with animal or abstract designs. Over 1000 modified beaver teeth have been excavated from the Prince Rupert sites, which suggest that they usually had wooden hafts such as the Ozette examples.

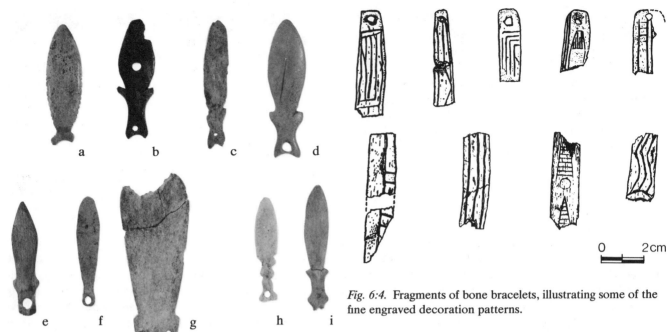

Fig. 6:3. Bone pendants.

Fig. 6:4. Fragments of bone bracelets, illustrating some of the fine engraved decoration patterns.

Bone Pendants

The bone pendants are of particular interest in the Prince Rupert area since they are numerous, span a significant period, occur at most sites and are relatively simple in form. They appear to be highly stylized human figures which are hung upside down. Inverted as in Figure 6:3, the "head" of the figure is a large oval or pointed form with a proportionally smaller body and variable number of appendages. Usually the space between the "legs" is gouged or drilled to form the suspension hole. There are no indications of interior details on the figures. One example *(Fig. 6:3b)*, which dates A.D. 800-900 has a hole through the middle of the "head." One of the earliest examples *(Fig. 6:3d)*, which dates between 1000 and 1500 B.C. has a pointed "head" and simple protruberances for limbs. A number of aberrant forms occur. The pendant figure which appears in Figure 6:3h has multiple limbs and the specimen illustrated in Figure 6:3f has no limbs at all. In Figure 6:3i, the "body" portion has been transformed into a jawed monster with the head rendered as a protruding tongue. The specimen illustrated in Figure 6:3g is much larger than the others and may not in fact be part of this class. There are two suspension holes and the "head" has become the dominant element. Further aberrant forms include Figure 6:3a which has no suspension hole and appears to be more fish-like, with multiple notches on both margins. Figure 6:5 shows two examples found together which also have notched margins.

The identification of these pendants as humanoid in form is of course speculative, but warrants further comment. The basic model of several highly stylized, almost

Fig. 6:5. Bone pendants.

abstract artifact types from the Northwest Coast is one that is basically humanoid. One example is the slate mirror with a head and body zone with highly abstract arms and legs *(Fig. 6:6)*. Another example is the copper that has carried the abstraction of the human form even farther with only a head and a body. The limbs have been eliminated altogether (Holm: pers. comm. 1973). Of course the copper, unlike the pendants or mirrors, has basic interior details such as the central backbone and ridge dividing the head from the body. The painted decorations on copper provide further interior details, for those who are skeptical of the humanoid interpretation for these forms, such as face and ribs in the appropriate panels of the copper.

A question which remains to be answered is why the pendant figures were hung upside down. Although it is too complicated an argument to go into here, I will simply offer the statement that it is because they represent ancestors. These pendants can be compared to the many examples of Thule human figure pendants, which are

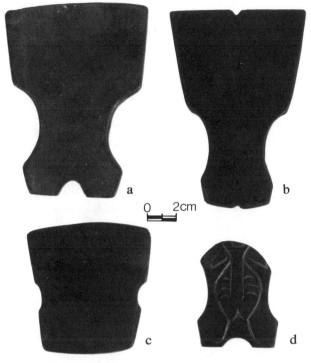

Fig. 6:6. Slate mirrors.

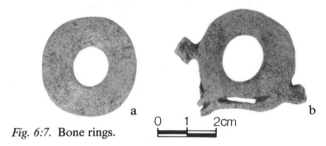

Fig. 6:7. Bone rings.

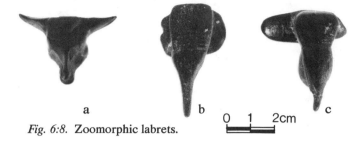

Fig. 6:8. Zoomorphic labrets.

Bone Rings

Although there are only a few bone rings from the North Coast sites they provide at least a glimpse with a possible cross-tie to the south. The first example is an incomplete carved ring *(Fig. 6:7a)* which dates between 1500 and 1000 B.C. that is similar to examples illustrated in Stewart (1973:143, V9). An example of a plain bone ring from the North Coast appears in Figure 6:7b.

Labrets

Although most stone labrets are plain, they are part of the category of items of personal decoration on the North Coast which spans a long period. The first example from the Prince Rupert area occurs about 1500 B.C. Dark grey slate is the favoured material although examples of coal, marble and a type of dull red slate also occur. Unfortunately, there are not enough sufficiently well-dated examples to suggest a sequence, although a few trends are obvious such as an increase in size toward the time of Christ when a few extremely large examples occur. The three late examples with bird heads protruding from the front have been mentioned previously *(Fig. 6:8)*. Only one was found in a site and it dates late in the sequence, after the first millenium A.D. All have beak-like protruberances and bulbous eyes, but otherwise are different stylistically from anything else from the North Coast. In the graves before A.D. 1 labrets occur with both males and females, although ethnographically they are restricted to females (Cybulski 1974).

On the Queen Charlotte Islands, Severs (pers. comm. 1976) has evidence from the occurrence of tooth abrasion for the possible use of dual lateral labrets from about 1000 B.C. as well as medial labrets similar to those from the Prince Rupert sites. Although labrets do not reveal much about art forms on the North Coast, their use as personal ornamentation, and their association with status differentiation makes them of some considerable interest.

Copper Ornaments

Prehistoric copper has been found in significant quantities only with the burials at the Boardwalk site which date to circa 500 B.C. Twenty pieces of cold annealed copper (including two flat copper bracelets *(Fig. 6:9)*, one pair of copper earrings, tubular rolled beads of copper and sheets of copper rolled around and preserved pieces of cedar rods *(Fig. 6:10)*) were found among the grave goods. The

much more realistically carved, that were hung upside down by a hole between the legs. The only possible analagous form I can see on the South Coast are the highly stylized pendants which are found in cross section rather than flat, but which often have the same template as these North Coast pendants (Stewart 1973:147).

Any attempt to answer the question of how these pendants were used must also be speculative. However, the closest analogy from ethnographic material appears to be the bone pendants fund on chiefs' and shamans' aprons through Siberia and northwestern North America. These aprons often have hundreds of pendants of a single type for each costume, such as deer or reindeer hooves, puffin beaks, incisor or canine teeth or pieces of bone or antler. There is further evidence in the vast literature on shamanism that multiple small human figures on shamanic paraphernalia represent the people of the community he served. These multiple pendants also provided him at the same time with their support when required, such as in conflicts between shamans.

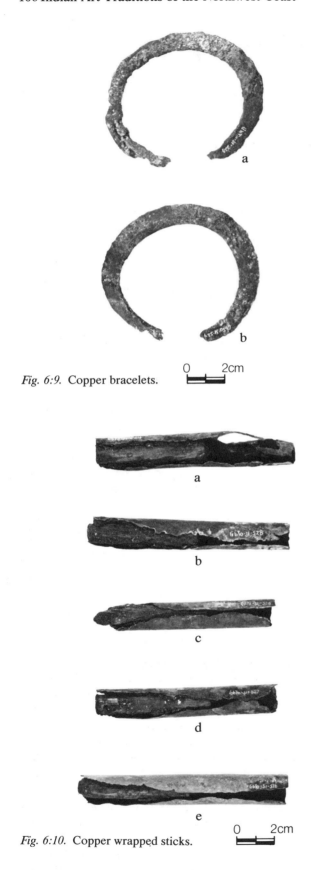

Fig. 6:9. Copper bracelets.

0   2cm

Fig. 6:10. Copper wrapped sticks.

0   2cm

alignment of the tubes in double, parallel rows, and their association with a cache of weapons including a slate dagger and three types of clubs, suggests that they may be all that remains of a suit of rod armour. None of the copper bears surface decoration. It is quite conceivable that this cache of weaponry represents an isolated example of booty captured from another tribe and disposed of in the cemetery area. A single female skull found nearby, and stained with copper from the cache, may have been a trophy head. Decapitation at this period is verified by a number of skeletons in the Boardwalk site and other contemporary burials that lack the skull and show cutmarks on the cervical vertebrae (Cybulski: pers. comm. 1976).

Sea Otter Teeth Mosaics

At one grave from 500 B.C. at the Boardwalk site, and a possibly contemporary grave from Dodge Island, large quantities of sea otter molars were found over a rectangular area covering the burials. Although no intelligible pattern could be distinguished in either case, they appear to have been used as decorative studs hammered into the lid of the burial box. The use of sea otter teeth inlay on box lids was common in ethnographic times along the length of the coast. The only prehistoric example, however, seems to be the whale saddle from the Ozette site that was inlaid with sea otter molars to form a thunderbird and Sisiutl design.

Beads

Shell disc beads were found in considerable quantities only in the Boardwalk site burials at 500 B.C., along with irregular drilled fragments of amber and jet. Dentalium shells also occurred as part of necklaces and ear pendants at this cemetery. The vast majority of burials excavated from other sites in the area are totally devoid of grave goods.

Bone Bracelets

Bone bracelets have not been found in the Prince Rupert deposits before the time of Christ, and appear to be entirely absent from known sites on the Queen Charlotte Islands. They are of particular interest, however, because of the fine engraved decorations which occur on them. The association of these bracelets in terms of age and sex affiliation is not known and I do not know of any in ethnographic collections of the Tsimshian or Haida. They do occur in Tlingit ethnographic collections however, with similar, predominantly geometric incised decoration, and are referred to as shamans' armlets (Harris: pers. comm. 1977). Most examples recovered from the Prince Rupert area *(Fig. 6:4)* are fragmentary but they still retain something of their original curvature. At either end of the bracelet one or two holes have been made for lashing

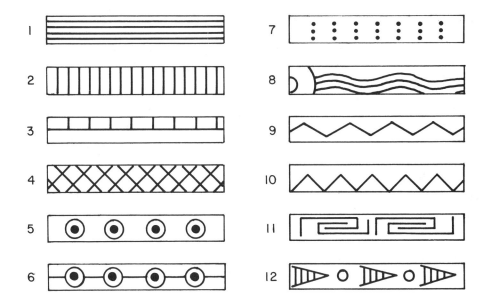

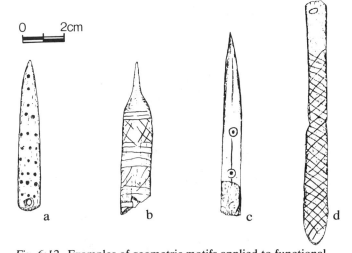

Fig. 6:11. Geometric motifs from bone bracelets.

together with sinew. The geometric decorations on brace-lets can be grouped into the following forms *(Fig. 6:11)*:

1 parallel longitudinal lines
2 ribbed lines
3 longitudinal lines, segmented along one edge like the backbone designs etched on siltstone concre-tions of fish and serpents
4 cross hatching, a design that also occurs on incised stone
5 concentric circles arranged in rows
6 concentric circles joined by a line
7 parallel rows of dots covering the surface
8 undulating parallel lines (with or without intermit-tent circular designs)
9 zigzag design (with single or multiple lines)
10 zigzag lines filled with parallel lines
11 continuous fret motifs
12 continuous devouring monster heads comprised of circular eyes and expanding mouths filled with lines

The common thematic element in the motifs appears to be stylized vertebral columns, eyes, teeth and scales that have their parallels in incised stone concretions. The concern in all cases seems to be with the stylized features of water monsters or fish, particularly their eyes, vertebrae and ribs. They are much simplified concerns that are also emphasized in the elaborate stone club complex of the region. Occasionally these same motifs are applied to awls and perforators, either singly or in combinations *(Fig. 6:12)*.

Bone Combs
Combs are the most highly decorated of all artifact classes

Fig. 6:12. Examples of geometric motifs applied to functional objects.

on the North Coast. It is unfortunate that only four combs have been found in the 20,000 artifacts. Only three of these are sufficiently complete to comment on. The most interesting and complete example (GbTo 23-850; *Fig. 6:13a)* dates around A.D. 800. An earlier date of A.D. 290 (MacDonald 1971) had been assigned to this piece but subsequent dates indicate the strata in which it occurred accumulated more rapidly than expected. The bridge of the comb depicts a wolf (or possibly a bear) in a profile hocker position, carved identically on both sides. The ribs are clearly indicated but the emphasis is mostly on the tongue, the ear and the eye, the primary organs of communication. The consistent emphasis on these fea-tures in the iconography of the coast may symbolize the superior powers of communication of animals over man

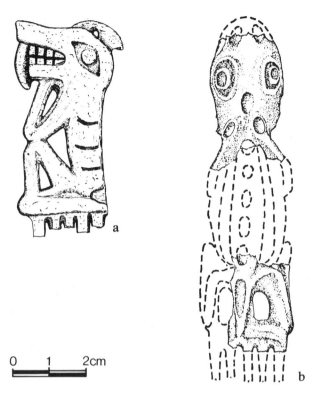

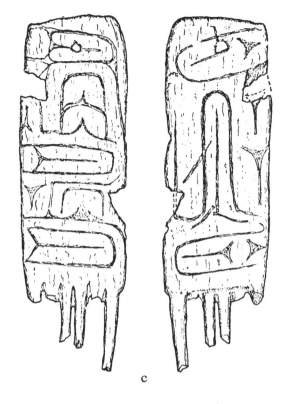

Fig. 6:13. Bone combs.

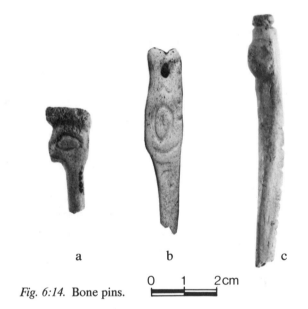

Fig. 6:14. Bone pins.

as emphasized in the circum-polar bear cult. Of stylistic importance is the extended tongue motif as well as the backward pointing ear, and the eye which slopes down at the back. All three features are prominent in the bear figures (and associated shaman) carved in the rocks of the Kitselas Canyon.

The second comb (GbTo 33-3985; *Fig. 6:13b*) dates somewhat later and portrays an animal with a long tail, possibly an otter or lizard. The stylistic importance of this piece is to be found in the use of many joint marks at the shoulders and along the spinal column and in the concentric ringed eyes and openwork between the limbs and the tail.

The third comb (GbTo 34-1805; *Fig. 6:13c*) is an example of flat design. The design relies heavily on ovoids, eye and U-forms and split U's. However, Bill Holm, who was sent a cast on it, was unable to see a meaningful figure in the design. The use of what Holm (1965) calls cuneiform (open Y-like) elements is much more characteristic of Straits Salish design in the historic period than it is of the North Coast. Nevertheless the importance of the piece is in its combination of several classic North Coast elements to completely fill the design field.

Bone Pins

Three examples of bone pins with carved heads appear in the Prince Rupert material between A.D. 1000 and 1500. They were possibly used as fasteners for cedar bark capes. It seems strange that no earlier examples

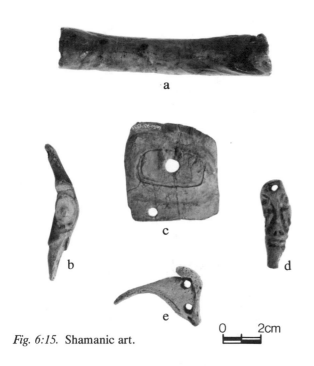

Fig. 6:15. Shamanic art.

0   2cm

eye forms on each side and four holes along the back for suspension *(Fig. 6:15a)*. This piece was found during the period the project was active in Prince Rupert by a private individual who turned it over to the Museum of Northern British Columbia in Prince Rupert. It was found during blasting operations for a fuel storage tank on Tuck Arm, a few miles from town. It was in a rock crevice with a human skeleton that was subsequently lost. The extent of blasting at the site destroyed all trace of the grave but I judged its isolated situation to be typical of a shaman's grave, well removed from village locations. Although there is no way of dating the piece, it appears to be characteristic of the carvings executed with beaver tooth chisels in the prehistoric period. If so it is the only prehistoric soul catcher from the North Coast. Although it is not as elaborate as the historic double killer whale type of soul catcher, it is stylistically closely comparable.

A number of carved bone charms from the Prince Rupert area are less definitely attributable to shamanism. The example in Figure 6:15c dates circa A.D. 1100 and is of interest as a classic North Coast eye form with a clearly incised double ovoid assymetrical pupil and ovoid eye zone. The next specimen (GbTo 31-4; *Fig. 15d*) is one of the only examples of a carved human face in a somewhat grotesque form. The last specimen (GbTo 34-910; *Fig. 6:15b*) is a bone pendant with a monster head in which the ears, eyes and tongue are enlarged to maximum dimensions. It is from a matrix that is yet undated and can only be attributed to the late prehistoric period.

The final example of shamanic art is the slate mirror *(Fig. 6:6)*. At one time I was inclined to view these items as paint palettes since there was some evidence to suggest they were used as abraders for faceted chunks of red ochre pigment, along with the fact they had very poor reflective properties, even when oiled. I am now inclined to see them as shaman mirrors, that were not true mirrors but objects for meditation. Widespread shamanic beliefs from Siberia and northern Canada lay heavy stress on shamans' mirrors as an essential tool for the location of lost souls which could only be seen as a reflection. A second well marked function for shaman mirrors was for looking into the future to predict the outcome of raiding or hunting expeditions. A decorated mirror handle from the Boardwalk site *(Fig. 6:6d)* depicts a human in frontal view. Unfortunately it was a surface find, and cannot be dated.

have appeared but it may be due to the very small sample.

The first example (GbTo 23-1205; *Fig. 6:14a*) dates circa A.D. 1000 and is decorated with a bird's head. The only distinguishing features are the beak, the eye and a serrated comb on the bird's head. Rooster-like combs are also encountered on a miniature bone club, mentioned later.

The second example (GbTo 33-2086; *Fig. 6:14b*) is an innovative one with a long snout, a slotted eye and a vague arc behind the eye zone that may indicate an ear form. The proportion of the head to the tapered pin suggest that it may portray a serpent or water creature of some sort.

The third example (GbTo 23-25; *Fig. 6:14c*) is a somewhat thicker pin which dates circa A.D. 1000-1200. It is decorated with a crude human face, in which the eyes and mouth are simple pits, and a bun-like knob at the top that may represent a hairdo.

Shamanic Art

A number of isolated finds from the North Coast relate directly to shamanism. The first is a bear claw bony element with double perforations *(Fig. 6:15e)* which has been ground flat at the proximal end presumably as a part of a shaman's crown of grizzly bear claws. A crown of this sort is a standard item of a shaman's paraphernalia for the Tsimshian speaking people, although it is rare among the Haida and Tlingit.

The second item is a bone "soul catcher" with double

Bone Clubs

Four decorated bone clubs were found in the Prince Rupert sites in addition to several plain bone clubs. Two were miniature while the other two were working models. By far the most spectacular of all decorated bone objects is the club in Figure 6:16a from the Boardwalk site burials. Stylistically the elements used in this piece are surprisingly close to those of the ethnographic period from the

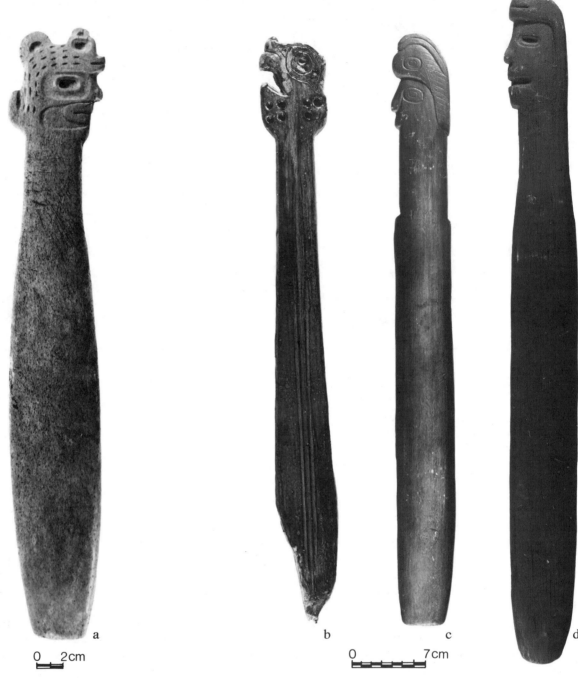

0 2cm

0 7cm

Fig. 6:16. Bone clubs.

South Coast as can be seen in the examples in Figure 6:16b-d which date at least 2000 years later.

The human face in the Boardwalk site example *(Fig. 6:16a)* is formed of ovoids and U-forms (Holm 1965). The eye zone and eye itself are ovoids while the mouth and mouth zone are U-forms. The upper lip is covered in front by a nose ring that is also a U-form. Surmounting the human head is an animal with fur (indicated with dashed lines) and a curved tail. The eye of the animal, possibly an otter, is similar, but somewhat rounder than

the human eye. The ear of the animal is small and notched, while on its back is a larger notched U-form that appears to be part of the animal but which I believe is the human's ear. If so, it is an excellent example of merging forms and visual punning typical of ethnographic art of the North Coast. The animal and the human have drilled nostrils and the cut away iris of both figures suggest inlays of shell or other material now gone. The attention devoted to the sense organs of both figures, that is the emphasis on the ears, the drilled nostrils and the inlaid

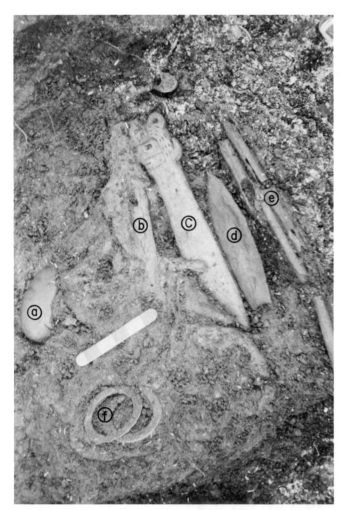

Fig. 6:17. Cache of warrior weapons, which date to 500 B.C., from the Boardwalk site. *a* stone club; *b* killer whale jaw club; *c* whalebone club; *d* basalt dagger; *e* copper wrapped sticks; *f* copper bracelets.

Several miniature clubs also occurred at the Boardwalk site. These obviously have no practical use as weapons and are therefore considered to be ceremonial in function. Shamans' kits often contained ceremonial weapons for fighting other shamans or witches in visionary encounters, which would be a possible explanation of these miniature clubs.

The first example (GbTo 31-211; *Fig. 6:18*) dates to circa A.D. 100. It is a miniature of the larger antler clubs that were common to the region in historic times. This example possesses the projecting branch of the larger antler original, even to the slot on the end that usually held a sharp stone inset. The top of the club is decorated with a bird's head with the suggestion of a crest. The segmented backbone is decorated with a bird's head with the suggestion of a crest. The segmented backbone of the bird extends down the handle. The base of the handle is stepped down and has an incised zigzag border and perforation. It appears significant that the slot in the branch, or 'beak' of the club ends in a carefully drilled circle that reflects the drilled eye of the bird. This can be interpreted as a second head in relation to the bird head at the top.

The second example (GbTo 31-1358; *Fig. 6:19*) which dates to circa A.D. 250, is another miniature replica of the antler club type. It also has a bird head finial and lightly incised wings on either side; the handle portion is missing.

Decorated Stone

By historic times the stone work of the North Coast had achieved a high degree of refinement on a par with that of classic civilization in Central and South America. Although the state of the art was highly developed, elaborate stone pieces were not produced in very large numbers, nor were large sculptural pieces made, in keeping with the fact there were no permanent cult centres. Localities of symbolic or ceremonial importance were often embellished with incised carvings of often major proportions. At least several thousand individual glyphs are found in the Prince Rupert Harbour and the life sized figure of "The Man Who Fell From Heaven" is possibly the most elaborate single figure from the coast.

The tradition of stone carvings appears in modest scale in the archaeological deposits by 1500 B.C. in the form of incised concretions of mudstone. These pieces are generally small, irregular forms whose natural shape suggests the figure for which details such as eyes, mouths, vertebral columns, ribs, limbs, wings or fins, are added by simple inversion. While a range of bird, animal and fish forms are found, salmon, killer whales and water monsters predominate in the iconography. Incised concretions continue through to the second millennium A.D.,

eyes, is a notable feature of all Northwest Coast ethnographic art. Only the tongues have been neglected. The rest of the club is undecorated.

The next example was found together with the above club in the cache of warrior weapons that date from 500 B.C. *(Fig. 6:17).* It was so fragile that it could not be preserved even in the laboratory (it was removed intact from the site in a wax jacket but proved to be only a paper thin shell of bone tissue when preservation was attempted). It was made from the jaw of a killer whale with the teeth forming the striking edge. In form it is very like a number of wood and stone clubs from the North Coast, having a row of large conical projections along one edge, which mimic the natural form of the killer whale jaw and teeth, although considerably modified in outline. The only decorations on this club were double rows of concentric circles joined by lines on either face of the club.

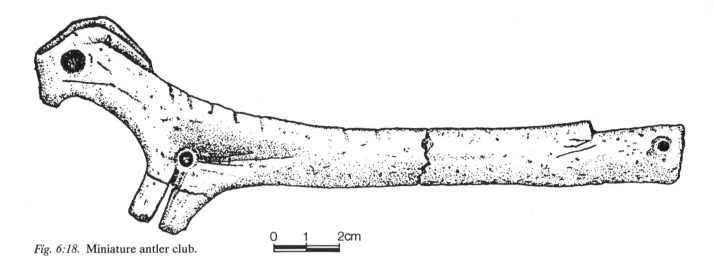

Fig. 6:18. Miniature antler club.

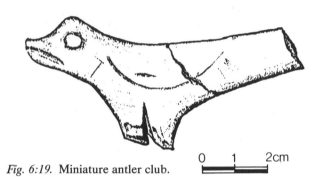

Fig. 6:19. Miniature antler club.

Fig. 6:20. Incised concretion.

Fig. 6:21. Stone pendant.

which indicates they may have had a particular function in ceremonialism where their inherent natural shape was significant. By 1000 B.C. however, it is clear that completely sculpted effigies were being carved, such as the small raven pendant *(Fig. 6:26)* from an early Boardwalk site grave.

From the core features of the concretion carvings of segmented backbone, ribs, eyes and mouth lines, a highly stylized tradition emerges between 1000 and 500 B.C. in which these features become the essential statement of the piece and the likeness to a particular species is completely lost. The single most important stylistic element is the segmented backbone. Small sandstone tablets appear which generally retain the longitudinal mid-line which divides the backbone from the ribs, divided on either side of the mid-line into deeply carved segments. Frequently the number of segments on one side of the mid-line is greater than on the other, referring I would suggest, to the lesser number of ribs to vertebrae in all species, and an artistic convention well established in the incised concretions of the earlier period. In fact, I believe these tablets have become the quintessential statement of the regeneration principle of animals and especially of fish. This segmentary principle in Northwest Coast art was applied to many other media such as carvings in wood and bone and is the implication behind the stacks of cylinders or "potlatch cones" used on human or crest animal figures in historic times. The backbone of these figures has literally been extended out through their heads and appears to have symbolic implications of favourable reincarnation, as for example, the tall segmented extensions on North Coast memorial poles.

Before discussing the next major development in stone art, the pecked and ground stone tool complex, a more detailed description of the earlier incised stone complex is in order.

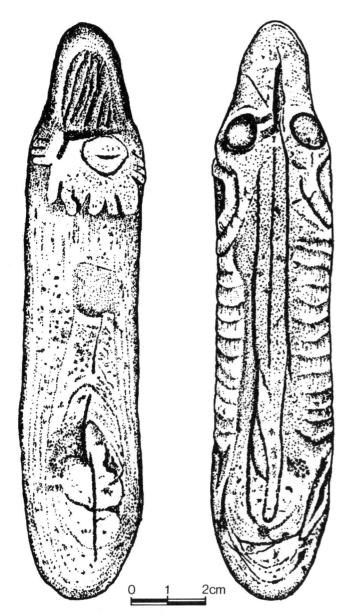

Fig. 6:22. Two views of zoomorphic concretion.

Incised Concretions

The earliest example (GbTo 31-2424; *Fig. 6:20*) is a long concretion in which the head is divided from the body by a natural construction emphasized by three parallel bands incised around the neck. The backbone is indicated by a pair of lines which merge at the head. Both the ribs and the vertebrae are expressed by open cross hatching over the body of the creature, a device which may also have the implication of fish scales.

Another example from roughly 500 B.C. is a pendant of a harder stone, that is more clearly distinguishable as a salmon (GbTo 33-3261; *Fig. 6:21*). The head has eyes and gills and the tail section has a deep groove that is worn smooth, probably by a suspension cord. Only the

Fig. 6:23. Segmented stone (2 views).

Fig. 6:24. Segmented stone.

backbone of the fish is indicated on the body. It is defined by a longitudinal line incised on both sides and divided into segments by deeply incised grooves. I believe this simple fish effigy relates the concept of segments to stylized animal or fish backbones which occur on earlier siltstone concretions, to the completely stylized segmentary forms.

A very elaborate incised concretion (GbTo 36-128; *Fig. 6:22*) dating from around the time of Christ, has the core elements such as the backbone of parallel lines continuing through the head, clearly defined ribs, eyes and mouth. In addition it has clearly defined force and hind limbs and paws, and on the underside an ovoid joint mark and tail or fin element composed of crude U-shaped elements. It is truly a monster figure combining limb features of several different creatures. An undated find from the Kitselas Canyon *(Fig. 6:23)* probably fits into the sequence about the time of Christ. It illustrates well the meaningless combination of core design elements such as backbone, mouth gash and eyes. Nevertheless, it still retains the appearance of a creature of some kind, or a monster, which is lost in the next series of segmented tabular forms.

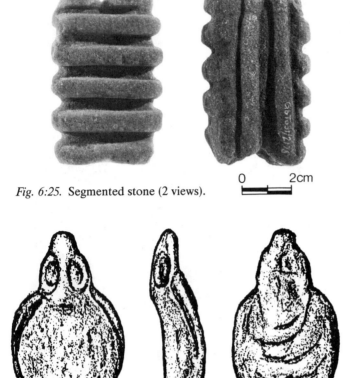

Fig. 6:25. Segmented stone (2 views).

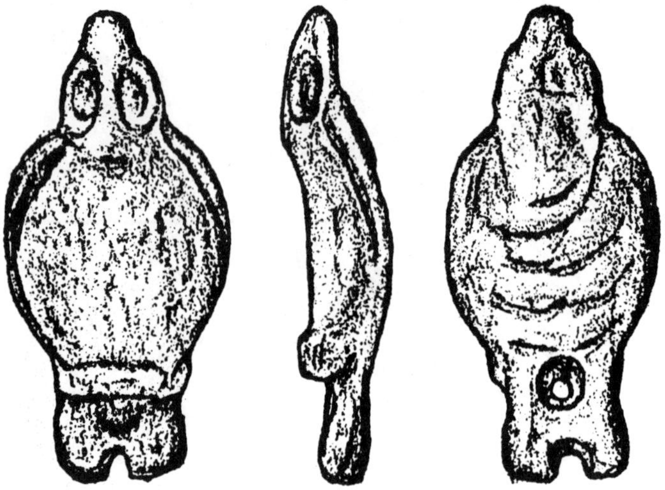

0   2cm

Fig. 6:26. Three views of a schist raven pendant.

Segmented Stones

Although the development of segmented stones begins in incised concretions and develops over a millenia, by about 500 B.C. it has achieved the level of a purely formal statement. In one example (GbTo 31-X717; *Fig. 6:24*), head and tail features are totally eliminated. The tabular body section is divided on both sides by a mid-line, and the rib and vertebral elements are matched except that they are interrupted on one side.

A second example (GbTo 31-2176; *Fig. 6:25*), lacks the mid-line, and the deeply carved segments completely encircle the form. Other examples of ribbed forms from the North Coast are illustrated in Stewart (1973:95), and many others were recovered from the site of Gitaus (GdTc 1) in the Kitselas Canyon. Since this major fishing station on the Skeena River produces an inordinate number of ribbed stones their association with fish ceremonies is strongly implied.

Carved Stone Charms

A beautiful carved raven pendant (GbTo 31-2178; *Fig.*

6:26) of micacious schist is a particularly subtle and refined statement of the art of stone carving at circa 1000 B.C. Rib-like crescentic designs on the underside of the bird, which is otherwise naturalistic in style, provides some link to the skeletal style which prevailed in the incised concretions of the period. The eye areas have been channelled out and once may have held inlays of shell or other animal.

Pecked and Ground Stone Tools

One of the major problems in the history of art and technology on the North Coast surrounds the problem of dating the appearance of the elaborate pecked and ground zoomorphic style. There is a high degree of consistency and integration in this style whether it occurs on stone bowls, hafted and hand mauls, adzes, plank abraders, etc. Unfortunately the extreme scarcity of dated archaeological finds compounds the problems of historical style analysis. A case can be made that the style, appearing together with new tool forms and hafting techniques, is a technological artistic complex derived from outside the area, presumably from the Maritime cultures of the north Asian coast. If, in fact, this is the case, it is more likely that it occurred by stimulus diffusion of a tool complex rather than by direct contact across the North Pacific, as the basic cultural pattern shows no significant change to coincide with the appearance of the tool complex. Some elements like stone bowls, 3/4 grooved adzes, and saddle type hand mauls have their counterparts across the North Pacific rather than further south on the Northwest Coast.

Pecked and ground stone clubs on the other hand may represent a specialized tradition with deeper roots on the North Coast than the massive stone tool complex with zoomorphic decoration. The Boardwalk burials and those from other sites in the Prince Rupert Harbour show skulls bashed with stone clubs of this complex has been found in datable context at circa A.D. 250. Elaborately decorated bone clubs, as noted previously, have been found in much earlier context (circa 500 B.C.).

The North Coast club style, particularly what Duff (1963) called the Skeena River style, will, in all probability, eventually be dated to at least 500 B.C. Leaving aside the strong sexual imagery described by Duff (1975), the club style is concerned very strongly with rib, backbone and scale designs carried to total abstraction that was noted in the earlier incised concretion and segmented tablet forms, and appears to at least have a strong indigenous element to it. I will return to this essential point of the origin of the massive stone zoomorphic style of the North Coast in the conclusion, but wish to pause here to review some of the pieces under discussion.

Stone Clubs

The only excavated stone club is from GbTo 34 *(Fig. 6:27)* with a date of circa A.D. 1-500. It is a very simple

Fig. 6:27. Stone club.

example compared to those in Duff (1969, 1975) but has the essential features of a phalliform head and ribbed blade.

Biconical Stones

Close examination of excavated examples of biconical stones from Prince Rupert appear to confirm Drucker's reasoning (1943: *op. cit.*) that they were abraders for smoothing adzed or split planks in preparation for painting. The knob-like extremities are highly variable, but in extreme examples approach in shape the phallic-like head of some stone clubs *(Fig. 6:28)*.

Barkshredders

Stone barkshredders are limited to the North Coast tribes, although they bear some formal relationship to the wooden barkshredders and mat creasers of the central and south coast tribes. While mat creasers were used for preparing reeds, an activity that was not important on the North Coast, barkshredders were used for shredding cedar bark for clothing, etc., a very important North Coast activity as elsewhere.

At least four stone bark shredders have been found in archaeological sites near Prince Rupert, but only one has zoomorphic decoration. Nevertheless, other decorated examples do occur in surface collections from the area. The decorated example (GbTo 18:297; *Fig. 6:29*) dates to circa A.D. 1 and is made of schist. It is not possible to identify the animal depicted but the head and tail appear to fit into a bird category.

Zoomorphic Hand Mauls

Plain hand mauls appear in the Prince Rupert sites about A.D. 500. The vast majority have the conical top; flat top examples common in the late period of the southern coast are quite rare. A number of examples with zoomorphic finials occur in surface collections from the area, but only one example has been found in stratified context. The bulbous eyes and curved snout of the very generalized animal figure are common features of the prehistoric examples, although ethnographic specimens occasionally are elaborately and completely carved (e.g., Duff, 1975: Figures 76, 77).

Zoomorphic Hafted Mauls

Stone mauls with 3/4 hafting grooves follow the same pattern as the hand mauls. Many surface collected examples with animal head finials exist in collections but only

Fig. 6:28. Biconical stones.

Fig. 6:29. Zoomorphic bark shredder.

a b c

0   2cm

Fig. 6:30. Zoomorphic hafted mauls.

Fig. 6:31. Fluted stone bowl.

three examples GbTo 34-1374 *(Fig. 6:30a)* and GbTo 23-118 and 1784 *(Fig. 6:30b and c)* were found in sites. All date to the second half of the first millennium A.D. The first example has very prominent eye bases with central pits, a round snout and a groove around the face of the maul. The second example also has the prominent eyes, round snout and mouth. The third, although in the process of being manufactured, appears to have the same basic features. Several examples of birds and animal headed forms are illustrated in Duff (1975: Figures 92, 93).

Decorated Stone Mortars

Stone mortars achieve a high state of development in the later period on the North Coast, and have often been described as tobacco mortars, which may indeed have been their main, if not exclusive, function. Fine examples are illustrated in Duff (1975) and MacDonald (1976). Two prehistoric decorative styles occur. The simplest is embellished with grooves which run around the bowl as rings or up the sides of the bowl as flutes. A single fluted example (GbTo 30-2000; *Fig. 6:31*) has been estimated to date to A.D. 1500. No zoomorphic stone bowls have been found in datable context although the style of decoration on examples such as that in Figure 6:32 from the Museum of Northern British Columbia collection has the same emphasis on massive simplified sculptural features as does the hafted mauls. I would therefore expect that they will eventually be dated to at least the first millennium A.D.

The view of northern Northwest Coast art derived from

Fig. 6:32. Zoomorphic stone bowl in the collection of the Museum of Northern British Columbia (from Duff 1975:152).

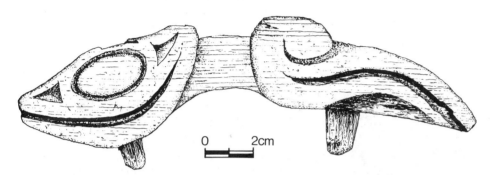

0   2cm

Fig. 6:33. Carved red cedar handle.

the bone and stone artifacts suggests that the art of a thousand years or more ago was stylistically simple and a relatively rare occurrence. In fact, we know that even in historic times the tribes of the northern coast used stone and bone sparingly and for relatively simple expressions such as amulets or shamans' charm figures, with the exception of Haida argillite carvings for the early tourist trade. The discovery of wet sites with preserved fibres and wood on the coast provides at least a glimpse of art in highly perishable (and easily worked) materials.

The Lachane site (GbTo 33) has produced a range of wooden and basketry artifacts including bentwood boxes, bowls, paddles, labrets, adze and chisel handles, bark containers, painted shafts and a range of basketry forms dating from 520 B.C. to A.D. 320 (Inglis 1976). The general impression obtained is that the wood and basket technology is remarkably similar to that at the time of contact. The bowls, for example, are unfinished discards, but demonstrate clearly the ability to carve wood with the stone and shell blade tools available. Only one object is elaborately carved (GbTo 33-C423; *Fig. 6:33*). It is made of red cedar and appears to be a handle of a bowl lid since it was evidently fixed to a curved surface with square pegs. It portrays an unidentified animal of fluid form, perhaps a sea creature. Stylistically it is interesting as it has no distinguishable limbs but does have a clear head portion with a well developed eye form and a whirl-like tail section. Another wet deposit, on the Boardwalk site, produced a small carving of a seal-like creature that was too eroded to retain any detailed features. There appears

to be no lack of wet sites in the Prince Rupert region or elsewhere on the North Coast which hold the best potential for solving the problems of prehistoric development of the art of the northern Northwest Coast. I would venture to guess that when such work has been done the basic elements of North Coast style wll be traced back at least as far as the second millenium before Christ.

Rock Art

Our knowledge of the extent of rock art on the northern coast is expanding rapidly. Until recently few examples had been reported from the Queen Charlotte Islands. Gessler and Gessler's work (1974) however, has yielded examples from Skidegate Inlet and other areas that have been examined. Other localities are reported from Higgins Pass, sites on Kitimat Channel, along the Skeena and Nass Rivers and other regions that have been adequately examined (Hill and Hill 1974). The Prince Rupert Harbour is particularly rich in petroglyphs, although less so in pictographs. In total there are at least several thousand individual glyphs at a dozen or more sites in the Prince Rupert Harbour, limited only by the availability of large boulders or suitable bedrock shelves on which to carve them. To judge from the degree of erosion of many figures, some of which are only barely discernible, the rock art tradition in the area must be several thousand years old at the minimum *(Fig. 6:34)*.

I will limit my comments to pertinent comparisons between stylistic features of the rock art in comparison with those of mobilary art in stone.

Fig. 6:34. Bedrock outcrop in front of GbTo 6, covered with glyphs, typical of the rock art in the Prince Rupert area.

Fig. 6:35. "The Man Who Fell From Heaven" petroglyph, Robertson Point (GbTo 4), Prince Rupert Harbour.

There are two extraordinary examples of rock art from the North Coast. The first is "The Man Who Fell From Heaven" petroglyph which is carved on a bedrock outcrop on the beach in front of the Roberson Point Site (Gb To 4; *Fig. 6:35*). In brief, the legend associated with the figure states that when Wegets (Raven) and his brother, who had human mothers and Sky people fathers, were expelled from the upper world for being half human, Wegets' brother chose to land on the kelp bed in the Prince Rupert Harbour and sank out of sight. Wegets observed this and chose the bedrock shelf that crosses Metlakatla Pass as his landing spot. Even he sunk into the rock from the force of his fall and had to enlist the aid of a marten to free him from the rock. Subsequent stories in the raven cycle of the region take Wegets up the Skeena and Nass Rivers, leaving his imprint on the rocks of the entire Tsimshian speaking territory.

In fact this is one of the best examples I know of in which rock art features are interrelated over a vast region by means of a mythological framework. No systematic study of the myths and rock art features has been done for the area but the potential for a structural study involving the Wegets myths, the rock art, economic territories and possibly social organization are outstanding. Without dwelling at length on this aspect, I would predict that at least some of the rock art of the region forms a cognitive map, via the Wegets legends for the territories of the Tsimshian, Gitksan and Niska. There is some evidence in fact that there are three cognitive maps, one for each dialect of the Tsimshian language. A cross linking of these cognitive maps is provided by the reference in the three systems of "The Man Who Fell From Heaven" as a point of common origin. The possibility of an overall cognitive map which transcends those of the three dialect groups, must also be explored.

Before leaving "The Man Who Fell From Heaven" example, I should note that H.I. Smith published a note on this feature in 1936, in which he cites ethnographic information which states that initiates for secret ceremonies reappeared on the morning on which their period of seclusion ended, lying in the depression of this petroglyph. In fact, some initiates claimed to have caused the feature. I view this as confirmation of the central importance of the feature, since initiates are themselves literally reborn from another cosmic zone, and typically such localities associated with cosmogenic acts are chosen for their reappearance.

A unique human figure of carved stone found in the midden at Metlakatla and presented to Israel Powell, the first Indian Commissioner in B.C. in 1879 is the only other known human figure of stone in the area *(Fig. 6:36)*, although in this instance the image is expressed in positive rather than negative terms. It is tempting to speculate that this figure also represents Wegets and its transfer to

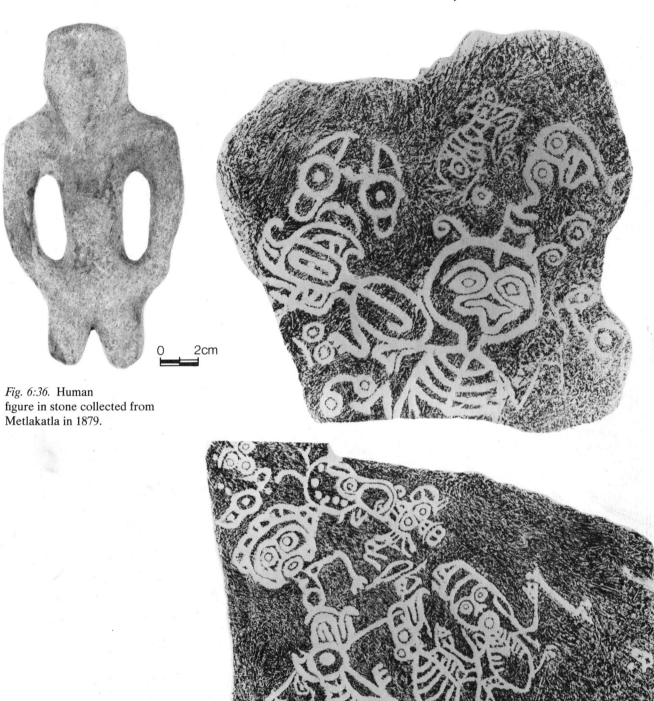

Fig. 6:36. Human figure in stone collected from Metlakatla in 1879.

0   2cm

Fig. 6:37. and *6:38.* Rubbings of the two major glyph panels from Ringbolt Island, Kitselas Canyon, Skeena River.

the first Indian Commissoner of the area was not entirely devoid of symbolic value.

The second important rock art feature is on Ringbolt Island in the Kitselas Canyon *(Figs. 6:37 and 6:38)*, access to which can only be gained during favourable levels of the Skeena River. When Dave Walker and his associates from Terrace found this feature it was covered by heavy layers of moss, implying at least a certain degree of antiquity. The number of individual glyphs in this panel are considerable, but two sets warrant special attention. Both depict human figures directly associated with bear figures. The humans have long curling ears, extended tongues and prominent eyes. The bears also have extended tongues, curved back ears and prominent eyes. Knowledge of Tsimshian beliefs suggests that both sets represent shamans communicating with bear spirits.

Several aspects of Tsimshian cosmology are worth mention here. The first principle is that all animals and fish are under the control of "chiefs" or "masters" of their species in exactly the same way that humans are organized. Further, different species and their corresponding chiefs are hierarchically organized in a system in which "bear" is the ultimate chief of all of the animals. The second principle is stated in terms of cosmic zones. The sea, the land and the sky are joined by an axis (in fact multiple axes, depending on the circumstances and the area) which interconnect the cosmic levels through "holes" in the respective zones. Rivers are transitional features since they carry water which falls from the sky, from the mountainous interior to the sea. Salmon, the sustenance of Indian life, are caught in this transitional river zone, as shellfish and other species from the coast are taken from the intertidal zone, a parallel transitional region. A third principle which is common throughout northern North America and Siberia, states that animals (particularly the bear as chief of the animals) are superior to mankind in terms of their ability to communicate. Specifically, they can understand mankind's every utterance, but mankind's understanding of animal languages is very limited. Consequently the tongues, ears and eyes of animal representations are emphasized to express the superior ability of animals to communicate, and therefore to control other creatures. These principles are exemplified in a common Tsimshian belief which equates the image of mankind looking down at the schools of salmon in the river, with that of bears looking down at human villages.

The fourth principle, also widespread in Siberia and northern North America, states that the ultimate reduction of a living creature is to its skeleton as a concrete form, and is to its spirit as a power form. The spirit itself can be alienated, or even destroyed by improper treatment of its remains (ultimately its bones). Skeletal parts are individually important, as an expression of *pars pro toto* or in anatomical order as an expression of the ordered relationships of the universe in ultimate terms. Throughout the coast much emphasis is placed on the spinal column as the prime structure of the animal, or human being, since it is the axis of the being. Its segmented structure is the ultimate cognitive form of all axes. It is particularly significant that the axial line on incised concretions, bone clubs, segmented stones, etc., project through the head and tail of the figure. This principle of segmented forms projecting through the heads of animals and humans as potlatch rings is conceptually a lengthening of their prime axis and hence their spirit power.

The fifth principle is that the most effective communication link between mankind and animal powers is through the shaman, who opens the channel for communication by ritual purification, dreams and visions. The importance and meaning of the Kitselas petroglyph is therefore its expression of the communication between the human and animal world represented in the exaggerated ears and tongues of the shaman and the bears. The location of this panel on an island with limited access in the first canyon of the Skeena is particularly appropriate.

Focusing on stylistic cross ties between the rock art and mobilary art of the Kitselas Canyon and the Prince Rupert Harbour respectively, the emphasis on extended tongues, prominent ear forms and other sense organs such as eyes and occasionally nostrils, has been noted in the Kitselas glyph as well as in the Prince Rupert artifacts, particularly the bear comb and the bone club.

Conclusion

Despite the pessimistic note in the introduction concerning the relative paucity of artifacts and other prehistoric features from the North Coast with which to attack the problems of origin and meaning of North Coast art, I feel there is sufficient material to throw light on at least some of these problems. Stylistic features of the art are discernable, such as the emphasis on skeletal structure as related to regeneration and access to food species, on sense organs as expressing communication between man and his food supply, via the shamans' spirit power in terms of axis of spirit power. Broader cosmological and cosmogenic concepts can be seen in the rock art of the tribal and linguistic areas.

I wish to express my sincere gratitude to Richard Inglis for information, critical comments and figures and figure captions he provided, and to Jerome Cybulski and Patricia Severs for their information and critical comments for this text.

CHAPTER 7

Prehistoric Art of the Central Coast of British Columbia

ROY L. CARLSON

A glance at any Northwest Coast art book attests firmly to the existence of a highly developed tradition of painting and carving wood during the nineteenth century by the ancestors of the Bella Bella and Bella Coola peoples of the central coast of British Columbia. Similarly, examination of the journals of Sir Alexander Mackenzie and George Vancouver carries this tradition backward into the last decades of the eighteenth century. The reading of McIlwraith's, *The Bella Coola Indians* (1948), or Boas', *Mythology of the Bella Coola* (1900b) and *Bella Bella Tales* (1932), provides some insights into the meaning of this art in the cultures which produced it. But what of the decades, centuries and millenia which preceded both the early explorers and the later ethnographers? What art was produced then? What techniques were employed and what styles were produced? What was the meaning of this art and what were its historical relationships? This paper is directed toward answering these questions, even though in spite of the considerable archaeological research over the last fourteen years, the data base is still very much limited.

Chronology

Archaeological research on the central coast since 1968 has resulted in the establishment of a cultural chronology spanning almost the last 10,000 years (Carlson 1979, Hobler 1982). Some thirteen sites have been tested by excavation, and others have been sampled by surface collecting. At the top of the temporal scale are the rotting house posts and burial caves of the Ethnographic Period with their mouldering testimonials to the artists creativity

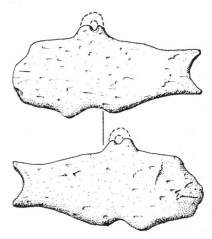

Fig. 7:1. Whalebone pendant resembling a rockfish from the site of Namu dating to about 3,500 years ago.

in wood. At the bottom—the beginning of time for this part of the world—archaeological evidence comes from a single component at the site of Namu (ElSx 1). The assemblage from the basal levels of this site is a chipped stone industry with relationships to both the Pebble Tool Tradition and the Microblade Tradition (Ch. 1). The evidence for artistic production in this Early Period assemblage is nil.

The following Middle Period between 5500 and 1500 years ago is almost blank as far as decorated objects are concerned. A single decorated item, a pendant fashioned from whalebone to resemble a rockfish *(Fig. 7:1)*, is the only art object discovered so far. It is from Namu and is about 3500 years old. Such pendants may have represented spirit helpers of their owners. Adze or chisel blades indicative of the knowledge of those same types of tools

	Item	Locality	Site	Phase	Date Estimate	Figure
1	Anthropomorphic figurine of antler	Kwatna	FaSu10 710	Anutcix	AD 200-1200	7:2
2	Zoomorphic pendant of antler	Kwatna	FaSu 10 978	Anutcix	AD1200	7:4a
3	Bird pendant of antler	Kwatna	FaSu 10 250	Anutcix	AD 200-1200	7:4b
4	Bone object fragment; line and dot design	Kwatna	FaSu 10 902	Anutcix	AD 200-1200	7:4c
5	Decorated antler valve, for sealing harpoon head	Kwatna	FaSu 2 3013	Anutcix	AD 1200	7:3b
6	Crude anthropomorphic figurine, stone	Kwatna	FaSu 2 3037	Anutcix	AD 1200	7:4d
7	Shuttle/spindle of whalebone	Kwatna	FaSu 2 2896	Anutcix	AD 1300	7:3a
8	Bone pin with eye design	Kwatna	FaSu 2 2960	Anutcix	AD 1200	7:4e
9	Bone object fragment with dot design	McNaughton Island	ElTb 10	Anutcix	?	-
10	Zoomorphic stone club fragment	Kwatna	FaSu 2 695	Kwatna	AD 1500 1800	-
11	Antler harpoon valve with incised line	Kwatna	FaSu 10 1035	Anutcix	AD 200-1200	-
12	Bone pendant with line and dot design	Kwatna	FaSu 1 514	Kwatna	AD 1500-1800	7:6a
13	Antler pendant with joined anthropomorphic figures	Kwatna	FaSu 1	Kwatna	AD 1500-1800	7:6b
14	Stone hammerstone-grinder with anthropomorphic figure	Kwatna	FaSu 1 1905	Kwatna	AD 1500-1800	7:6c 7:8
15	Bone spoon handle with perforated design	Kwatna	FaSu 10 964	Kwatna	AD 1800	7:6d
16	Wooden spoon handle with perforated design	Kwatna	FaSu 1	Kwatna	AD 1500-1800	-
17	Circular stone with incised design	Koeye River		Surface find		7:7
18	Soapstone hammer with zoomorphic sculpture	Bella Coola Valley		Found in plowed field		7:5
19	Grooved maul with zoomorphic design	Bella Coola Valley		Found in plowed field		-
20	Frog bowl of vesicular basalt	Kwatna		Kwatna	AD 1500-1850	7:8
21	Whalebone pendant shaped like a rockfish	Namu	ElSx 1	Unnamed	1500 BC	7:1

Table 7:1. Art Objects From Central Coast Archaeological Sites

as used ethnographically in woodworking have been found also beginning about 3500 years ago, and suggest the presence of an art tradition in that medium. No waterlogged site in which specimens might be preserved has yet been found that dates this early.

It is only in the Late Period between about A.D. 500 and A.D. 1800 that there is clear and direct evidence for a tradition of decorative and ceremonial art. This evidence comes from three sites at Kwatna excavated by Philip Hobler and myself between 1969 and 1972, from one object from the McNaughton Island site (ElTb 10) investigated by J.A. Pomeroy in 1971, and from surface finds from the Bella Coola valley and the Koeye River. There are only 16 decorated objects (Table 1) out of nearly 7000 artifacts from these four excavated sites. Within the Late Period we have defined two sequent phases, the Anutcix phase followed by the Kwatna phase. Radiocarbon dates on these phases are not entirely satisfactory (Table 2), but do suggest that the Anutcix phase persisted from about A.D. 200 to A.D. 1400, and

Date A.D.	Lab Number	Site	Cultural Association
1 190 ± 90	Gak 4333	FaSu 10	Anutcix phase, oldest layer
2 480 ± 100	Gak 3210	FaSu 2	Below Anutcix phase house floor
3 670 ± 100*	Gak 3207	FaSu 1	Burned wood in Kwatna Phase associations in waterlogged deposit
4 1140 ± 70	Gak 4931	FaSu 10	60 cm deep in Anutcix phase associations
5 1270 ± 75	Gak 4932	FaSu 10	110 cm deep in Anutcix phase deposits
6 1280 ± 80	Gak 3211	FaSu 2	Anutcix phase house floor
7 1590 ± 90	Gak 3208	FaSu 1	Fish weir stake in water-logged Kwatna phase deposit
8 1710 ± 80	Gak 3209	FaSu 1	Fish weir stake in water-logged Kwatna phase deposit
9 1620 ± 80*	Gak 3909	FaSu 2	Anutcix phase
10 1920 ± 80*	Gak 3908	FaSu 2	Kwatna phase
11 1950 ± 90*	Gak 3213	FaSu 2	Kwatna phase
12 1950 ± 120*	Gak 3212	FaSu 2	Anutcix phase

* These dates are unacceptable, and are the result of either contamination or error in the dating system. C[14] dates within the last 500 years tend to be generally unreliable.

Table 7:2. C[14] Dates on Sites With Kwatna and Anutcix Phase Components at Kwatna.

the Kwatna phase from about A.D. 1400 to A.D. 1800. There is continuity in many of the common artifact types between the two phases.

The site of Nutlitliquotlank (FaSu 2) exhibits an Anutcix phase house followed by a Kwatna phase occupation in the upper 60 cm of the site. A C[14] date of A.D. 480 ± 100 from below floor level, and a date of A.D. 1280 ± 80 from the floor itself would appear to date the Anutcix phase (Carlson and Hobler 1972). The Kwatna phase occupation is stratigraphically above this and contains only a single European trade object, a rolled copper bead. There are also several far too recent dates from this site (Table 2).

At Axeti (FaSu 1) there is both a waterlogged midden and a land midden. Since artifacts diagnostic of the Kwatna phase occur throughout, I am considering the site to be solely Kwatna phase in time even though one early C[14] date of A.D. 670 ± 100 is in contradiction to the two younger dates of A.D. 1590 ± 90 and 1710 ± 80.

At Anutcix (FaSu 10) there is an Anutcix phase occupation followed by a short Kwatna phase occupation which extends into the historic period. The oldest C[14] date is A.D. 190 ± 90 which comes from the very bottom of the deposit. The shell layer immediately above produced a date of A.D. 1270 ± 75, and the layer midway in the deposit 60 cm above the preceding date, and 60 cm

below the surface gave a reading of A.D. 1140 ± 70. The dates listed in Table 1 are approximations based on where the listed artifacts were found relative to the accepted C[14] dates in the respective sites.

Late Period Art Objects

Of the 16 decorated objects found in archaeological context, 10 are from the Anutcix phase, and 6 from the Kwatna phase. I will discuss the art of the Anutcix phase first.

Anutcix Phase Art

A glance at Table 1 shows that the art of this phase is preponderantly anthropomorphic aad zoomorphic as opposed to geometric in style, although both styles occur. The most common material is antler, followed by bone and stone. Several of the objects are utilitarian items, others are ornaments.

The earliest decorated object is an antler figurine *(Fig. 7:2)* from the lowermost layer at FaSu 10. This layer was dated at A.D. 190 by C[14] although the layer immediately above was dated at A.D. 1280. These dates bracket the potential time span for this figurine, although it actually should date closer to the earlier C[14] estimate. I was very surprised to discover this figurine at Kwatna, as my first

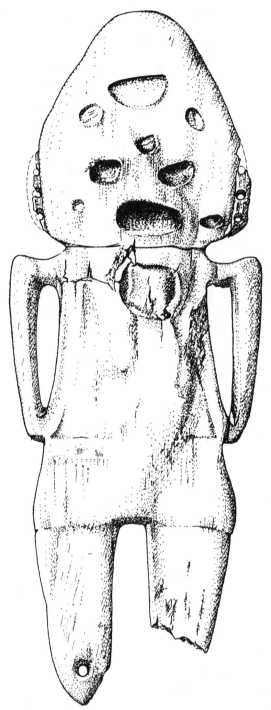

Fig. 7:2. Anthropomorphic figurine made of antler from Anutcix (FaSu 10) at Kwatna. This figurine dates between A.D. 200 and 1200 with present evidence favouring the earlier date. Actual size.

acquaintance with figurines of this type was in the San Juan Islands far to the south almost 30 years ago where a similar figurine had been found in a cave on Sucia Island (Carlson 1954). Since that time two other figurines have been found, one by Onat working at the Fishtown site (45-Sk-33) at the mouth of the Skagit River, and one by Munsell at the Conway site (45-SK-59) also in northern Puget Sound. A close look at the figurine found by H.I. Smith (1904) in a grave at Tampico indicates that it is of the same type. Another has been found on the beach at Montague Harbor in the Gulf Islands. Hence there are now six of these figurines with a distribution from near Yakima, Washington through northern Puget Sound to Kwatna Bay off Burke Channel, with the greatest frequency found in Puget Sound. Onat (pers. comm.) estimates the dates of the Conway and fishtown figurine at about A.D. 1000 which is within the time span of the Kwatna figure. The Sucia figure is undated, as is the Tampico figure although Warren (1968) places the grave associated with the Tampico figure in his Plateau pattern of Interior prehistoric culture which begins after A.D. 300 and persists into the Ethnographic Period.

The question of meaning in respect to these figurines is perhaps of greater interest. Three are possibly female, at least they all wear what is possibly a fringed cedar bark skirt (fringed skirts are also worn by Shamen, however). The Montague Harbor Figure is a male. The head shape of the Kwatna and Sucia figures suggests head deformation which would indicate a high status female, although the facial configuration of the Kwatna figure may indicate a mask. From a stylistic viewpoint, the Tampico and Sucia figures are interesting as both exhibit "joint ovals," and as such suggest that they might figure into the ancestry of classic style northwest coast art. Their overall configuration, however, is Salish and the more likely interpretation is that these ovals are the result of influence from northern classic styles. The Kwatna piece may actually be a trade object from the south as I know of no elk remains anywhere nearby large enough to provide an antler for local manufacture of this object. The total style of the Tampico figure is in keeping with Plateau styles of rock art, and as such suggests local manufacture. These figurines are similar to shamanic spirit helpers from Siberia. They are illustrated and discussed further in Chapter 11.

The other Anutcix phase objects are more firmly dated to about A.D. 1200. While the information is actually meagre, it seems clear that classic Northwest Cost art was in existence along this part of the coast by this time, and that even some distinctive elements we see in Bella Coola ethnographic art may also have been present. The evidence for the first statement is based on two items *(Fig. 7:3)*, a whalebone hand spindle or shuttle and the valve of a sealing harpoon head, both of which exhibit an artistic device which Holm calls a T-form which in classic

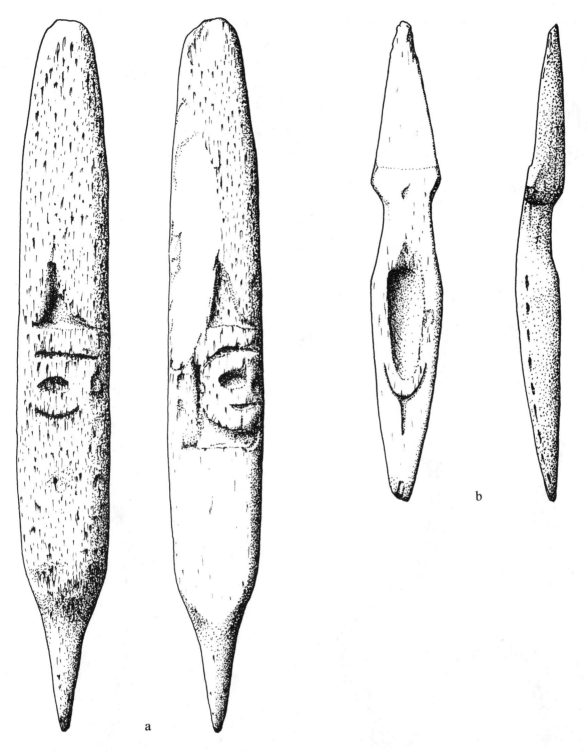

Fig. 7:3. Artifacts from the Anutcix phase suggesting the northern style of Northwest Coast art. *a* Spindle or shuttle of whalebone. *b* Valve from a sealing harpoon head of bone. Note the T-forms on both pieces. A.D. 200-1300 (actual size).

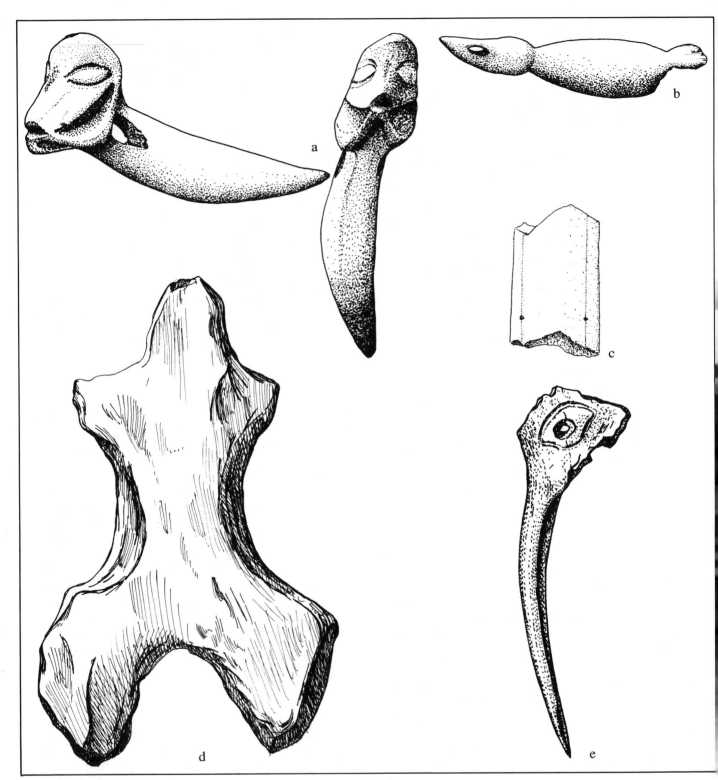

Fig. 7:4. Decorated objects from Anutcix phase components at Kwatna dating between A.D. 200 and 1300. *a,b* bird pendants of antler. *c* bone object fragment with incised geometric design. *d* crude stone figurine. *e* bone pin with incised eye. *a* twice actual size; *b-e* actual size.

Fig. 7:5. Soapstone hammer from a ploughed field in the Bella Coola valley. This object is about 12 cm tall.

Northwest Coast art is used for relieving monotony on plain surfaces. This element seems simple, which indeed it is, but it is also highly sophisticated and not an element which would come about at the very beginning of stylistic development. The eye form of the bone pin *(Fig. 7:4)* is suggestive of classic art also, but is too crude to be definitive.

Evidence for the statement about the presence of a Bella Coola style at this time rests on this smiling antler pendant *(Fig. 7:4a)* from Anutcix which dates to about A.D. 1200. The deep relief carving is more reminiscent of Bella Coola than of any other art style with which I am familiar. The head is clearly skull-like and somewhat bird-like. There is a circular hole in the top of the head. Is there a Bella Coola myth about a bird skull with a hole? (I haven't found one, yet.) A soapstone hammer *(Fig. 7:5)* found in a ploughed field in the Bella Coola valley is reminiscent in style of this pendant, but is obviously not a depiction of the same being. Who this smiling creature, this prehistoric Mona Lisa is, I don't know, but I'll bet he/she's somebody.

The other Anutcix phase art objects *(Fig. 7:4)* consist of a small bird-form pendant of antler, a crude anthropomorphic figurine of stone, the valve from a salmon harpoon head with an incised line outlining its edges, a bone object fragment with a series of drilled dots and another fragment with a line and dot design. These objects offer little in the way of information beyond their mere presence, although if one can imagine these motifs combined and recombined in wood and on a grander

scale than that in which they survive in bone, one would probably have a truer picture of the art of the Anutcix phase than that shown here.

Kwatna Phase Art
The majority of the art objects of the Kwatna phase come from the waterlogged midden at Axeti (FaSu 1) (Hobler 1970:87; Carlson 1972:41). Even though this is a site with excellent preservation of wood and basketry, the only decorated wooden objects are portions of two spoons, one with a textured surface pattern produced with a porcupine or beaver tooth incising tool, and one with incised outlining on the handle with a perforated slit down the centre of the handle. The circumstances of the waterlogging phenomena at Axeti are not absolutely clear, but we seem to have been excavating trash caught in the silt at the end of the fish trap, which likely emanated from houses on the island directly above the end of the fish trap.

Bone objects from the Kwatna phase consist of a pendant with an incised line and drilled dot design, and a bone spoon handle *(Fig. 7:6)* with the same kind of T-form perforated slit as the wooden one.

The single antler object from the Kwatna phase is a pendant with two anthropomorphic figures, back to back, and holding hands. The style is more naturalistic than anything else. As with the earlier anthropomorphic beings, it is difficult to speculate as to the meaning of these figures. Are they the twins widespread in North American Indian mythology, and here associated with procuring

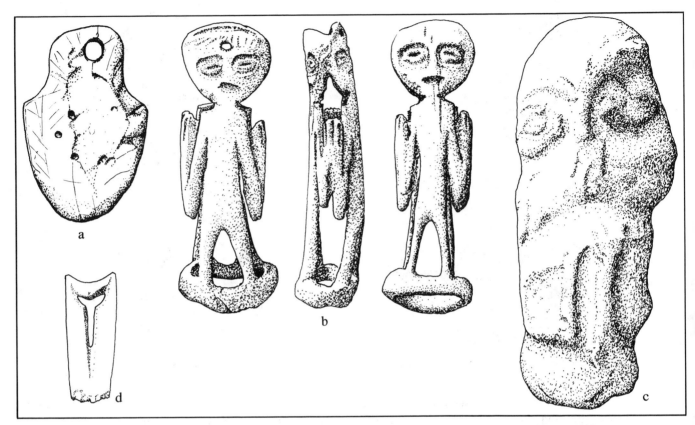

Fig. 7:6. Decorated objects from Kwatna phase components at Kwatna dating between about A.D. 1400 and 1800. *a* bone pendant (2 times natural size). *b* antler pendant (actual size). *c* stone hammerstone-grinder (actual size). *d* bone spoon handle (actual size).

salmon? Or is this simply man (any man or all men) and the fact that there are two of them, only to balance the composition? What they remind me of are the little men one sees in the rock art of this part of the coast. We don't know what he means in those contexts either.

Mobiliary sculpture in stone is also present in Kwatna phase associations. The head of a club from FaSu 2 is nearly identical to the head of a complete club from Powell River (Duff 1975, #113). The source of these clubs is unknown. A hammerstone-grinder from FaSu 1 *(Fig. 7:6c)* bears a sculptured figure reminiscent of coastal petroglyphs; it is quite surely local in origin as the hammerstone-grinder is a typical Kwatna implement. Inverarity (1950 Fig. 50) illustrates a stone figure of similar style from the Bella Bella region. This completes the description of those items with good archaeological context. There are a few pieces without good context: a grooved zoomorphic maul from a ploughed field in the Bella Coola valley which is possibly a trade item from the north at least it would be more at home there; a perforated stone *(Fig. 7:7)* found by a logger at a site on the Koeye River. The style on the latter with its little stick men also occurs in pictographs in the central coast region, and belongs to what Lundy (Ch. 5) calls the Interior Intrusive Style. We have yet to find this style in an archaeological context, but consider it quite recent.

The final piece of art from this area is a large stone bowl of vesicular basalt shaped to represent a frog *(Fig. 7:8)*. This bowl is known only from a photograph in the Smithsonian Institution. The bowl can be ascribed to the Kwatna phase as objects of vesicular basalt are found only in that phase.

Conclusions

In terms of the questions posed in the introduction to this paper, some conclusions can be offered. The first and most obvious is that, although limited in quantity, there indeed is art from the central coast that is definitely prehistoric. The earliest art, the fish pendant from Namu, is characterized more by crude realism than by any definable style. The next art to appear (A.D. 200-1200) is related to both classic northern coastal art, and to Salish art to the south. The final art style of the region attested to by painted and sculpted objects of the Ethnographic Period is in northern classic style. Considerably more archaeological research is required to augment this small, but fascinating sample of prehistoric art from the central coast of British Columbia.

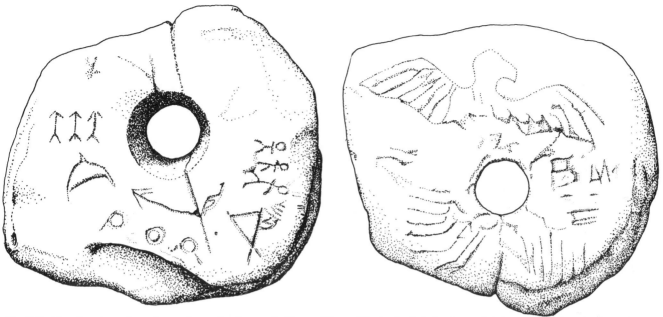

Fig. 7:7. Circular stone from the surface of a site on the Koeye River. The incised design is reminiscent of Interior pictographic style which also occurs on this part of the central coast.

Fig. 7:8. Pecked stone artifacts. *a* Frog bowl and *b* hammerstone-grinder from the late prehistoric or early historic period at Kwatna. *c* Grooved maul from the Bella Coola valley. Variable scale.

CHAPTER 8

Prehistoric Art of the Lower Fraser Region

CHARLES E. BORDEN

The present paper attempts to delineate the sequent manifestation of prehistoric art in the Lower Fraser valley. Located on the southwestern mainland of British Columbia, the study area extends from a few kilometres above the terminus of the Fraser Canyon at Yale to the mouth of the river. At the time of White contact this part of the Fraser Valley was inhabited by tribes of the Halkomelem-speaking Stalo Indians (Duff 1952), a major division of the Coast Salish *(Fig. 8:1)*. Although a study of early art may help to shed light on various problems of local prehistory, this paper will be mainly devoted (a) to analytical descriptions of some of the known regional art forms, and (b) to presenting these as closely as possible in proper chronological sequence.

Part of the basic chronology to be employed is that developed for the Milliken-Esilao locality about four kilometres upriver from the settlement of Yale, B.C. The chronometric data, phase names and other details of this framework are shown in the right column of Figure 8:2 (cf. also Borden 1960, 1961, 1965, 1968b, 1975). Developments at the mouth of the river, though somewhat similar to those in the Canyon, are by no means identical. Investigations by the University of British Columbia (Borden 1950, 1951, 1954, 1968b, 1969b, 1970, 1976) have traced developments in the Delta region back to about 1000 B.C. Thanks to other investigations, especially by S. Gay Calvert-Boehm (Calvert 1970, Boehm 1973) and by R.G. Matson (1976), the prehistory of the Fraser Delta has now a known time depth comparable to that in the Canyon region. Phase names, chronometric and other data pertaining to developments in the Delta region are entered on the left of Figure 8:2. Research in the Fraser valley between the Canyon and the Delta is progressing (e.g. Crowe-Swords 1974, Hansen 1973, Kidd 1968, LeClair

1976), but is as yet not sufficiently advanced to permit the construction of detailed local chronologies.

I have divided the manifestations of artistic expression into five provisional periods on the basis of their association with various radiocarbon-dated components and/or phases. The sequent periods, their respective duration stated in approximate calendric dates, and the culture phases encompassed by each period are presented in Figure 8:3. These are provisional periods and subdivisions, and modifications of this chronological scheme may be expected in future.

It is desirable at this point to note that the term "phase" is used here in the sense defined by Willey and Phillips (1958:22). A useful feature of the concept as defined here is that a phase has both a temporal and a spatial dimension. Moreover it is well to point out that "it is quite possible for more than one archaeological phase to occupy a region at the same time". As will become evident from stylistically distinct but contemporary art forms there appear to be several instances of the simultaneous presence in the Lower Fraser region of different cultures or sub-cultures.

The Early Period

This period encompasses the Milliken and Mazama phases in the Canyon and Component I (i.e. Early Glenrose) at the Glenrose site in the Delta. The upriver and downriver components dating to this time appear to be closely related culturally. The main hints of possible artistic activity during this period are the extensive use of ochre as well as of the requisite grinding tools documented at the Milliken site, and the occurrence at the

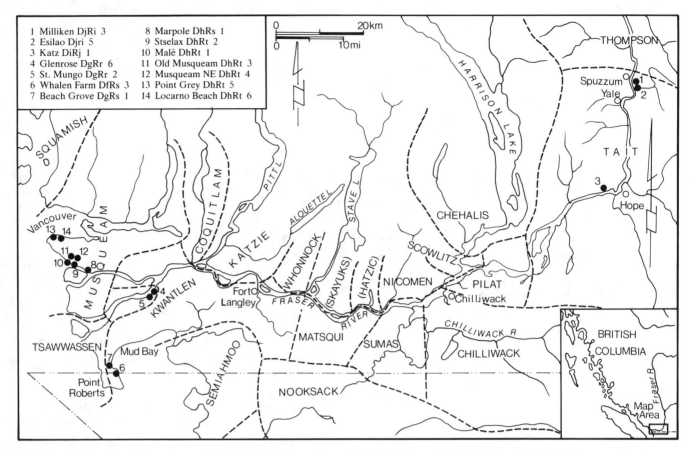

Fig. 8:1. Map of the Lower Fraser region, showing the territory of Stalo Indian and adjoining Coast Salish tribes as well as the location of archaeological sites mentioned in the text. (Based in part on Duff 1952:Map 1).

same site of fragments of abraded and polished steatite. Present also are modified quartz crystals, quartz crystal chips, burins and abraders all of which would have enabled these groups to work not only steatite, but also antler and bone. However, because of soil acidity bone and antler artifacts are not preserved in any of the Canyon phases. No art work has been recovered from the early deposit at Glenrose, even though bone is preserved there.

The Developmental Period

This period is represented in the Lower Fraser region by several components, some of which have been assigned phase names, among which the Eayem phase in the Fraser Canyon and the St. Mungo phase in the Delta are the most important. This period is characterized by increasing technological complexity. The ground slate industry is introduced early in this period (c. 5000 B.P.), bone ornaments are perforated with chipped stone drills, and bone, antler and soft stone are incised and shaped with stone and rodent incisor tools. In this period we find the first definite known manifestations of art, including the first sculptures in the round.

A small fragment of a siltstone plaque with smoothly finished surfaces, one of which is engraved, was recovered from an Eayem phase stratum radiocarbon dated to about 5000 B.P. *(Fig. 8:4a)*. The incised straight lines appear to be deliberately cut to different depths and widths and intersect, seemingly again deliberately, at different angles. Because of the smallness of the fragment, the full extent of the pattern of these various lines is not discernible, but obviously we are not dealing here with simple cross-hatching.

Both components of the St. Mungo phase in the Fraser Delta have produced fragments of ground slate plaques. Calvert reports two specimens incised with a simple feather design from early in this phase, the beginnings of which date to about 4300 years ago at the type site (Calvert 1970:57,70). Of similar age are ground slate fragments incised with lines arranged and combined in various ways from the type site *(Fig. 8:4e)* and the St. Mungo component at Glenrose *(Fig. 8:4b-e)*. Design elements include drilled pits, notched or scalloped edges and a rudimentary curvilinear design in which a series of lines run more or less parallel to the curving edge of the specimen. The function of these plaques is as yet unknown, nor can we say anything definite regarding the

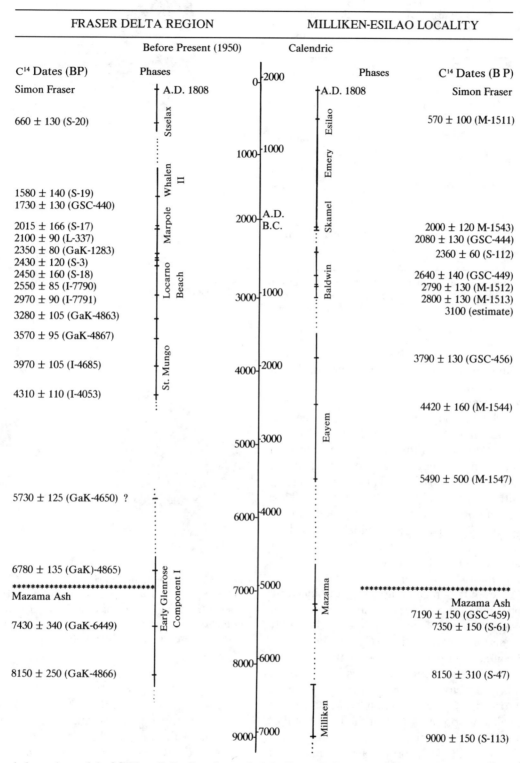

Fig. 8:2. Cultural chronology of the Milliken-Esilao locality and of the Fraser Delta region. Chronometric chart of named phases: their age and duration. Dates in radiocarbon years before the present (B.P., that is A.D. 1950). Based on Borden 1960, 1961, 1965, 1968b, 1969, 1970, 1975, 1976; Calvert-Boehm 1970, 1973; Matson 1976).

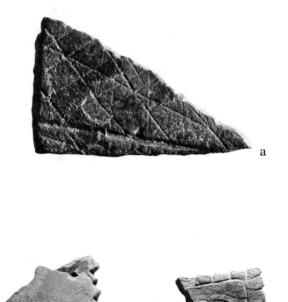

Period	Approximate Calendric Dates (Based on C¹⁴ Estimates)	Culture Phases	
		Fraser Canyon	Fraser Delta
Late	c. A D 1200 - Historic (1808-)	Esilao	Stselax
Post Climax	c. A D 350-1200	Emery	Whalen II
Climax	1100 B C - A D 350	Skamel Baldwin	Marpole Locarno Beach
Developmental	3500 - c. 1100 B C	Eayem	St. Mungo
Early	7000 - c. 4000 B C	Mazama Milliken	Glenrose

Fig. 8:3 Outline of the prehistory of art in the Lower Fraser Region. Main periods and the phases encompassed by each period.

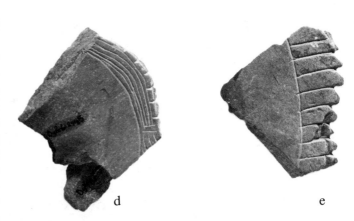

Fig. 8:4. Developmental Period art from the Eayem and St. Mungo Phases. *a* enlarged fragment of incised siltstone plaque from the Eayem phase at Esilao. *b-e* incised and notched ground slate plaques of the St. Mungo phase. *b-d* Glenrose site. *a* St. Mungo site. Maximum dimension of *a:* 2.46 cm.

possible meaning of the various design elements found on them.

"Decorations" were also applied to bone and antler objects during the Developmental Period. Although no artifacts of these materials have been preserved in the acid soils of the upriver sites they do occur in the shell strata of coastal components. Several fine examples were recovered from the St. Mungo site. The most interesting is a broad, flat, originally pointed antler object, perhaps a ceremonial knife or dagger, from an early level in the deposit *(Fig. 8:5a)*. The handle is provided with a scalloped margin, each rounded projection having a rather large circular perforation. In addition, a cruciform element has been boldly incised through the middle of the handle. The edges of two fragmentary bone artifacts from the same component at St. Mungo feature notched or serrated edges, and the surface of another is delicately incised with a series of parallel lines *(Fig. 8:5b-d)*.

Among the most intriguing objects of this time are small spindle-shaped, segmented carvings in the round fashioned of bone or easily worked soft stone *(Fig. 8:6)*. Evidently not ornaments, these carefully crafted creations appear like realistic representations of the larvae of flies or similar insects. It is worth noting that until recent times insect larvae, grubs, and worms played an important role in the mythology of various Northwest Coast groups and others along the Pacific rim. They were believed to be endowed with supernatural powers and the ability to grow into huge size or to change into other beings (Barbeau 1951; de Laguna 1934: 116, 204, Plate 52 no. 5; Nelson 1899: Fig. 158, Nordenskiöld 1882:507). The earliest of these little carvings was found at Esilao in deposits of the Eayem Phase and radiocarbon dated to about 5000 B.P. *(Fig. 8:6a)*. They are also found in components of the St. Mungo phase at the mouth of the river *(Fig. 8:6c-e)*. Similar carvings and variations on this theme persist into later periods.

Certainly the most remarkable art object from the Developmental Period is an anthropomorphic sculpture from the St. Mungo component of the Glenrose site *(Fig.*

The recovery of this skillfully sculptured human figurine from an early context like the St. Mungo phase comes as a surprise. It is the oldest anthropomorphic sculpture known in the Pacific Northwest to date. The available C^{14} dates on the St. Mungo phase deposits at Glenrose range from 4240 ± 110 (GaK-4648) to 3280 ± 105 B.P. (GaK-4683), that is, from about 2290 to 1300 B.C. In sum, we perceive during the Developmental Period the appearance of certain important technological innovations as well as others of an aesthetic and perhaps cult significance which presage the startling and almost explosive cultural developments of the ensuing centuries.

The Climax Period

The Climax Period encompasses several regionally and temporally separable phases. Virtually coinciding in time are the Baldwin phase in the Canyon and the Locarno Beach phase in the Delta region. Both probably had their inception shortly before 1000 B.C. The earliest C^{14} date on a mainland component of the Locarno Beach phase is 2970 ± 90 B.P. or 1020 B.C. (I-7791). The earliest available dates on the Baldwin phase fall in the ninth century B.C. but since the samples were obtained at some distance above the bottom of the Baldwin phase deposit the phase must have come into operation somewhat earlier. Both the upriver and downriver phases seem to have lasted until well into the later half of the last millennium B.C. The beginnings of the ensuing Marpole phase in the Delta at around 400 B.C. seem to have overlapped with the later stages of the Locarno Beach phase. The same may have been true with respect to the onset of the Skamel phase which in the upriver region follows upon the Baldwin phase at approximately the same time *(Fig. 8:2)*.

Although the archaeological manifestations of the Baldwin and Locarno Beach phase cultures have certain traits in common they also exhibit significant differences (cf. Borden 1968b). This statement also applies to their art forms. Because by contrast with the Locarno Beach phase the Baldwin phase seems to have retained more traits which probably had their inception at an earlier time it seems advisable to discuss it first. Among definitely persisting traits are, for instance, insect-larva-like carvings very similar to those of the proceeding period as well as incised feather-like designs.

New in the Baldwin phase are carvings of vertebrate animals, both real and fantastic in soft stone, such as phyllite, steatite and fine-grained sandstone. Some are simple outline carvings *(Fig. 8:7)*, others are sculptures in the round. Occasionally no details other than the outline are rendered, as, for instance, in a flat, cut-out cookie-like representations of what is probably meant to be a bear *(Fig. 8:7a)*. More often a few additional features, external and/or internal are shown.

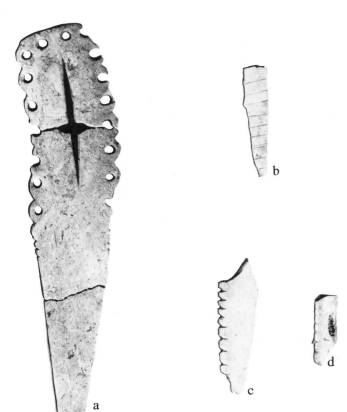

Fig. 8:5. Art of the St. Mungo Phase. Developmental Period. *a* antler "knife" with elaborately embellished handle. *b-d* selection of variously decorated bone artifacts. All from St. Mungo site. Length of *c:* 5.1cm.

8:6f; Matson 1976:183, Fig. 8-30f). Based on the antler tine, the sculpture depicts the head and legless torso of a human figure carefully carved in considerable detail with special emphasis on the face. Deeply gouged almond-shaped eyes slant upward and outward. Eyebrows and nose together form a single unit, which is carved in prominent relief. Broad lips in low relief form an oval, slightly open mouth, and excessively long jaw lines converge to form a sharply pointed chin. The hair is drawn firmly upward over the rounded crown of the head into a flat-topped knot which is tightly constricted at the base. The resulting groove may have served for the attachment of a thong. Demonstrating a long persisting trend in Northwest Coast art is the emphasis on the head which, together with the top knot, accounts for well over half of the entire figure. By contrast, the torso seems to have been of little importance to the artist. The only details shown on it are the tightly flexed arms and flat open hands, both firmly pressed against the chest. Gouged into the distal end of the back of the artifact is an open socket, the dimensions of which suggest that the object was intended as a haft for a beaver-incisor carving tool.

a   b   c   d   e

f

Fig. 8:6. The earliest known sculptures in the round.
Developmental Period. Eayem and St. Mungo Phases.
Segmented insect-larva-like carvings. *a, b* of phyllite from
Esilao and Milliken. *c, d* of bone from St. Mungo. *e* of one
from Glenrose site. *f* human figurine of antler from
Glenrose. Front and side views, and rear view showing
open socket for hafting beaver incisor carving tool. Note
also perforated ear lobe. Length of *c:* 2.7 cm, of *f:* 10.35 cm.

Fig. 8:7. Flat outline carvings in stone of animal figurines. Climax Period. Baldwin Phase. *a* Bear (?). *b* Anterior fragment of an unidentifiable quadruped. Note X-ray representation of ribs and esophagus or spinal column. *c* Pendant showing the head and neck of a bird (?), tip of beak missing. *d* Figurine of some fantastic segmented creature. *e* Another fantastic animal. All specimens from the Milliken site. Length of *d*: 11.43 cm.

The carving illustrated in Figure 8:7b may have been intended to be a realistic representation of some actual four-legged animal although the species is unidentifiable. The rear half of the creature is missing, yet deliberate smoothing of the fractured area indicates that the figure continued to be used even after it was broken. Noteworthy are the peculiarly shaped head, the deeply incised mouth, and the x-ray representation of ribs and what may be the esophagus which extends inward from the mouth toward the stomach (?). The latter may have been present on the missing half. The same features appear on both flat sides of the creature. The figurine thus begins to approach a carving in the round.

A pendant in the form of the neck and head of a bird (?)

lacking the broken tip of its beak *(Fig. 8:7c)* is like the preceding specimens a flat outline carving, but unlike them it is provided with a large circular perforation which served both for suspension and to indicate the eyes.

Figure 8:7d shows a peculiar, segmented creature which seems to be a large fantastic elaboration in outline form of the insect-larva-like carvings of the Developmental Period. Unlike these earlier creations, this creature has a head and a tail end. The head is provided with a large bilaterally incised fish-like mouth, and the eyes are represented by a circular perforation which, as in the bird pendant, may have served for suspension. The considerable weight of this specimen argues against its having been used as a pendant. Another fantastic segmented creature is illustrated in Figure 8:7e. The head has a pointed snout and small pit eyes.

Whereas the foregoing animal figurines from the Baldwin phase are all essentially outline forms with more or less flat surfaces true carvings in the round also occur in this phase. An at first glance unprepossessing sculpture in phyllite of a plump mammal *(Fig. 8:8a)* is of special interest because it anticipates several features which persist in later Northwest Coast art. The large head takes up more than one third of the total length of the creature, and the excessively large eyes, here represented by incised circles, presage the subsequent emphasis on animal and human eyes, a stylistic trait which is so characteristic of later Northwest Coast art. These are not the only features which persist into later times. The spinal column is clearly indicated on the back of the animal by two finely incised parallel lines, divided into a series of squares by transverse incisions. Further, barely visible along the flanks of the much handled sculpture are several incised chevrons indicating ribs. The animal species is uncertain, but the round eyes, large voracious mouth and the short limbs (flippers?), dragging the belly along the ground suggest that the beast is meant to represent a seal. Seals used to range far up the Lower Fraser in pursuit of the annual salmon runs. Found at the very bottom of the Baldwin phase component, this little work of art is at least 3000 years old.

Also of great interest is a steatite sculpture in the round of a bear's head *(Fig. 8:8b)*. Considerable attention has been focused on depicting various features of the animal: the short rounded ears, the eyes, as in the outline carvings represented by drilled pits, and vertical incisions around the mouth, an early attempt to indicate teeth. Small pits at the front of the snout represent the nostrils. However, the most intriguing aspects of the carving are the deeply incised grooves around the elongate snout and over other parts of the head, a strong suggestion that the artist meant to show the animal in a muzzled state. The practice of muzzling was still in vogue among some recent North Pacific groups who raised young bears in connection with bear ceremonialism.

Fig. 8:8. Stone sculptures in the round. *a* Carving in phyllite representing a seal (?). View of right side (photograph by Hilary Stewart). Left side. Note incised chevrons indicating ribs. Top view showing vestige of incised backbone. *b* Side and top view of a muzzled bear's head. Steatite. Both figures from Milliken site. Length of *a:* 5.78 cm, of *b:* 7.52 cm.

Fig. 8:9. Miniature death mask carved in sandstone. Climax Period. Baldwin Phase. *a* Left side, *b* and *c* front and rear views. Milliken site. Height: 2.49 cm.

Figure 8:9 shows three views of the striking sculpture of what is very likely a miniature human death mask. Noteworthy are the hollow eyes with their raised centres, the large triangular nasal cavity, the exposed teeth indicated by incisions around the front of the upper jaw and along the margin of the drooping mandible. The side view reveals incised lines across the cheek which suggest tattoo marks. Indications are that a small top knot was once affixed to the crown of the head. The fact that the bear and the base of the carving are hollowed out further supports the suggestion that we are dealing here with the miniature representation of a mask.

These sculptures of the Baldwin phase artists reflect a growing interest in depicting the natural and imaginary creatures that dominated the thoughts and anxieties of their society. Bear ceremonialism is clearly indicated. Suggested also is a ritual preoccupation with death

although the nature and significance of this cult must remain unknown. Despite certain incipient stylistic traits that become important in later Northwest Coast art, such as the x-ray representation of internal organs and skeletal structures, the occasional emphasis on the eyes and the head at the expense of other parts of the body, on the whole, Baldwin phase art seems still considerably removed from what one would readily recognize as Northwest Coast art. It seems highly likely that Baldwin phase groups also used other materials such as bone, antler and wood for their artistic creations. Since none of these materials have survived in the acid soil it is fortunate indeed that these people also turned to various stones as media for their artistic endeavours as well as for their numerous and varied personal ornaments.

We shall now move downriver and examine some of the artistic expressions of Locarno Beach phase groups. Except for one or two simply incised siltstone concretions, all their known art is in organic materials.

During investigations at Musqueam Northwest (DhRt 4, *Fig. 8:1,* No. 12) excavators came upon a cache of four wapiti antler tine spoons, each spoon provided with a decorated proximal end. According to stratigraphic evidence and chronometric data, this cache dates between 600 and 700 B.C. (Borden and Archer 1975). The best preserved of the spoons features at the proximal end a complicated set of subrectangular perforations of enigmatic significance *(Fig. 8:10a).* Unfortunately, the second spoon is quite fragmented. Carved in low relief on its proximal end is the head of an unidentifiable animal. The proximal end of the third spoon, illustrated in Figure 8:10b, bears a magnificent anthropomorphic carving showing a man wearing a ceremonial fur (?) cape and headdress tipped with two short, pointed animal ears, the inside surface of each ear bearing an "inverted U" symbol, a design element which recurs frequently in recent Northwest Coast art. The raised lenticular eyes of the figure are set in large circular, deeply carved hollows. This type of eye configuration is somewhat reminiscent of the eyes on the miniature death mask of the Baldwin phase. the cheeks and nose, including the alae, are well modelled. Unfortunately, the front of the face, particularly the mouth region, has been so badly marred by a small rodent that details are no longer clearly discernible.

The sculpture of an animal head on another spoon is truly a masterpiece and can be readily recognized as being in the best Northwest Coast tradition *(Fig. 8:10c).* The conformation of the head, the absence of teeth characteristic of carnivores as well as the long ears suggest that the animal represented is probably a deer, perhaps a doe. The exaggeratedly large almond-shaped eyes and again the "inverted-U" symbol on the inner surface of the ears combine to impart to this sculpture in the round an air of early Northwest Coast art.

On contemplating these 2600 year old spoons, skilfully

Fig. 8:10. Carved antler tine spoons from Musqueam Northeast. Climax Period. Locarno Beach Phase. *a* Spoon with a set of oblong perforations. *b* Proximal end of a spoon showing a man wearing a cape and headdress tipped with two short animal ears. *c* Spoon whose proximal end features the head of a mammal with long ears. Note the "inverted-U" symbol on the ears of *b* and *c*. Length of *b:* 7.0 cm.

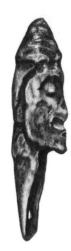

Fig. 8:11. Three views of an anthropomorphic atlatl hook. Climax Period. Locarno beach Phase. Note cone-shaped basketry (?) hat, depression for insertion of medial labret, and hair-do. The protruding chin of the figure served as the hook of the atlatl. Material: tip of a wapiti antler tine. Locarno Beach site. Illustrations by Mrs. Nan Cheney. Length: 7.5 cm.

fashioned and sculptured of wapiti-antler tines, it is difficult to escape the conclusions that they are somehow conceptually ancestral to analogous recent manifestations on the northern Northwest Coast: the mountain goat hornspoons whose handles feature the stylized carvings of crest animals and other mythological figures. Somewhere in the archaeological deposits of the intervening coast may still lie hidden the intermediary manifestations that bridge the long temporal gap between the 7th century B.C. and the 19th century of the Christian era. Unfortunately, whereas antler is usually well preserved in the coastal shell deposits the horn of the mountain goat rapidly decays without a trace. Thus, this hoped-for intervening evidence may forever elude discovery.

Locarno Beach (DhRt 6, *Fig. 8:1,* No. 14), the type site of the Locarno Beach phase, has yielded several fine examples of early Climax-Period art, dating to around 500 B.C. (Borden 1970:96-100). Among the specimens from this site is an anthropomorphic atlatl hook *(Fig. 8:11).* Based on an antler tine tip, the artifact shows a human figure wearing a cone-shaped basketry (?) hat and in the lower lip a medial labret. Similar to other human carvings from the early Climax Period discussed above, this figure has large circular hollow eyes with a raised centre. When the artifact is attached to the distal end of the atlatl shaft, the prominent chin of the figure served as the hook which engaged the pit at the proximal end of the spear or harpoon shaft. Other artifacts and faunal remains indicate that these groups engaged in sea-mammal hunting.

A small effigy of a human skull from the Locarno Beach site is fashioned from the split distal end of deer metapodial bone *(Fig. 8:12a).* Salient features of the specimen

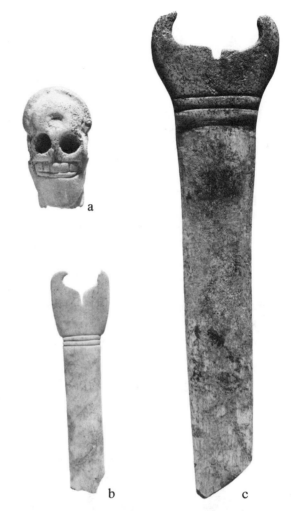

Fig. 8:12. Art of the Locarno Beach Phase. Climax Period. *a* Human skull effigy sculptured from the split distal end of a deer metapodial bone. *b, c,* Bone knives decoratively carved with a distinctive whale-tail motif. Locarno beach site. Length of 12 *c:* 15.61 cm.

are the deeply drilled eye sockets of even bore, the nasal cavity, the prominent row of teeth and the ingenious utilization of the natural contours of the bone. Like the miniature stone death mask of the Baldwin phase, this skull effigy may hint at ceremonials associated with the widespread belief in the coastal area that the dead had power over animals of the food quest and in this case especially over marine game (Drucker 1955b:73). On the other hand, it should be noted that the human skull effigy closely resembles the carved skulls attached to the ceremonial costume of the cannibalistic hamatsa and ghost dancers of recent Kwakiutl groups (Hawthorn 1967:129-132). The possibility of a relationship of this ancient skull effigy with similar ceremonials at an early time cannot be ruled out. Provision for attachment of the effigy to another object is made through a transverse perforation of even bore from one side of the skull to the other.

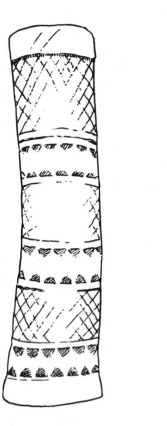
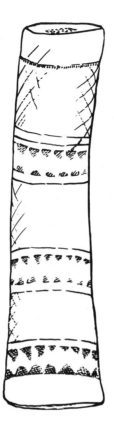
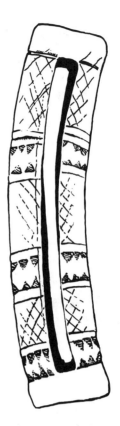
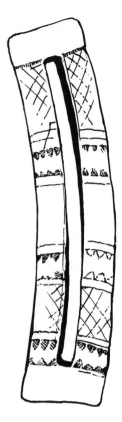

Fig. 8:13. Four views of a slotted antler cylinder decorated with geometric motifs, both incised and in low relief. Climax Period. Locarno Beach Phase. Locarno Beach site. Drawings by Mrs. Nan Cheney. Length: 9:9 cm.

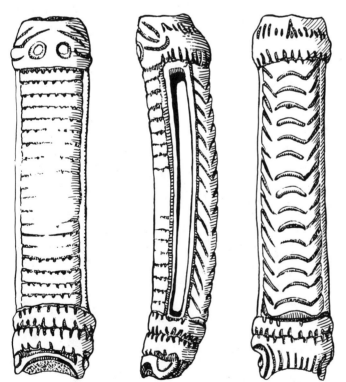

Fig. 8:14. Three views of a slotted antler cylinder combining zoomorphic with geometric decoration. Climax Period. Locarno Beach Phase. Locarno Beach site. Drawings by Mrs. Nan Cheney. Length of specimen: 9:55 cm.

Fitting once more into the context of sea-mammal hunting are two bone knives *(Fig. 8:12b,c)*, each decorated with a distinctive whale-tail motif, set off from the handle and blade by three transverse lines. The same motif, characterized by the inward turning of the tips of the flukes recurs on the tail of a sea monster carved on a yew-wood atlatl that was dredged from the Skagit River. Persuasive indirect evidence suggests that this artifact with its magnificent wooden sculpture dates to the time of the Locarno Beach phase (Borden 1969a:13-19).

Found so far only in components of the Locarno Beach phase are slotted antler cylinders. Three of the four available to date are elaborately decorated. Of significance no doubt regarding their use and function is the heavy wear on these artifacts which on the specimen illustrated in Figure 8:13 has nearly obliterated the purely geometric decoration in the medial portion of the design. Distinguishable are rectangular fields filled with finely incised cross-hatching. The fields are bordered by transverse lines and broad zigzag motif in low relief. This combination of motifs is repeated three times on both faces.

Another slotted antler cylinder is of special interest in that it combines zoomorphic with geometric decoration *(Fig. 8:14)*. Clearly carved in low relief at one end is the head of an animal with closely set circular eyes. On the bottom side of the legless animal is a series of segments which unquestionably are meant to depict the relatively

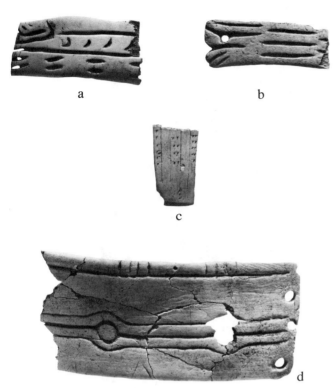

Fig. 8:15. Fragments of browbands *a, b* and other wapiti antler artifacts, decorated with incised geometric designs. Climax Period. Marpole Phase. Marpole site. Length of *a:* 5.57 cm.

large ventral scales of a serpent. The geometric decoration on the dorsal side consists of a series of spurred transverse lines which in an abstract way represent the small scales on the back of the snake.

Clearly, some of the art forms of the Locarno Beach phase reflect in significant ways the general spirit, concepts, and style of later Northwest Coast art. The recent recovery of basketry and wooden artifacts from water-saturated Locarno Beach phase deposits raises the hope that we may eventually find impressive works of art in wood dating to this phase (Borden 1976; Borden and Archer 1975). On the other hand, we may also note certain important limitations in the creative efforts of Locarno Beach phase groups. Thus, whereas wood requires certain special conditions for its preservation, stone does not. It is noteworthy, therefore that groups of this phase, by contrast with their upriver contemporaries of the Baldwin phase, failed to apply their skill and imagination to the creation of works of art in stone, unless one includes here certain of the enigmatic small artifacts of the so-called "Gulf of Georgia complex" (Duff 1956a), isolated examples of which have been found in Locarno Beach phase components of the Fraser Delta. But all of these are either ornaments or devices of unknown function and none are zoomorphic or anthropomorphic. Moreover, although these people were familiar with the techniques of pecking-and-grinding stone they used these techniques very rarely. Only few stone mortars or bowls and girdled

sinkers of igneous rocks have been found in their deposits and none of these artifacts are sculptured or geometrically decorated. Still absent also are pestle-shaped hand mauls of tough stone which had to be fashioned by a long and painstaking pecking, grinding and polishing process. The lack of this extremely effective tool for pounding chisels and wedges probably placed significant limitations on the nature and the scale of what artisans of the Locarno Beach phase could produce in wood. It is among other things such limitations which set off these earlier groups from those of the ensuing Marpole phase whose artistic creations reflect their delight in the creative manipulation of a wide range of raw materials.

The Marpole Phase (2350 - 1600±B.P.; 400 B.C. - 300±) represents the apogee of the Climax Period and thus of all local art history. Marpole phase peoples perfected techniques of fashioning artifacts out of a wide range of local and imported raw materials, including igneous and volcanic rocks that had been generally shunned by earlier groups along the Lower Fraser. A favorite raw material for a great variety of manufactures was the antler of wapiti (*Cervus canadensis*), the largest deer on the southern Northwest Coast. As we noted previously, some artwork in wapiti antler had been created earlier by Locarno Beach phase groups and even by craftsmen of the St. Mungo phase; but the artists of the Marpole phase exploited the possibilities of this medium with greater skill and imagination than any one had done before. Especially useful to them was the thick hard cortex of the huge antler beam of the wapiti. When separated from the soft cancellous core the cortex provided an excellent medium not only for common artifacts of every day use, but also for artistic creations. Manifest in many of their manufactures is a fine sense of form, a pride in craftsmanship, and an obvious delight in representing the creatures of their environment and the supernatural beings of their myths. Mention should also be made of the importance Marpole phase groups placed on personal ornaments, including labrets, nose ornaments and a great variety of pendants and beads. Some caches contained tens of thousands of disc beads.

Fairly common among artifacts of the Marpole phase are browbands of wapiti antler to hold the hair in place. Since many of these artifacts were worked down to a thickness of only a few millimetres, nearly all of the recovered specimens are fragmentary. A single complete browband for a child's head was found in the Marpole phase component of the St. Mungo site (Calvert 1970:61). Many browbands and other antler artifacts are decorated with incised geometric designs *(Fig. 8:15)*, but zoomorphic designs also occur. Figure 8:16a illustrates a fragmentary browband incised with a series of leaping spotted toads, probably the common northwestern toad (*Bufo boreas*). Noteworthy is the extraordinary economy of line employed in the simple yet lively representation of these amphibians.

The head of a sinister-looking animal, perhaps a super-

Fig. 8:16. Incised and sculptured animals on antler artifacts. Climax Period. Marpole Phase. *a* Browband fragment incised with a series of spotted toads. *b* Head of a horned serpent (?) carved on the proximal end of a broken artifact. *c* Sea monster bifacially engraved on the basal portion of a barbed harpoon head. *a, c* Marpole site. *b* Old Musqueam (DhRt3). Length of *a:* 6.75 cm, of *b:* 4.80 cm, of *c:* 11.57 cm.

natural serpent (?) is carved in low relief at the end of a broken antler artifact *(Fig. 8:16b).* Pointed appendage-like extensions rise upward and outward from the closely-set, sharply slanting oval eyes. It is these eyes that completely dominate this creation. Their fixed piercing gaze is bound to hold the attention of any onlooker.

Figure 8:16c illustrates the basal portion of a broken barbed harpoon head, which is bifacially engraved with the head of some mythical animal, probably a sea monster. The back of the head is bordered by a fringe of radiating appendages, while the first or proximal barb of the harpoon may have been conceived as a horn-like appendage rising from the creature's nose. The relatively small oval eyes have small dot-like centres.

Birds of various species were favourite subjects of Marpole phase artisans. Like most of their representations of animals, all of the birds illustrated in Figure 8:17 and 18 are conceived as parts of utilitarian artifacts. Interest-

ingly, it is especially in these representations of birds that we note the first appearance of open-work, that is, sizable portions of the carvings are not merely outlined, but excised completely.

Figures 8:17a and b are basically outline carvings representing the heads of two species of raptorial birds, perhaps of owl and eagle. These two creations are reminiscent of similar outline carvings in stone of the Baldwin phase in the Fraser Canyon, particularly the Baldwin phase pendant representing the head and neck of a bird *(Fig. 8:17c).* Even the double function of the large perforation on Figure 8:17a which, in addition to representing the eye of the bird probably also served for the passage of a cord, recalls the eye perforation on the Baldwin phase bird pendant which likewise doubled as a means for suspending the ornament. The two bird heads of the Marpole phase have in addition the maxilla and mandible of the beak separated by an excised slot. The function of

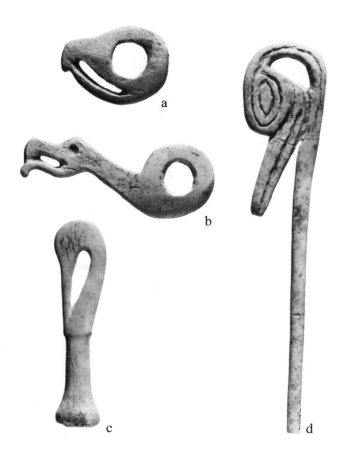

Fig. 8:17. Bird forms incised and sculptured in antler. Climax Period. Marpole Phase. *a, b* Buckles or cord adjusters in the form of two species of raptorial birds (owl and eagle?). *c* Miniature pestle featuring the sculptured head and neck of a water bird preening its breast feathers. *d* Long-shafted pin with the head of a long-beaked bird on the proximal end. *a, b* Beach Grove site. *c, d* Marpole. Length of *d*: 13.0 cm.

Judging from the long beak, the carving probably represents another water bird, but because of the semi-abstract execution of the piece the species is indeterminable. The design is simple but nonetheless very effective. The ascending shaft of the pin passes without a break into the bird's neck which then proceeds to curve in what is virtually a semicircle until it reaches the head. The outside perimeter of the neckline then continues downward to outline the top and front of the head as well as the long, downward pointing, tapering beak. A centre line, incised in the neck, follows the latter's curve until it reaches the head from where it continues to form the outer outline of a large lenticular eye. In doing so it effectively frames the lenticular iris. Basically, the creation is a flat outline carving with incised details, the same details appearing on both sides of the artifact. A distinctive aspect is imparted to the piece through the careful excision of antler between the straight rear of the bird's head and the curving upper part of the neck, thus creating a semilunar aperture. This open work interrupts the otherwise continuous flat surface thereby greatly enhancing the aesthetic appeal of the design. At the same time the aperture provides a means by which the pin could be suspended, the other end of the cord being perhaps attached to a robe worn around the shoulders. In sum, this zoomorphic artifact is another masterpiece of early Northwest Coast art which clearly anticipates "classic art" of later times.

Perhaps the finest example of Marpole phase antler sculpture is a partly realistic though nevertheless stylized rendering in the round of the complete figure of a great blue heron (*Ardea herodias*), standing on the bulbous form of a miniature pestle *(Fig. 8:18)*. The sculpture is carried out in remarkable detail. The toes of the feet are outlined in low relief, and the individually carved legs are separated by an open space between them. The legs support a well proportioned rounded body which is thicker than any other part of the animal. A short tail protrudes from the folded wings each of which exhibits long individually incised feathers. The long rather sturdy neck supports in classic Northwest Coast style an exaggeratedly large head and beak. The over-sized eyes occupy the greater part of each side of the head, indeed, they are the most dominant aspect of the entire sculpture. In form they represent one of the classic Northwest Coast eye styles: a large ovate, set in an elongate, bi-pointed, raised outline. The pointed proximal extension of the eye points almost straight downward, thus forming in effect an "angled eye." Crowning the head is the majestically raised crest of the male heron. Behind the head and below the rear of the crest is a small eyelet, indicating that this artifact was to be worn like the preceding miniature bird pestle, as a pendant. Perhaps they were used to mix small amounts of pigment for painting face and body.

these two Marpole phase pieces is not clear; they may have served as buckles or cord adjusters.

The miniature pestle shown in Figure 8:17c is one of the most exquisite creations of the Marpole phase. The proximal end of the artifact features the gracefully curving neck and head of a water bird. The tip of the downward pointing beak is shown preening the bird's breast feathers. Unfortunately, the almond-shaped eyes of the much-used artifact are so worn as to be barely visible. An elongate portion between the head and the neck of the bird has been cut out. This open work combined with the well rounded neck and head, considerably enhances the aesthetic appeal of this creation. At the same time the perforaton served for the attachment of a cord so that the artifact could be worn as a pendant.

Another example of a zoomorphic artifact utilizing a bird motif is a large antler pin, the proximal end of which has been carved in the shape of a bird's head *(Fig. 8:17d)*.

Fig. 8:19. Anthropomorphic sculptures in antler. Climax Period. Marpole Phase. *a* Pendant in the form of a human head with a mask-like face. *b* Miniature pestle topped by a human head with huge orbits dominating the face. *c* Human figure with a miniaturized body and a large head. *a, c* Marpole. *b* Old Musqueam. Length of *b:* 5.52 cm.

Fig. 8:18. Miniature pestle carved in antler, the handle featuring the sculptured full figure of a great blue heron *(Ardea herodias)*. Climax Period. Marpole Phase. Marpole site. Height: 11.2 cm.

Anthropomorphic sculpture in antler is relatively rare in the Marpole phase, and individual examples vary greatly in style. A small pendant in the form of a human head is carved with a mask-like face *(Fig. 8:19a)*. An eyelet on top of the sculpture crumbled during excavation. Basically prismatic in shape, the head has three flat planes, one of which forms the rear of the head, while the stylized features of the face are carved and incised on the two converging anterior planes. The brow arches are boldly incised over the large almond-shaped eyes. The nose is slightly arched, and a long line curves from the well-formed alae down each cheek and past the protruding mouth to the chin. Perhaps this little carving with its distinct Northwest Coast cast is a small replica of a mask representing some mythological character.

There can be no doubt about the mythological nature of the next specimen, which is another example of a miniature pestle *(Fig. 8:19b)*. The apex of the cone-shaped shaft of the implement is topped by a human head with a flat face whose most prominent feature is two enormous round eyes or rather orbits. Other facial

Fig. 8:20. Animal figurines in stone. Climax Period. Marpole Phase. *a* Siltstone concretion slightly modified to resemble a fox. *b* Siltstone concretion engraved to represent a fish, probably a salmon. *a* Beach Grove. *b* Marpole. Length of *b:* 11.3 cm.

margins of the head indicate that the figure was part of a composite object. Interestingly, this caricature of the human figure bears a marked resemblance to a figurine on a "soul catcher" used by a northern Kwakiutl shaman during the nineteenth century (Inverarity 1950: No. 163).

Artists of the Marpole phase also worked in stone. They often used relatively soft kinds of rock such as local siltstone and sandstone as well as steatite imported from upriver. However, they did not shrink from also utilizing less easily tractable local rocks like vesicular lava, andesite and even granite.

The peculiar natural shapes of siltstone concretions occasionally stimulated the imagination of artists to modify them slightly or sometimes more extensively into animal forms. The specimen illustrated in Figure 8:20a is based on a siltstone concretion which has been altered only slightly through abrading to create an animal form whose pointed head, short legs and long bushy tail suggest the figure of a fox. No attempt has been made to indicate other details such as eyes and mouth. It is essentially an outline carving not much different in character from those of the Baldwin phase.

Some concretions were modified more extensively into fish effigies, as shown, for instance, in Figure 8:20b. The overall outline of the flat stone has been left unchanged, but external and internal details of the head and body have been elaborately engraved on both sides of the stone in a conventionalized naturalized style which anticipates that of later Northwest Coast art. Boldly incised on the oversized head, which occupies more than one third of the effigy's length, are large lenticular eyes, each superimposed by a prominent, arching browline. The wide tooth-filled mouth extends from the blunt anterior of the head downward to a point beneath the eyes. A strong straight line runs from the proximal corner of the eyes across the length of the body to the tail. Closely spaced rib-bones extend downward from the front portion of this line, while the backbone is indicated by bilateral rows of overlapping chevrons. The effigy, most likely that of a salmon, was intended for suspension by means of perforations through the back near the centre of gravity. The care devoted to the creation of this effigy suggests it was meant for use in some ritual.

Marpole phase components have yielded numerous stone bowls fashioned of vesicular lava, andesite, and other igneous rocks. Sandstone was used relatively rarely; some were made of steatite. Many are plain, like the few stone bowls fashioned of vesicular lava, andesite and derable number of Marpole phase vessels are zoomorphically or anthropomorphically carved.

A zoomorphic stone bowl from the Marpole phase component of the Point Grey site (DhRt 5, *Fig. 8:1*, No. 13) is based on an ovate boulder of vesicular lava *(Fig. 8:21)*. The face of an animal is pecked petroglyph fashion on the narrower end of the stone. Faint grooves on the

features are only perfunctorily indicated. Still visible in the hollows of the orbit is a greenish tinge, the vestige of a greenish substance which most likely was cupric oxide. Since we know from other evidence that native copper was used for ornamental purposes during the Marpole phase (Borden 1970: 96, Fig. 29; p. 102, Fig. 31o). It seems reasonable to infer that the orbits were originally inlaid with two shiny circular sheets of native copper. An eyelet on top of this remarkable composite sculpture indicates that, like the other miniature pestles described above, this piece was meant to be worn like a pendant.

The small figurine shown in Figure 8:19c is executed unifacially in low relief on a thin curving piece of antler. In this specimen some of the major stylistic traits of Northwest Coast art are carried to an extreme: a huge head with large bulging eyes and a prominent forehead and nose surmounts a body and limbs so reduced in size that it is difficult to distinguish individual parts. The figure lacks a neck and all that remains of the body is the rib cage to which vestigial arms and legs are attached to the sides and lower corners respectively. Perforation on the

Fig. 8:21. Zoomorphic stone bowl of vesicular lava, probably representing a seal. Climax Period. Marpole Phase. Point Grey site. Overall length: 19.62 cm.

sides behind the head as well as on the posterior suggest the front and rear limbs of the animal, perhaps the flippers of a seal. As in many recent stone and wooden bowls of the more northern Northwest Coast the entire artifact is conceived as representing the animal. Similar zoomorphic vessels as the one described are fairly common in the Marpole phase. Another good example is illustrated by H.I. Smith (1903, Fig. 54a).

Space limitations make it impossible to describe all zoomorphic vessels from the Marpole phase in detail, hence a brief summary must suffice. Other examples of such vessels known to be from or attributable to the Marpole phase include a heavy sandstone bowl in the shape of a mammal whose cloven feet suggest some ungulate, perhaps a mountain goat. The specimen was found in situ at the Beach Grove site (DgRs 1: U.B.C. Museum of Anthropology); a "paint mortar" of hard igneous rock, probably from Marpole, depicting a diving porpoise (Provincial Museum No. 618; Duff 1956a:63, No. 22, 1975 No. 16; H.I. Smith 1903, Fig. 54b); a bird bowl from the Marpole site showing an inverted bird

with a bowl on the ventral side and supported on the back by a cylindrical pedestal (Duff 1956a; Plate 17G); and finally another sculptured vessel from Marpole described by H.I. Smith (1903: 184, Fig, 56:186) as "a mortar with four legs, and a handle in the form of an animal. The head seems to be that of a bird, probably an owl, while the mortar itself gives the impression of being the body of a quadruped."

In addition to zoomorphic stone vessels from the Marpole phase there are a number of anthropomorphic bowls which originated in Marpole phase components. The artifacts fall into three types:

Head Mortars
Bowls with Head on one End
Seated Human Figure Bowls

Head Mortars. The Marpole phase component of the Beach Grove site which yielded the bowl in the form of a mammal with cloven feet also produced a massive head mortar laboriously sculptured from tough red granite *(Fig.*

Fig. 8:22. Human head mortar from the Beach Grove site, sculptured in red granite. Climax Period. Marpole Phase. (Specimen in private hands). Height: 21.3 cm.

8:22). As in a number of other human sculptures from this phase the face is based on two planes which converge in the middle, the centre ridge being dominated by the broad, downward expanding, slightly beaked nose. Arching brows meet in a prominent wedge over the depressed bridge of the nose. Great care has been devoted to the oversized eyes, each consisting of a raised oval ridge which completely surrounds a raised centre. The artist seems to have experienced some difficulty in shaping the mouth which is slightly askew and off-centre. Moreover, the perhaps unfinished lower lip protrudes unnaturally beyond the upper lip. On the whole, however, this head mortar is one of the more impressive works of art from the Marpole phase.

Bowls with a Human Head at one End. The head from the end of a bowl of this type was recovered during systematic excavations at the Marpole site *(Fig. 8:23).* Sculptured of vesicular lava, this head resembles the head mortar from Beach Grove in some details, particularly in the arching brows which converge in the middle to form

a prominent descending wedge above the nose. The most startling aspect of this sculpture is the huge thick-lipped, wide-open, almost circular mouth, a feature which strongly suggests that the figure is represented as shouting or singing.

Harlan I. Smith (1903: Fig. 53a) illustrates a "stone mortar" which he excavated at Marpole. Carved of sandstone, the piece features a small realistically sculptured human face protruding from the rim of one end of the bowl. This specimen is unique in that, apart from the carved face, the flat rim of the bowl and the outer surface immediately below it are each incised with a simple zigzag line.

Seated Human Figure Bowls. Duff (1956a) lists a total of fifty seated figurines from the entire area of their distribution, and since then a number of additional specimens have been found. Unfortunately, evidence on their provenence is lacking, incomplete or questionable in nearly every instance. It is all the more important that the most reliable contextual and chronometric data come from the Marpole site where no fewer than three of these sculptures were recovered. Two were excavated and one was found entangled in the roots of a large tree, that had grown on the shellmound after the site was abandoned. Statements alleging that one specimen "was found on the surface of disturbed deposits" (Duff 1956a; 43, 94; 1975:173) are in error. All of these sculptures originated at depths of from 1 to 1.5 m within the deposits of this village site. Since radiocarbon assays on samples from this component of the Marpole phase range from about 350 B.C. to A.D. 200 it seems likely that at least the known specimens from the type site date to sometime within this time span.

One of the seated figures was recovered at Marpole in 1930 by Herman Leisk, This "Marpole Image" *(Fig. 8:24)* is one of the larger seated figurines. It is 28 cm high, 18.8 cm wide, 25.5 cm from front to back and weighs about 18 kg. Apparently made of local sandstone, the figure appears unfinished, that is, of having been merely blocked out by pecking. No part was smoothed by abrasion. The massive, grossly oversized head comprises about two-fifths of the total height. The face is composed of two slightly excurvate planes which meet in the middle at an obtuse angle forming a convex ridge which extends from the crown to the mouth. The nose is merely a part of this median ridge and lacks other details. Two large shallowly pecked oval grooves form the eyes. The mouth consists of a large deeply pecked rectangle with rounded corners and a raised oblong centre. A form of headdress appears to be framing the face. The neck is short and massive. Carved in low relief, the arms extend forward from the shoulders, holding a slightly dished "bowl" which is fused with the chest and abdomen. Hips and buttocks are also outlined in low relief, merging with barely indicated outstretched legs at the base of the figure. Both hands and feet are omitted. The seated figure is leaning backward slightly with face and eyes raised, and perhaps singing as suggested by the open mouth. With a remarkable economy of effort, but motivated by a powerful drive, the ancient sculptor has wrought a work of art which exudes an air of impressive solemn reverence.

The largest of all known seated human figure bowls was found in 1913 in the "Eburne shell heap" (that is the Marpole site) among the roots of a tree three feet (ca. 1 m) below the surface. The height of the sculpture *(Fig. 8:25)* is 53.3 cm and the width 25.4 cm. Since the head with its headdress is 22.8 cm high it comprises well over 40% of the total height. Fashioned, like the preceding figure, of local sandstone by pecking only, the statue exhibits relatively few parts that are worked out in detail, most of the attention as usual being devoted to the head and especially to the face. The thick, nearly parallel lips are slightly parted as though the figure were singing.

By contrast with the preceding largest of all known seated human figure bowls, the third specimen is one of

Fig. 8:23. Human head broken from the end of a stone bowl of vesicular lava. Climax Period. Marpole Phase. Marpole site. Height: 10.28 cm.

the smallest. Indeed, it *is* the smallest in the Lower Fraser region *(Fig. 8:26)*. In view of repeated statements made by Duff (1956a:43, 94; 1975:173), alleging that this figurine had been found in disturbed surface deposits of the Marpole site it is important to set the record straight and to describe briefly the circumstances of the recovery of this specimen.

In 1949 an archaeological field crew from the University of British Columbia was conducting excavations on a back lot of the Marpole site. This work inspired a next-door neighbour to dig a test pit in his own backyard. In the process the man found the small statue at considerable depth in stratified shell deposit well beneath the thick cultivated topsoil. There can be no question either about the assignment of this specimen to the Marpole phase or about its creation and use prior to the abandonment of the Marpole site. The figurine is now in the Museum of Anthropology, U.B.C.

Only 10.2 cm in height, this seated human figure bowl is the smallest of all the specimens known to have originated in the Lower Fraser valley. It is fashioned of a good grade of steatite, but because the stone is fairly

Fig. 8:24. The so-called "Marpole Image," a seated human figure bowl carved in sandstone, excavated at the Marpole site. Photograph by Hilary Stewart. Height: 28 cm.

Fig. 8:25. The largest of all known human figure bowls. Climax Period. Marpole Phase. Found at the Marpole site in 1913 among the roots of a tree approximately 1 m below the surface. Height: 54.5 cm.

Fig. 8:26. Front and side view of the smallest human figure bowl of the Lower Fraser and the Strait of Georgia region. Climax Period. Marpole Phase. Dark brown steatite. Excavated at Marpole in 1949. Height: 10.2 cm.

Fig. 8:27. Pestle-shaped handmauls of dense, tough stone illustrating variously finished tops. Climax Period. Marpole Phase. *a* DgRs4, *b* DgRs5, both located near Beach Grove site (DgRs1) *c* Marpole. Height of *b:* 21.17 cm.

hard, the artist, working only with stone tools and perhaps sharpened beaver incisors, may have had some difficulty in rendering certain fine details. Nevertheless, despite minor flaws and its smallness the figure has a powerful, dynamic quality about it.

As is common in late and, as we have seen repeatedly also in early Northwest Coast art, the head is accentuated out of all proportion to the rest of the figure, the part below the stout column-like neck comprising only a little more than half of the total height. The trunk is short and stocky. Rudimentary, loosely flexed, footless legs are shown in low relief extending forward from the buttocks. Scapulae and shoulders project outward like shelves, and long attenuated arms extend forward from them and embrace a bowl-like container while vestigial hands overlap in front. The deep, carefully hollowed-out bowl is not conceived as a separate entity, but as an integral part of the body.

Rising vertically from the sturdy neck is the disproportionately large head, the obviously dominant part of the sculpture. The artist has devoted much care to delineating

many of its features. As often in Marpole phase sculpture, the face is based on two converging planes which in this case meet at an obtuse angle. Both planes are quite flat, and the details of the face are engraved on them. Most prominent are the two relatively huge lenticular eyes whose flat centres are outlined by deeply engraved grooves. Above the eyes are clearly marked eyelids, and above these, browridges arch in low relief forming an acute "V" as they meet in the centre. The median ridge formed by the converging facial planes serves for most of the nose, except for the laterally incised alae and two small pits which indicate the nostrils. Two furrows curve from the nose down the cheeks toward the chin.

The artist has devoted considerable effort to sculpting the mouth into a pursed, open, rounded shape with the lower lip slightly protruding. No doubt this configuration is intended to suggest that the mythological figure represented is shouting or singing like a number of other seated figurines and human sculptures from the Fraser River-Strait of Georgia area.

The face is framed by a raised line which marks the

limits of a curious headdress which rises to a crest-like formation and ascends above the face when seen from the front. Attached to the rear of the crest is an elaborate form which is divided into segments by eight transversely incised lines. This strange configuration is strikingly reminiscent of the segmented insect-larva-like carvings of the Eayem-St. Mungo phases.

The recovery of three seated human figure bowls from deposits of the Marpole site and the possibility of placing these particular specimens within a certain time range, that is, from about 350 B.C. to A.D. 200, a time range which begins and terminates much earlier than the formerly assumed time-span of A.D. 1-1000 for the occupation of the important Marpole settlement (Duff 1956b:95), raise questions regarding previous attempts to assess the age of the entire seated human figure bowl complex and to estimate for how long the cult of which it was a part, played a significant role in the life of the Indians living along the Lower Fraser. All other known seated human figure bowls, as mentioned earlier, are random finds without contextual or radiometric data. Hence, up to now, there exists no concrete evidence for assuming that the seated human figure bowl complex and the practices associated with it persisted long beyond the early centuries of the Christian era. As will become evident, the same may be true of much of the impressive artistic activity which lends such glamour to the remarkable Marpole phase.

Present evidence of the impressive efflorescence of graphic and plastic art during the Marpole phase is confined to creations in bone, antler and various kinds of stone. The question naturally arises as to whether the artists of this phase also used wood as a medium of artistic expression. This question can with reasonable certainty be answered in the affirmative, for not only are many of the techniques applied to antler similar to those used on wood, but in the Marpole phase the entire complement of tools requisite for both small- and large-scale wood working is present for the first time (Borden 1970: Figs. 29 and 31). Aside from adzes and wedges, this complement included for the first time in local cultural development the highly efficient pestle-shaped hand mauls, the tops of which were finished in various decorative ways *(Fig. 8:27)*. The presence of these stone pounders which are so very effective for driving wedges and chisels with minimum damage to the polls of these tools must have greatly stimulated large-scale wood working, including perhaps the creation of sculptures of much larger size than was possible in antler or stone.

Compared to the glorious efflorescence of art during the Marpole phase there is a marked dearth of evidence of artistic activity during the contemporary Skamel phase as well as during later phases of the Fraser Delta and perhaps along the length of the Lower Fraser. This dearth of evidence may in part be attributed to inadequate

sampling of critical components, to the vagaries of preservation, and especially to the paucity of excavations at crucial sites in the region between the Fraser Canyon and the Delta. Distribution studies have shown that this intervening region produced numerous excellent and fascinating stone sculptures of various categories (Duff 1956a). Unfortunately, because of lack of contextual and chronometric data we do not know whether these creations are contemporary with the Marpole phase or whether they date to later or perhaps even to earlier times.

The upper component at Katz and the component at Milliken-Esilao following upon the Baldwin phase together comprise the Skamel phase, *skamel* being the Upper-Stalo word for pithouse. The Skamel phase differs markedly from the preceding Baldwin phase. Whereas the latter was rich in stone sculpture and a great variety of stone ornaments the two known Skamel phase components are completely devoid of any decorative items and carvings in stone. Moreover, as usual in the upriver region soil acidity has destroyed all faunal remains including artifacts of bone and antler that probably were present. Nonetheless, the Skamel phase has produced evidence of quite remarkable artistic creativity in another medium, and has been included within the Climax period.

Among the debris of a burnt, collapsed and subsequently buried pithouse at Esilao were in addition to cordage and wooden objects, the fragmentary remains of two carved wooden artifacts. One of the latter comprises portions of a carefully smoothed board one surface of which is engraved with an elaborate curvilinear design, executed with great care and high technical skill *(Fig. 8:28)*. No obvious animal or other representation is discernible. The design is unique for no closer parallels are known from any time at any other locality in the Lower Fraser or the Strait of Georgia region. Perhaps it was a design and a technique which were used mainly on suitable wooden surfaces, that is surfaces which were larger than those that could be worked on antler or stone.

The second engraved wooden artifact comprises highly fragmentary remnants of a rectangular box, gouged and carved from a single piece of wood. One end and most of the sides were consumed by the conflagration that destroyed the pithouse. The approximate dimensions of the box were: length over 30 cm, width at the rim over 11 cm and the total present height, including four small oblong feet near the corners, about 10.5 cm. Whereas the outer surface of the remaining outward leaning end is plain, the long sides of the box are elaborately engraved in a style apparently similar to the one on the illustrated board fragment. Since the design is executed with the same care and skill it seems likely that the two objects, which were found in close association, are the product of the same artisan.

Two radiocarbon assays on wood charcoal from the

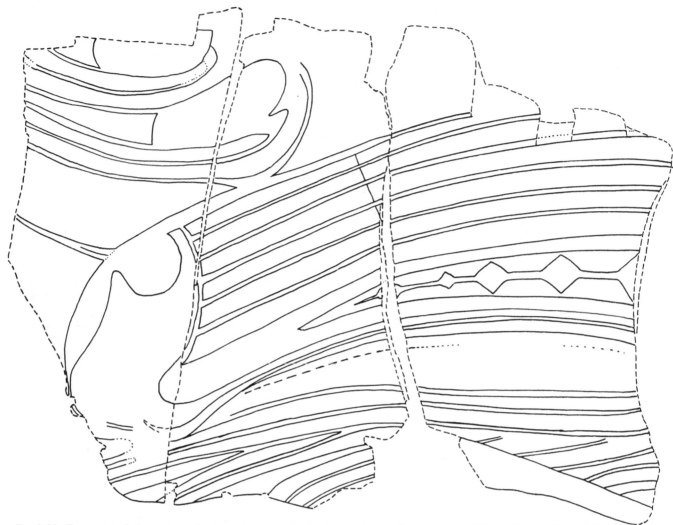

Fig. 8:28. Fragment of charred wooden board engraved with elaborate curvilinear design. Climax Period. Skamel Phase. Esilao site. Longest dimension: 21.3 cm.

fire-ravaged pithouse place these wood engravings fairly accurately in time. One sample yielded a date of 130±130 B.C. (GSC-444) and the other 50±120 B.C. (M-1543). Very likely, then, these artistic expressions date to early in the last century B.C. They are not only the earliest such artifacts along the Lower Fraser, but until now they are the only preserved manifestations of artistic activity of wood for the entire prehistoric period of this particular region.

Post-Climax Period.

The end of the Skamel phase and hence also the beginning of the ensuing Emery phase are uncertain. Perhaps it was a gradual transition from one to the other. A date of about A.D. 200 *may* fall within the period of this transition. Moreover, the Emery phase is still poorly defined because extensive earthmoving activities by the pithouse-dwelling Indian occupants of the Milliken-Esilao locality scrambled much of the deposits. The only presently available way of obtaining some notion of the cultural content of the Emery phase component is by subtracting from a mixed assemblage of artifacts those items that definitely belong in either the preceding Skamel phase or the ensuing Esilao phase. At least some of the remaining items may be tentatively assigned to the intervening Emery phase. Such a tentative assignment applies, of course, not only to the general artifact assemblages of the Emery phase components at Esilao Village and the Milliken site, but more specifically also to the artistic manifestations of the Emery phase. Because of the slender evidence it is not entirely clear what happened during the Emery phase, but the few available data suggest a possible merging at this time of Skamel phase culture with traditions characteristic of the Baldwin and Marpole phases. Among indications in support of this conclusion is an "apparent" resurgence in the Canyon at this time of

Fig. 8:29. Art of the Emery Phase. Post-Climax Period. *a* Human-effigy pipe. *b* Cigar-shaped effigy pipe. *c* Bird-effigy pipe. *d* Bird-effigy mouth-piece of tubular pipe. *a-c* Milliken site. *d* Esilao. Length of *d:* 10.56 cm.

sculpture in steatite and phyllite. Other factors may have contributed to this resurgence. Indicative of strong outside stimuli from afar during the Emery phase, for instance, is the first evidence of pipe smoking. Both fairly simple and magnificently carved effigy pipes, evidently of local manufacture appear to date to this time.

Figure 8:29b illustrates a cigar-shaped pipe. Near the margin of the bowl may be seen what was probably an abortive attempt to create a small zoomorphic carving. This assumption is supported by a similar soapstone pipe from the Thompson Indian area. This pipe has a small, well sculptured animal head in the same position (H.I. Smith 1913, Plate VXc).

A small zoomorphic pipe-bowl exhibits the rather rudimentary carving of a bird's head and wings *(Fig. 8:29c)*. Very likely the sculpture is unfinished because through an error of the artisan one side of the bowl became too thin and was pierced. The bowl no doubt was intended to be mounted on a wooden stem.

Long-stemmed steatite pipes were also made. These required an expertise in the technique of drilling stone, such as had not existed earlier. The mouth piece of one such pipe is very effectively modelled in the shape of a raptorial bird's head with circular eyes and a curving beak.

One of the most striking works of art, apparently dating to the Emery phase is an effigy pipe in the form of a seated human figure, strongly reminiscent of the seated human figure bowls although there are no indications that this figure was holding a bowl *(Fig. 8:29a)*. Fashioned of light grey steatite, the figure is realistically carved in a sitting position with legs sharply flexed and the lower legs close to the body. Feet are absent. Issuing from carefully modelled shoulder blades, the arms are extended forward loosely flexed with the elbows resting on the knees. Unfortunately, the front of the figure is badly damaged. The back, however, is complete. Four pairs of ribs are incised beneath the shoulder blades, but details of the spinal column are omitted. Only part of the rear and a portion of one side of the head are preserved. The head is supported on a short neck, and the one remaining ear is pierced. Somewhat elongate vertically, the head forms the bowl of the pipe. A fairly large bore passes from the flat base of the figure to the bowl. A wooden stem must have been fitted to the base. Carefully smoothed and polished, the entire sculpture is executed with consumate skill and careful attention to detail, one of the few masterpieces of the Post-Climax Period.

Despite the high quality of some of the art work during the Emery phase we cannot escape the fact that beginning with the Skamel phase such manifestations become rare in the upriver region. This paucity is in sharp contrast to the obviously intense artistic activity during the Baldwin phase. Moreover, this decline in artistic creativity is paralleled by a disinterest in personal ornament, a social attitude which is again in glaring contrast to that reflected by the numerous and varied beads, pendants, labrets and other ornaments of the Baldwin phase. One is tempted to attribute this apparent waning in cultural intensity in the upriver region to inadequate sampling if it were not for two important facts: (1) There is even less evidence in the available archaeological record of the Esilao phase, the last prehistoric phase in the Canyon, of work in stone for artistic or ornamental purposes, and (2) cultural developments in the Fraser Delta during the last two millennia are quite similar to those upriver although the decline in artistic creativity in the Delta region appears to begin somewhat later and by contrast with upriver sites, artifacts of bone and antler are well preserved in the shell middens of the Delta.

Whereas the termination of the Baldwin phase in the Canyon appears to coincide with the advent in the region of Skamel phase groups around 400 B.C. it is a curious fact that this date also marks the approximate beginning of the expansion of Marpole phase peoples in the Fraser Delta and the concomitant efflorescence of their remarkable culture which seemingly continued until at least the third century A.D. and at some localities (e.g. Beach Grove, DgRs 1) perhaps a little later. The demise of the Marpole phase culture seems to coincide more or less with the appearance in the Delta of the Whalen II culture identified at the Whalen Farm site, Fig. 8:1, No. 6, (Borden 1950, 1951, 1968b, 1970) which so far has only a single C^{14} date of A.D. 370 ± 140 (S-19) based on a sample collected from approximately the middle of the total depth of the Whalen II deposit so that the beginning of the phase may have been early in the fourth century. One of the most important aspects of the Whalen II phase, and one which distinguishes this stage from all preceding phases, is the fusion in this phase of two important complexes that were present in either the Locarno Beach or the Marpole phase, but which these two earlier cultures did not share, namely (1) sea-mammal hunting and fishing with composite toggling harpoons, first encountered in the Locarno Beach phase, but not adopted by Marpole phase groups; and (2) large-scale wood-working with the full complement of heavy-duty tools, including, aside from wedges and adzes, the extremely effective pestle-shaped stone hand maul which as we have seen, first appeared during the Marpole phase. The fusion of these important complexes in the Whalen II phase is part of the highly adaptive cultural synthesis which persisted into the Late Period and thus became an integral part of the efficient food procurement and manufacturing systems of the recent Coast Salish.

Notwithstanding these important developments during the Whalen II phase, certain other cultural aspects which had added lustre to Fraser Delta cultures of the Climax Period, such as the abundance and great variety of personal ornaments in both the Locarno Beach and

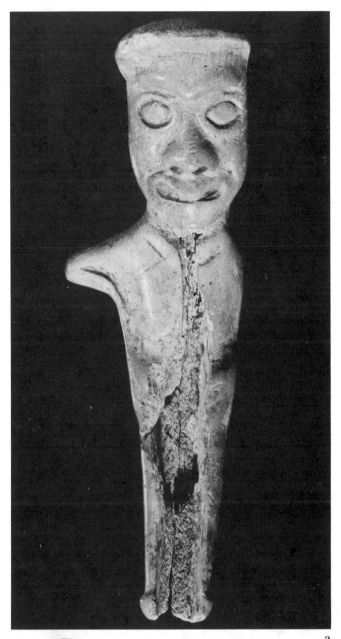

Marpole phases and stone sculpture during the Marpole phase appear to be rare or even lacking in the Whalen II assemblage. In part, this impression of cultural impoverishment may have been created by inadequate sampling. On the other hand, we may perhaps discern here the beginning of a trend toward a diminishing interest in representative and decorative art. A similar trend as we noted, had begun in the upriver region somewhat earlier. But, as in the Canyon, evidence of artistic activity is by no means totally absent during this Post-Climax stage of the Fraser Delta.

Proof that some master carvers were still present during the Whalen II phase is an expertly sculptured anthropomorphic haft for a beaver-incisor carving tool *(Fig. 8:30a; Duff 1956b Plate Ib)*. Salvaged by Wilson Duff during a pause in bulldozer operations which levelled the nearly four-metre deep shell mound of the Whalen Farm site, the haft was one of several grave additions associated with a burial found partly exposed within the Whalen II component of the site. In true Northwest Coast tradition, the head of the man depicted is disproportionately large, comprising somewhat more than one third of the figure's total height (13.3 cm). The artist devoted much effort to modelling the features of the face and other details of the head, but he showed little interest in delineating much detail on other parts of the figure. Legs are not indicated at all. Instead, the figure tapers, and an open socket to accommodate the beaver incisor carving tool is gouged into the distal end.

Whereas the antler figurine from Whalen II is a fine example of Post-Climax art in the Fraser Delta region other known manifestations of artistic activity dating to this period are of a more modest quality. Also found among the grave additions of the same burial which yielded the sculptured antler haft was a dagger with a large chipped basalt blade inserted in a haft fashioned from the tapering distal portion of a wapiti antler tine (Duff 1956b, Plate Ia). The haft is laboriously incised with fifteen pairs of encircling lines, each line consisting of short, closely spaced "spurs."

Two additional artifacts recovered from the Whalen II component (Borden 1970:107, Fig. 32h,i) need to be considered. Perhaps functionally related to the miniature antler pestles of the Marpole phase is a small pestle-shaped object of siltstone *(Fig. 8:30b)*. The artifact consists of a cylindr-cl shaft with an expanding basal end. The top third of the shaft features a complex of four incised

a

b   c

Fig. 8:30. Art of the Whalen II Phase. Post-Climax Period. *a* Anthropomorphic haft of deer antler for a beaver incisor carving tool. *b* Small geometrically incised pestle-shaped object of siltstone. *c* Bone artifact fragment carved in low relief. All specimens from Whalen II deposit. Length of *a:* 15 cm, of *b:* 7.29 cm.

encircling lines. The two lowermost lines, which are spaced more widely apart than the others, are linked by a series of vertical lines. Similar simple arrangements of encircling and vertical lines persist into the Late Period of the Fraser Delta.

Finally, mention must be made of a tantalizing fragment of calcined bone, meticulously carved in low relief *(Fig. 8:30c)*. Unfortunately, the specimen is too fragmentary for adequate description. Visible are eight slender pinnate elements framed by a curving border of closely spaced radiating lines. The style of this intriguing fragmentary design has no close parallel in any other Lower Fraser period.

The items described above comprise all that is known about artistic activity during the Whalen II phase, the duration of which is unknown. There is some justification, however, for postulating a "Pre-Stselax phase," which may have intervened between Whalen II and the latest phase in the Fraser Delta region (Borden 1970:110).

Late Period

This final prehistoric period is represented by two spatially distinct and in part culturally differentiated phases which virtually coincide in time: the Esilao phase in the Canyon and the Stselax phase in the Delta. Radiocarbon assays and other evidence suggest that both began around A.D. 1250 or perhaps a little earlier, and both ended in 1808 when Simon Fraser made his perilous journey down the river which now bears his name. This event signified the terminatio along the Lower Fraser of prehistoric time and the onset of the Historic Period (Borden 1965, 1968b, 1970; Lamb 1960).

Excavations at both Esilao Village and at the Milliken site have produced no concrete archaeological evidence that the occupants engaged in artistic activity during the Esilao phase. Yet, decorated artifacts of bone and antler similar at least to those recovered from shell midden deposits at the mouth of the river were almost certainly also in use in the Canyon at this time. These artifacts from the Stselax phase will be described below. Moreover, Simon Fraser's journal makes repeated references to zoomorphic carvings in wood observed on mortuary houses and on houseposts, thus documenting that local craftsmen created sculptures in this medium at least in late prehistoric time.

At Spuzzum, which Fraser recognized as "the boundary line between the Hacamaugh (Lower Thompson) and Ackinroe (Upper Stalo) Nations" (Lamb 1960:97), he noted mortuary houses at the mouth of Spuzzum Creek and went to inspect them. This description fits Upper Stalo practices rather than those of the Thompson Indians. With some grudging admiration Fraser comments:

> These Tombs are superior to any thing of the kind I ever saw among the savages. . .Upon the boards and Posts are carved

beasts and birds, in a curious but rude manner, yet pretty well proportioned. The monuments must have cost the workmen much time and labour, as they were destitute of proper tools for the execution of such a performance. (Lamb 1960:97-98).

The next day, when Fraser was well within Upper Stalo territory he described a plank house, the construction of which he found "excellent." Among other things he observed that the "very strong" posts, which support the rafter beams, are "rudely carved" (Lamb 1960:99). In the afternoon of the same day (June 28, 1808) Fraser's party arrived at an Indian camp not far from the Indian village at present-day Yale. At this place Fraser examined "a new tomb. . .supported on carved posts. . .the sculpture is rudely finished." (Lamb 1960:100). Three days later, when the party arrived at a village in the vicinity of today's Langley (Duff 1952:49), Fraser described a large plank house "640 feet long by 60 broad all under one roof." In one of the large frontal house posts, he continues, "is an oval opening answering the purpose of a door. . .Above, on the outside, are carved a human figure large as life, and there are other figures in imitation of beasts and birds." (Lamb 1960:103-104).

Fraser's brief but tantalizing observations, made at the very threshold of the Historic Period leave no doubt that the Stalo Indians of the Late Period possessed a well established tradition of wood sculpture and that representative carvings of beasts and men were relatively common. Unfortunately, no examples of these prehistoric carvings have been preserved. Photographs and examples of zoomorphic and anthropomorphic figures created much later in the nineteenth and twentieth centures by Stalo Indians *do* exist, but considering the rapid changes which occurred during the Historic Period it is uncertain how closely these later sculptures reflect the earlier tradition.

Whereas we may invoke lack of preservation as a likely reason for the absence of objects fashioned of organic materials we cannot do so for work in stone during the Late Period at Esilao village and the Milliken site, especially since the Esilao phase components have produced a considerable assemblage of artifacts fabricated of various lithic materials. The apparent absence of stone ornaments and art work in stone is, therefore, all the more significant. There is, however, one possible though unfortunately, uncertain exception. The artifact in question is an elaborately engraved spindle whorl of dark brown steatite *(Fig. 8:31)*. The whorl might have provided direct evidence as to its antiquity had it been found in proper context. However, it was recovered from material that had sloughed off from the wall of an excavation unit so that no completely reliable contextual data are available. The area of its discovery at the Milliken site evidently was used as a cemetery by inhabitants of the nearby Esilao pithouse village for many centuries, probably from late in the Emery phase onward to Historic time. Charred material from one burial, a partial cremation, yielded a C^{14} date of A.D. 1380±100 (M-1511) placing this burial early in the Late Period. Repeated burial activity in this area caused many graves to be disturbed, and no dates on other graves are available. Circumstantial evidence make it seem highly likely however, that the spindle with the attached stone whorl was a grave addition. The crucial question is "When was it made and used?"

The artifact's general resemblance to recent elaborately decorated spindle whorls of wood dating to the Historic Period is obvious. Yet, there are also differences whose temporal significance is difficult to assess.

In a summary presentation of Lower Mainland prehistory I tentatively assigned the steatite spindle whorl to a late stage in the Emery phase (Borden 1968b:22). However, I have felt uneasy about this assignment ever since. A consideration which perhaps overrides all the others is the fact that the artistic manifestations on the flat surface of the steatite whorl represent a true composition, that is, in this instance the carefully planned arrangement on a flat plane and in a given limited space of several separate animal images as well as part of such animals as design elements. Such true compositions we find among the Halkomelem-speaking Salish only on recent, that is, historic spindle whorls. We have no evidence that such compositions were made in the Lower Fraser region during any of the prehistoric periods. On available evidence it is perhaps best to consider this steatite whorl more or less contemporary with the carefully designed compositions on some of the elaborately carved spindle whorls of the nineteenth century, bearing in mind, however, that future data and deeper insight may eventually justify placing this remarkable artifact into an earlier period.

Skillfully engraved on the flat plane of the steatite spindle whorl *(Fig. 8:31a)*, that is, the surface on which the spun yarn accumulates (Lane 1951:Fig. 3), we behold the dramatic confrontation of two powerful serpents with huge heads, large baleful eyes and relatively diminutive bodies arranged around the centre like two partially concentric circles. The typical Northwest Coast emphasis on the head at the expense of the body is so great in the left one of the two serpents that the length of the head equals that of the rest of the animal. In surface area the head actually exceeds that of the body. There is also considerable distortion in the right serpent, but because of the markedly greater length of the body it is less severe. The reason for the great difference in body length of the two facing serpents is not clear. A third rather small serpent encircles the central perforation in such a way that its large inverted head is positioned on the opposite side of the perforation but midway between the heads of the two snakes on the other side. Despite the different sizes of the three reptiles they are disposed in such a way

a

b

Fig. 8:31. Zoomorphically engraved spindle whorl. Context uncertain. Perhaps Late Period, Esilao Phase, but more likely Historic Period. *a* Flat face. *b* Convex face. Dark Brown steatite, Milliken site. Diameter: 11.45 cm.

as to achieve an admirable balance in the given circular field. It seems obvious that the artist was striving for balance rather than for bilateral symmetry. Eight adroitly spaced isolated eyes are arranged along the periphery of the circle. A ninth isolated eye fills the space between the tail and head of the innermost serpent. The heads and bodies of the three serpents are spotted with pits in diminishing rows of three and two and finally one. It is worth noting that a number of isolated pits are used as fillers in some of the vacant spaces of the circular field on both surfaces of the artifact.

The elongate, basically lenticular eyes are outlined by an upper and lower eyelid which encloses an oval centre. The converging ends of the eyelids are drawn out into thin tapering lines. Two other features of these eyes are noteworthy. The oval centre of all of them, whether part of a serpent or isolated, is partly covered by the upper eyelid, a fact which imparts to these eyes their peculiar baleful appearance. Another aspect of these eyes is that most of them are at least partially "angled," some markedly so, that is, their extended proximal ends are turned downward thus forming an angle with the main axis of the eye.

The composition of the convex face of the spindle whorl is no less dramatic than the one just described. No fewer than fifteen disembodied serpent eyes of varying sizes are whirling around the central perforation, all with their convex sides facing outward toward the rim, while the concave inner sides are turned toward the centre. Curiously, by contrast with the eyes on the obverse face, the eyes on this convex face are all wide open, that is, the oval centres are all completely uncovered. This consistent difference in the depiction of the eyes on the two faces of the whorl appears to be deliberate although the significance of this contrasting portrayal remains obscure. On the other hand, just as on the obverse face, all the eyes are "angled," some more so than others. There is a link here with the Climax Period since we first encountered this "angled-eye form" on the sculptured great blue heron of the Marpole phase *(Fig. 8:18)*. The angled eye also occurs on some of the seated human figure bowls (cf. especially Duff 1956a; Nos. 11 and 17). However, the same eye form is also found on the secondary figures attached to the top of certain recent *sxwaixwe* masks of Halko-melem-speaking Coast Salish groups (e.g. Inverarity 1950: No. 62; Wingert 1949: Plate 34) of Vancouver Island and the Lower Fraser River. The "angled eye" is thus one of the longest persisting local stylistic traits.

The perforation for the spindle shaft is also engraved like an eye on the convex face of the steatite whorl. The centre of this eye is circular rather than oval because the perforation had to accomodate the round shaft of the spindle. It is possible that at one stage in the development of the design this central "eye" was intended to double as a mouth for a human face, the deeply incised outline of

Fig. 8:32. Art of the Stselax Phase. Late Period. *a, b* Incised drinking tubes of bird bone. *a* Malé village site. *b* Stselax. *c* Comb with geometric carving in low relief. *d* Anthropomorphic comb. Both combs from Stselax. Length of *b:* 7.49 cm, of *d* 7.35 cm.

which is clearly discernible. The symbolism underlying the designs of this spindle whorl is enigmatic. One of the most fascinating questions is why this potent assemblage of serpents and serpent eyes was affixed to a woman's implement.

Stselax, a segment of the Coast Salish winter village of Musqueam (DhRt 2, *Fig. 8:1* No. 9) at the mouth of the Fraser's North Arm, has given its name to the latest culture phase in the Fraser Delta region (Borden 1970:110-112). A C[14] date of 660±150 B.P. or ca. A.D. 1290 (S-20) on charcoal from *near* the bottom of the village deposits suggests a beginning date for this occupation and by inference perhaps for the Stselax phase and the Late Period at around A.D. 1250 or possibly somewhat earlier (Borden 1968, 1970).

Extensive investigations at Stselax and other parts of

Musqueam Village, including excavations outside and inside of old Indian houses still in existence until recently, supplemented by systematic surface collecting have produced some 5000 artifacts, most of them assignable to the Stselax phase, but others of recent Historic origin. The Prehistoric assemblage includes a wide range of manufacturing tools, food procurement devices, household utensils and so forth. Despite this large sample from a winter village, inhabited continuously for the last six prehistoric centuries, the assemblage from this site includes only a relatively small series of artifacts that can be said to manifest some artistic activity. It is important to note moreover that not one of such artifacts is made of stone; all are made of either bone or antler, and with the exception of a few isolated anthropomorphic and zoomorphic items, all others are limited to rather simple and for the most part geometric designs.

Incised Drinking Tubes. During her first menses a Coast Salish girl was enjoined to use a bone drinking tube, allegedly to protect her teeth (Barnett 1955:151) or, according to one Musqueam informant, "because her lips were not supposed to touch water." Commonly made of bird bone, such tubes were provided near one end with a lateral perforation for suspension. A considerable number of drinking tubes have been found at Musqueam, most in fragmentary condition *(Fig. 8:32a,b)*. Several of these bear a few or occasionally numerous fine lines seemingly incised at random without any deliberate arrangement or discernible design. Such manifestations can only barely be included under the rubric "art."

Combs. Combs are rare in archaeological deposits of the Fraser Delta region, a major reason probably being that, as in recent times, combs were usually made of wood and hence are not preserved. One *plain* comb of wapiti antler was excavated at Old Musqueam (DhRt 3), dating to about the third or fourth century B.C. of the Marpole phase. The only other two combs, also of wapiti antler, are from Stselax phase deposits (DhRt 2) and thus are examples of the Late Period.

Both of these Late Period combs are essentially rectangular in outline. The larger of the two *(Fig. 8:32c)* is provided with eight long tines, six of which are still intact. Topping the handle or bridge of the comb is a large semicircular (?) loop, the upper portion of which is now missing. Rectangular in shape, the bridge features a simple configuration consisting of rows of horizontal and vertical geometric design elements carved in fairly high relief. In addition, a number of forms are carved on the reverse face of the bridge, but their original shape is obscured by the advanced corrosion of the soft cancellous antler tissue of this face. The execution and finish of this comb seem rather casual.

The second, somewhat smaller and thinner comb is

anthropomorphic in a very simple way *(Fig. 8:32d)*. A flat nearly square head with rounded corners and tapering only slightly upward is set directly on a short limbless "body," separated from it only by slight lateral indentations at the "shoulders." Originally the comb had seven tines, four of which are still complete. The tip of another is missing. Details of the head and face are executed in a rudimentary yet stylistically distinctive fashion. No hair and ears are indicated. Four straight, horizontal, equidistant lines are incised horizontally across the face. A somewhat greater distance separates a lowermost fifth line from the fourth. Moreover, this fifth line dips bilaterally towards the middle, where a small isolateral triangle, incised somewhat askew, and a short vertical line, running upward from the baseline of the triangle, serve to indicate both mouth and nose. Two minute circles interrupting the third line from the top mark the eyes.

On pondering this artistic expression of the Late Period one is struck with the realization that it would be difficult to depart further from what one would normally recognize as Northwest Coast art style than is exemplified by this anthropomorphic comb from the Stselax phase at Musqueam.

Blanket Pins. Fairly common among carved and/or engraved artifacts of the Late Period (Stselax phase) are blanket pins, a fact which reflects the importance among the Coast Salish of spinning and weaving mountain goat and/or dog wool into blankets. Such blankets were commonly worn around the shoulders and fastened in front by means of a pin. The function of the large, usually carved and/or incised head of the pin no doubt was to prevent the pin from slipping through the blanket. Most of the pins are fashioned of antler and only the occasional one of bone. They are most conveniently grouped and described according to the form of the head. Blanket pin heads with simple geometric designs are shown in Figure 8:33a,h. Zoomorphic blanket pin heads *(Fig. 8:33i,j)* suggest the heads of birds or of some other creature without actually revealing the animal's identity. Details are left perhaps intentionally too vague for specific identification.

Historic Period

Contrasting with the generally stark and sober artistic manifestations in the archaeological record of the Late Period at Musqueam are a few fragmentary bone and antler artifacts whose execution is patently more in the "classic Northwest Coast style." One example is the impressive zoomorphic blanket pin illustrated in Figure 8:34a. This impressive bifacial carving features the head of some mythical animal with a small backward slanting crest and large "angled eyes" with large oval centres.

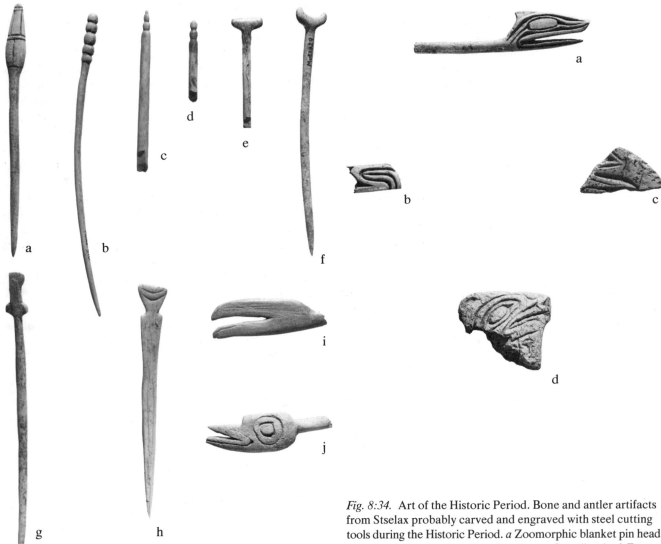

Fig. 8:33. Stselax Phase blanket pins. Late Period. *a-h* Pins with heads of simple geometric design. *i* Pin with an abstract zoomorphic (?) carving. *j* Pin topped by a bird's head. All from Stselax site. Length of *a:* 10.87 cm.

Fig. 8:34. Art of the Historic Period. Bone and antler artifacts from Stselax probably carved and engraved with steel cutting tools during the Historic Period. *a* Zoomorphic blanket pin head executed bifacially in "classic Northwest Coast" style. *b* Fragment of bone artifact deeply engraved with a curvilinear design. *c* Marginal fragment of an elaborately and bifacially engraved spindle whorl fashioned from the epiphysis of a whale vertebra. *d* Fragment of a zoomorphic antler artifact (comb?) executed in "classic Northwest Coast" style. Length of *a:* 8.23 cm.

The truly masterful execution of this piece with its meticulous attention to fine detail contrasts sharply with that of the previously described blanket pins. Moreover, the deep, sharply cut lines even in narrow spaces, such as the creature's mandible, suggest the use of steel tools in its creation, a circumstance which necessitates assigning it to the Historic rather than the Late Period.

Another of these historic specimens is a small fragment of a beautifully finished bone artifact, simply but precisely incised with a curvilinear motif *(Fig. 8:34b)*. The third is a small marginal fragment of a large spindle whorl fashioned from the epiphysis of a whale vertebra *(Fig. 8:34c)*. Judging from the design elements on this fragment, the entire surface of the whorl apparently was as intri-

cately engraved as some of the more magnificent recent spindle whorls of wood. The fourth speciment is the proximal end fragment of an unidentified wapiti antler artifact *(Fig. 8:34d)*. Again judging from what remains, the speciment was bifacially and skillfully engraved with an animal form which is identical in style and virtually identical in detail to the "otters" on the splendidly designed and beautifully engraved and carved spindle whorl collected by C.F. Newcombe at Cowichan, B.C. in 1912 *(Fig. 8:35)*. The resemblance in design and execution of the animal on the antler specimen from Musqueam with that of the supernatural "otters" on the spindle whorl is so close as to compel the conclusion that both of these artifacts were created by the same artist *(Fig. 8:35)*. This

which originated from disturbed surface deposits of the Historic Period whereas examples from the various classes of artifacts executed and decorated in the simple geometric style of the Late Period have been uncovered during excavations in undisturbed prehistoric deposits of the Stselax phase at Musqueam.

From the above discussion it seems evident that during the nineteenth century Coast Salish artists of the Lower Fraser and southeastern Vancouver Island were subjected to strong outside stylistic influences of radically different character from the simple geometric style that had been in vogue during the Late Period. This new style was more akin to that of the recent "classic art" of coastal groups living to the north of Coast Salish peoples.

Herewith ends our overview of 9000 years of art along the Lower Fraser.

Fig. 8:35. The two sides of the fragmentary zoomorphic antler artifact from Stselax illustrated in Figure 8:34 *d* are superimposed here to show the virtual identity in design, style and execution with that of the so-called "otters" on the nineteenth century spindle whorl from the Cowichan district on Vancouver Island. Diameter of whorl: approx. 20 cm.

spindle whorl obviously was carved and engraved with steel cutting tools probably around the middle or in the latter half of the nineteenth century. This being so, it seems an obvious corollary that the fine detail and sharply cut lines of the closely similar animal figure on the fragmentary antler artifact also must have been engraved with the aid of steel tools and that this art object thus must date to about the same time as the Cowichan spindle whorl. Furthermore, it seems highly likely that the aforementioned zoomorphic blanket pin, which is so reminiscent of the traditional style of the more northerly Northwest Coast, as well as the other specimens in this small group also date to the Historic Period. Supporting this suggestion is the fact that all these object are finds

CHAPTER 9

Prehistoric Mobile Art from the Mid-Fraser and Thompson River Areas

ARNOUD STRYD

The study of ethnographic and archaeological art from interior British Columbia has never received the attention which has been lavished on the art of the British Columbia coast. This was inevitable given the impressive nature of coastal art and the relative paucity of its counterpart. Nevertheless, some understanding of the scope and significance of this art has been attained, largely due to the turn of the century work by members of the Jesup North Pacific Expedition (Teit 1900, 1906, 1909; Boas, 1900; Smith, 1899, 1900) and the more recent studies by Duff (1956, 1975). Further, archaeological excavations over the last fifteen years (e.g., Sanger 1968a, 1968b, 1970; Stryd 1972, 1973) have shown that prehistoric Plateau art was more extensive than previously thought, and that ethnographic carving represented a degeneration from a late prehistoric developmental climax.

This paper will attempt to review current knowledge of mobile art with known archaeological provenience from the mid-Fraser and Thompson River areas. Inclusion of this region of the Columbia-Fraser Plateau in a volume on prehistoric Northwest Coast art is fully justified, as there is great similarity between the art of this region and that of the Lower Fraser River and Strait of Georgia. Parietal art, that is, art which cannot be moved, has been excluded for consideration here for several reasons, notably the existing pictograph study by Corner (1968) and the poor age estimations usually available for petroglyphs and pictographs. To avoid spurious distributional conclusions only mobile art with secure archaeological provenience and context will be included. Lastly, this study is restricted to the mid-Fraser from just above Yale in the south to Williams Lake in the north and the Thompson River area including the Nicola River valley *(Fig. 9:1)* because these areas not only have witnessed

the majority of archaeological work in the Plateau but also appear to be the "heartland" of Plateau art development as predicted by Duff (1956). Special attention will be focused on the previously undescribed carvings recovered in recent excavations by the author along the Fraser River near the town of Lillooet.

Reports and collections from seventy-one archaeological sites were checked for mobile art. They represent all the prehistoric sites excavated and reported as of Spring 1976, although some unintentional omissions may have occurred. The historic components of continually occupied sites were deleted and sites with assemblages of less than ten artifacts were also omitted. The most notable exclusions from this study are most of Smith's (1899) Lytton excavation data which are not quantified or listed by site. Thirty-six of the seventy-one sites yielded mobile art. The locations of all sites are shown in Figure 9:1. Mobile art includes all art which is not fixed to any one place. Two categories of mobile art are recognizable: (1) decorated utilitarian and ornamental objects; and (2) carvings in the round. Each is discussed separately.

Carvings in the Round

This category includes all portable objects sculptured in three dimensions as well as a few two-dimensional pieces (Table 9:1). Thirteen sites yielded thirty-eight specimens with two sites (EeRk4, EeQw1) accounting for twenty-two of the carvings. Many other carvings of unknown or questionable provenience are known but are not included in this study. Two basic kinds of carvings are evident. Most of the carvings incorporate the entire object so that the form of the subject and the carving are synonymous.

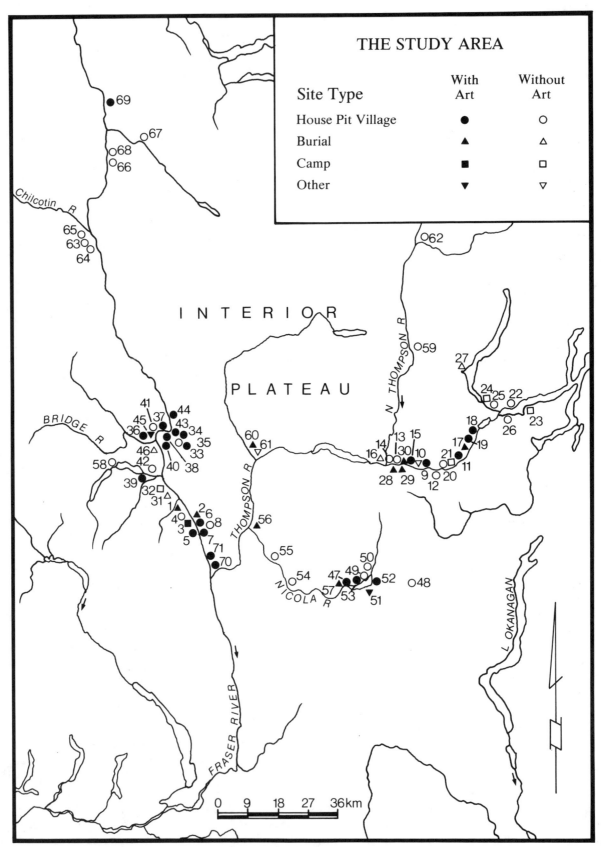

Fig. 9:1. The mid-Fraser and Thompson River areas of the interior Plateau of British Columbia locating the 71 prehistoric archaeological sites included in this study.

Table 9:1. Types of Carvings in the Round from the Mid-Fraser Thompson River Region.*

TYPE	Number
STONE	
Complete Sculptures	
Clubs	2
Bear figurines	6
Human figurine bowls	4
Bird figurine bowls	1
Vulviform bowl with 2 faces	1
Snake figurine	1
Lizard figurine	1
Fragmentary human face	1
Partial sculptures	
Zoomorphic mauls	2
Anthropormorphic mauls	1
Tubular pipes with carved bowls	2
Pendant with face and headdress	1
BONE & ANTLER	
Complete Sculptures	
Anthropomorphic figurines	4
Pendant or pre-form	1
Comb with bird figures	1
Hafts	2
Partial Sculptures	
Handles with human faces	2
Whalebone clubs	4
Fragmentary and undescribed	4
WOOD	
Masks	1

*Those pieces not illustrated here are in Sanger (1968 a, b), Duff (1975), and Smith (1900)

In some cases it is obvious that the shape and size of the sculpture are due to the form of the raw material (e.g., an antler tine) or to the morphology of the tool which is being carved (e.g., stone club). In other instances, however, the size and shape of the sculpture seem to be free of such constraints. A few specimens constitute a second category of carvings in which only a small portion of an object, usually a formed tool or ornament, is sculptured.

Half of the carvings are made of stone. The mauls and clubs are made of a dense material, probably greywacke, and were shaped by pecking. The phallic (?) club *(Fig. 9:2)* is further decorated by several long parallel lines incised by a fine-pointed tool around the circumference of one of the enlarged ends. The other stone carvings were executed in steatite by grinding and polishing which has erased much of the evidence for any earlier shaping

Fig. 9:2. Incised bi-phallic club of dense stone. Site EeRl 167 near Lillooet, B.C.

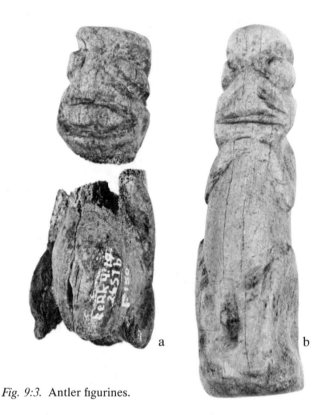

Fig. 9:3. Antler figurines.

Fig. 9:5. Anthropomorphic figurine.

Fig. 9:4. Antler figurine.

by cutting or incising. Facial and other features were formed primarily by incising although bas-relief carving was also employed, especially for depicting eyes.

Nineteen of the carvings were expressed in organic media including eleven of antler, seven of bone and one of wood. Deer antler appears to have been the favoured material. The small figurines were made on antler tines and all show the taper of the tine, three with the taper towards the head *(e.g., Fig. 9:3)* and two with the taper towards the feet *(e.g., Fig. 9:4, 9:5)*. Relatively wide, concave facets can still be seen on some of the bone and antler carvings attesting to the use of a whittling or cutting process in shaping the carvings to be followed in most cases by a light grinding. Like the steatite carvings, the features were usually incised, often in combination with some fine chiselling, with the occasional bas-relief carvings. Although I have been able to inspect only about one-third of the pieces the general impression is that most are well executed.

Recent archaeological excavations by the author at several house pit village and burial sites along the Fraser River near Lillooet, B.C. have yielded thirteen carvings of prehistoric age. Some of these have never been described whereas others have only been described in the author's unpublished doctoral dissertaton (Stryd 1973). The vulviform steatite bowl with two faces was included in the *Images Stone B.C.* exhibition and was discussed in the accompanying guide by Duff (1975).

Bi-phallic (?) club *(Fig. 9:2)*. This club was found in association with a double adult female and newborn/fetus burial at a small prehistoric cemetery known as the Bridge River burial site (EeR1 167). The site appears to be of late prehistoric age but the small artifact assemblage remains undated. The club is made of diorite and was "roughed out" by pecking. Diagonally oriented grinding marks are clearly visible and attest to the finishing method employed. Several small areas, notably parts of the smaller, proximal end, were missed and still exhibit the rough pecked surface. The club measures 31.9 cm in length and the shaft has a maximum width of 4.80 cm. The larger distal end displays an oval cross-section and measures 6.20 x 6.87 x 7.76 cm. Slight battering is evident on the distal end. The other end is also oval in cross-section but is considerably smaller: 3.80 x 5.42 x 3.27 cm. No battering is present on the proximal end. Both ends are slightly wider than they are long. The distal end is decorated with several finely incised lines. Two sets of almost parallel lines encircle the distal end; one set of two lines near its junction with the shaft and another set of three lines near its distal extremity. Along both lateral margins there is a row of short parallel incisions between the two sets of lines, eight on one side and six on the other. The meaning, if any, of these designs is not known although the long paired lines could represent a trench (Boas 1900:377). The club has a somewat phallic form and may be a bi-phallic representation (Duff Ch. 3).

Anthropomorphic figurine *(Fig. 9:3a)*.   Number EeRk 4:19-2658.   This small anthropomorphic figurine of antler was found in direct association with a second anthropomorphic figurine (number EeRk 4:19-2657) on the floor of house pit #19 at the Bell site house pit village (EeRk 4). Like the burial from this house pit, the floor assemblage is assigned to the early Kamloops phase (see below for the radiocarbon dates). Made on an antler tine which tapers towards the head, the 5.7 cm high figurine can "stand" erect on its flat circular base which has a diameter of 16 mm. The figure has a squarish, anthropomorphic head with a chin resting on two joined and fingerless hands (or two handless arms) held against the upper chest. The arms are flexed along the sides of the trunk but the elbows do not rest on the legs which are also flexed and without feet. The spinal column is marked by a row of five, short, horizontal lines incised into the figurine's back between the legs and the shoulders. Below the slightly distended abdomen is an 8 mm long notch which, considering its location and similarity to other figurines (numbers EeRk 4:19-554 and EeRk 4:5-213), probably represents a vulva. Facial features are marked by wide, carved lines. Two oval eyes with pronounced low relief irises almost meet above the nose which simply consists of two slanted nostrils, one more deeply incised than the other. A straight, horizontal line forms the mouth which has no teeth, lips or tongue.

Fragmentary anthropomorphic figurine *(Fig. 9:3b)*. Number EeRk 4:19-2565.   This anthropomorphic antler figurine was found next to the figurine just described (number EeRk 4:19-2658) on the floor of house pit #19 at the Bell site. Unfortunately, it was recovered in several pieces and is not complete, missing both the upper torso and the base. Nevertheless, it is apparent that the figurine resembles the one with which it was found and the two may have been a functioning pair. This figurine was also made on an antler tine which tapers towards the head. When intact, the figurine was probably slightly larger than its "mate" based on the dimensions of the two major fragments. Two eyes and a mouth are the only features cut into the squarish head. Both eyes are lenticular and have pronounced irises and the mouth is also lenticular, unlike any of the other figurines. No nose is shown and both the top and the back of the head are flat. The trunk fragments show a somewhat rounded belly and a straight back incised with at least fourteen short, unevenly spaced, horizontal lines which presumably represent the spinal column. Two bent elbows lie in low relief against the

sides of the body and the dangling arms deviate from the more common depiction of jointed hands in front of the chest by hanging downwards. Unfortunately, the lower abdominal area is missing and there is no way of knowing whether or not a vulva may have been present.

Rattlesnake-woman figurine *(Fig. 9:4)*.   Number EeRk 4:19-554. This antler figurine was found with the infant burial in house pit #19 at the Bell site. The infant, who was less than one year old but not newborn at the time of death, had been placed in a shallow oval pit dug into the house floor. Numerous grave inclusions were found in addition to the comb including several figurines described below. The burial is associated with a large artifact assemblage attributable to the early Kamloops phase (Sanger 1968:146-9; Stryd 1973:33-8) with dates of 1430±60, 1515±90, and 1250±200 radiocarbon years ago (the last two dates came from the same sample).

The figurine is 7.3 cm long by 1.3 cm in diameter and shows a possibly masked face on a slender snake-like body. Legs have been replaced by a rattlesnake tail with the rattles marked by six encircling grooves. Explicit female genitalia is depicted immediately above the tail and below the abdomen. The latter is slightly rounded but there is no strong suggestion of pregnancy. The arms lie against the side of the body and join in fingerless hands (or handless arms) in front of the upper chest. Much of the upper torso was cut away by removing the antler between the forearms, between the forearms and the chest and between the upper arms and the body, leaving but a thin spinal column and narrow shoulders.

The face or mask shows two long and narrow curved eyes carved in low relief from the top of the nose to the back of the head. A thin incised slit extends along each eye and may represent the iris. An open, toothless mouth marked by a wide groove gives the impression of an unhappy or edentulous figure. The incised cheek furrows extend into the hooked triangular nose and accentuate the nasal alae. Ears are absent and the head may be crowned with a notched headdress with a small perforation at the back just above the eye. Short parallel incisions in longitudinal lines cover the entire figurine except for the face, the genitalia and the tail, with six lines of incisions on the body and a single row on each of the upper and lower arms.

The head has been hollowed from the top to a depth of 17 mm, leaving but a thin outer wall for carving. Unfortunately, part of this wall has broken away, thereby partially removing one side of the face. It appears, however, that there probably never was a back to the head, leaving a gap which leads directly into the hollowed interior cavity. Originally I called this sculpture a haft (Stryd 1973:397-8) but, upon reexamination, I now consider the thin outer wall of the head to be too fragile to have held a tool. Further, the binding would have obscured the carved face and would probably have left wear marks on the figurine, for which there is no evidence. Considering that much of the upper torso has been hollowed out for no apparent functional reason, it seems likely that the head could have been similarly carved simply for representational purposes.

Lastly, we should note the possibility that the figurine may be wearing a mask. The highly stylized and artificial facial features, the relationship of the possible headdress to the upper face and the absence of a forehead are all suggestive of a mask. The hole above the eye may have been used for attaching the mask to the head although we cannot confirm the existence of a matching hole on the other side because of its fragmentary condition. If the figure was wearing a mask there would possibly be no need to depict the head, thereby accounting for its absence wherever it was not covered by the mask, i.e., the top and the back of the cranium.

Anthropomorphic figurine *(Fig. 9:5).* Number EeRk 4:5-213. Another antler figurine came from the floor of housepit #5 at the Bell site. Dated at 1380 ± 65 radiocarbon years ago, this house is assigned to the early Kamloops phase. The figurine was found close to four articulated fish vertebrae, a small Douglas fir twig with needles, and an angular rock measuring c. 18 x 8 cm, and may be functionally associated with them.

This figurine, although reminiscent of the other figurines which were recovered, is distinctive in several ways. It consists primarily of an anthropomorphic face with only a minimal representation of the torso. Arms and legs are not shown. The face occupies more than half the figure and so dominates it that it gives the impression that the body was of little or no importance. An exception to this may be the moderately deep, oval recess near the base of the figurine which probably represents a vulva. The face shows two oval, almost lenticular, eyes which are joined across the bridge of the nose by a shallow groove. The upper margins of both eyes extend down and back to form a spur 6 mm long. The eyes and oval nose are carved in bas-relief whereas the concave, smiling (?) mouth is depicted by a shallow, V-shaped whittled groove. Twelve short incised lines oriented longitudinally near the top of the head may represent a headdress. Broad, concave cut marks cover much of the figurine surface and may indicate that the piece was never finished. It is 5.94 cm long and 1.65 by 2.0 cm wide at the top, tapering to a rounded point at the bottom. The downward taper of the antler tine on which it is made is also unique to this piece.

Anthropomorphic or zoomorphic maul (?) *(Fig. 9:6).* Number EeRk 4:5-67. The carved proximal end of a pecked stone maul, pestle or club was also recovered

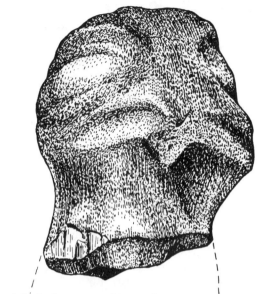

Fig. 9:6. Anthropomorphic maul.

from house pit #5 at the Bell site. Made of gabbro, the carving represents an anthropomorphic or zoomorphic head with an occiput and a slight facial projection (snout?). Two oval eyes have been pecked into the sides of the head, along with a faint groove below one of the eyes which may represent a mouth. At the base of the head the sculpture contracts to form a hand grip which can also be viewed as the neck or trunk of the figure. Extensive battering is evident on the top of the head. It measures 6.7 x 6.3 x 5.6 cm.

Zoomorphic ornamental comb *(Fig. 9:7).* Number EeRk 4:19-555. An intricately carved antler comb measuring 15.8 x 4.1 x 0.54 cm was associated with the infant interment in house pit #19 at the Bell site. Six long and slender pointed teeth with rectangular cross-sections and averaging 74 mm long form one end of the comb. Four of the teeth had been broken, probably due to the weight of the overlying fill, although one distal end may have been missing prior to the comb's placement in the burial pit. The other end of the comb depicts two crane or loon-like birds, 5.7 cm high, facing one another and touching at the beak. Both birds have a lenticular eye with a double spur, one spur slanting towards the beak and the other down the neck. A small drilled hole in each eye marks the iris. The mouths of both birds are represented by a single, continuous incised line which pierces the antler at both ends. Each bird also has two relatively long legs and a pronounced belly but wings and feet are not shown. One surface of the comb is partially decorated by pairs of incised narrow lines with short wide cross ticks which may represent trenches with earth or sacrifices piled to one side (Boas 1900:377, Fig. 298e), snakes, worms or

Fig. 9:7. Zoomorphic ornamental comb of antler.

Fig. 9:8. Bear figurine of siltstone.

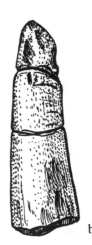

a   b

Fig. 9:9. a Anthropomorphic haft fragment. *b* Pendent.

woodworms or the skins of snakes or worms (Smith 1899:156). These decorations cover the medial section of the comb between the proximal end of the teeth and the feet of the birds and are also found on the bodies of the birds between the top of their legs and their necks. Short parallel lines oriented transversely to the long axis decorate the entire length of all six teeth but these lines are hard to see because of the deteriorated surface of the teeth. The reverse side of the comb is not decorated except for two incised eyes and the interconnected mouth of the birds.

Bear (?) figurine *(Fig. 9:8).* Number EeRk 4:19-553. A zoomorphic siltstone figurine depicting a seated bear (?) with outstretched arms and legs was also associated with the infant burial in house pit #19 at the Bell site. The proportionally large head is tilted downwards and sits atop a distended belly. Two small, circular ears, notched by a short line, are set off from the back of the head at the base of the skull. A narrow groove outlines two lenticular eyes with low relief irises. The open mouth shows neither teeth nor tongue but two short grooves directly above the mouth mark two nostrils separated by a septum. A small tail is tucked between the two hind legs (one of which is broken), forming a flat base on which the figure can "stand." The bear (?) measures 6.5 x 4.4 x 2.3 cm, is undecorated, and has been given a smooth finish by fine grinding.

Anthropomorphic face fragment *(Fig. 9:9a).* Number EeRk 4:23-268. A small and fragmentary anthropomorphic face of antler came from house pit #23 at the Bell site. It was found on the house floor in an early Kamloops

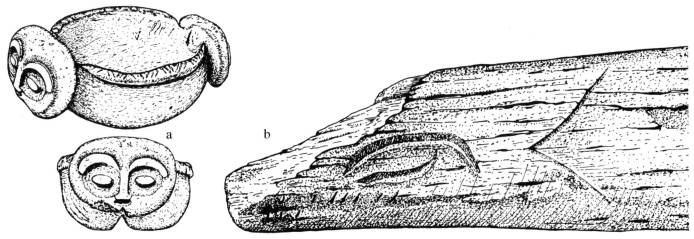

Fig. 9:10. a Vulvaform bowl. *b* End section of zoomorphic whalebone club.

phase context dated at 1560±90 radiocarbon years ago. Its overall size (5.1 x 2.2 x 1.4 cm), hollow interior cavity and worn exterior surface (due to handling?) suggest that it may be the proximal end of a small haft. The face consists of two circular, recessed eyes with round, raised irises and a nose marked by an oval groove with a raised centre, similar to the eyes. The object is too fragmentary to accurately describe the mouth although this feature may have been depicted by a short, concave groove directly below the nose. The grooves average 2.8 mm wide and are about 2 mm deep.

Anthropomorphic face pendant *(Fig. 9:9b).* Number EeRk 4:19-551. The infant burial from house pit #19 at the Bell site also yielded a carved steatite pendant. The low relief carving occupies about half of the piece and depicts a rectangular anthropomorphic face crowned by a notched headdress. The incised eyes have large irises and the mouth is represented by a straight incised line. The lower face is formed by a wide circular groove which encloses the mouth and divides the upper lip from a triangular nose without nostrils. The pendant measures 4.58 x 1.25 x 0.38 cm and has a convex-concave cross-section. A small hole, 3 mm in diameter and showing signs of wear, has been drilled through the uncarved end. Several long, thin lines had also been incised into this end but no pattern was apparent.

Figurine preform (?) (not illustrated). Number EeRk 4:19-815. The floor of house pit #19 at the Bell site also yielded an incised and shaped antler object which may be an unfinished figurine. It, too, was made on an antler tine which tapered towards the "head" and it measures 5.29 cm long, 1.77 cm wide at the base, and 0.76 cm wide at the "head." Incised lines have blocked out the major figure segments such as the head but detail and decoration are completely absent. Although it could have been a

pendant, its overall size and shape is reminiscent of a figurine.

Vulviform bowl with two faces *(Fig. 9:10a).* Number EeR1 21:13-1. This steatite bowl came from the fill on the floor of house pit #13 at the Seton Lake house pit village site (EeR1 21). The small, nondiagnostic artifact assemblage associated with the bowl cannot be assigned to any cultural phase but a date of 1220±85 radiocarbon years ago was obtained on charcoal from the house floor. The small carving measures 10.51 x 5.67 x 3.10 cm. The bowl is 7.37 cm long and 4.38 cm wide with a maximum depth of 2.48 cm. A shallow groove runs parallel to the top of the bowl, creating a raised outer edge around the entire bowl except at the ends. Short parallel lines have been incised into the top of this raised edge. These poorly executed incisions occur in sets of three (and one set of five) and form a zigzag pattern. A V-shaped groove with a maximum width of 6.4 mm has been sawn longitudinally into the bottom of the bowl on the outer surface.

Both ends of the bowl display a carved, anthropomorphic or zoomorphic face. The two faces are similar in design but differ somewhat in size. The larger face measures 4.32 x 3.30 cm and projects 1.66 cm from the bowl whereas the smaller face projects 1.23 cm and is 3.60 cm wide by 2.75 cm high. Both faces show an open mouth marked by a small, almost oval notch; two oval recessed eyes with oval or lenticular irises carved in bas-relief; a thin, vertical nasal ridge with a flared tip directly above the mouth; and two curved eyebrows carved in bas-relief which merge with the nose at one end and which stop abruptly at the other end. Part of the small face has broken off and the V-shaped cleft, which had been sawn into the bottom of the bowl, extends into the chin of the larger face. Duff (1975:172) thinks that the bowl is a female sexual symbol representing an open vulva when viewed from the top and a closed vulva when seen from below. He has also suggested that the faces may represent owls or generic humans (Duff 1975:49). The meaning, if any, of the short incised lines is not known.

Zoomorphic club *(Fig. 9:10b).* Number EeR1 19:1365. A zoomorphic club of whalebone was one of the grave inclusions associated with adult burial #1 at the Fountain site (EeR1 19), a large, plowed house pit village with a long occupation sequence and badly disturbed stratification. The burial probably belongs to the extensive but undated Kamloops phase component at this site. The club was exposed in three sections and must have been broken at least once prior to its placement with the burial because of the location of the pieces.

The club's morphology must have been largely determined by the shape of the rib on which it was made. It is narrow relative to its length and it is thin relative to its width and it has an elliptical cross-section. One end has been rounded whereas the other end has been modified into the head of a fish. A carved three-dimensional snout provides overall form whereas deeply incised grooves indicate various anatomical features. A long, wide groove filled with red ochre marks the mouth while numerous shorter incisions (some with red ochre) above and below this groove represent an upper and lower set of teeth. The eye consists of two wide grooves which do not meet, a lower concave groove filled with red ochre, and an upper convex one filled with black ochre which extends back and down below the bottom of the eye. Behind the eye an unlined V-shaped groove depicts a gill, its apex pointing towards the front. Because of the deterioration of the club's surfaces, the eye and gill are visible on one side only. The mouth and teeth are present on both surfaces but they are best seen on the surface without the eye and gill. The elongated snout resembles that of a sturgeon but the presence of teeth suggests that a salmon may be depicted.

Context. Carvings have been primarily recovered in a burial context. Only thirteen of the thirty-eight pieces were not associated with human interments and these all came from house pit deposits along the Fraser River. Carvings have been recovered from isolated, individual burials both within and outside house pits as well as from prehistoric cemeteries of all sizes. The placement of carvings with the dead does not appear to be age or sex specific as carvings have been recorded in association with males and females as well as with immature and adult interments. All the house pit carvings came from fill directly on top of living floors, and none were cached or placed in such a manner as to suggest any kind of special treatment or disposal.

Spatial distribution. Carvings have been found in the valley of the South Thompson River where seventeen pieces are known from burial sites, primarily the Chase Burial site, EeQw 1 (n=12) and along the mid-Fraser River where twenty-one carvings have been recovered from between just above Lillooet in the north to a few miles below Lytton in the south. Duff's (1956) study of the steatite carving complex indicated that the Fraser River distribution may extend further southward, possibly to the Fraser delta, but secure archaeological evidence is currently missing between Lytton and Yale. The complete absence of carvings in the Nicola Valley as well as the Williams Lake area may mark the maximum geographic extent of prehistoric Plateau carvings. It would be prudent to exercise some caution here, however, in that the current spatial distribution of carvings may be a product of the archaeological research that has been carried out to date. The location and extent of field work, the kinds of sites investigated and the preservation conditions for objects of bone, antler and wood are all variables which could skew our distributional results. Nevertheless we have to work with what we have and it is interesting to note how the emerging archaeological picture seems to fit with the distributional pattern observed by Duff (1956), viz., with a major centre of art along the mid-Fraser and a secondary centre along the Thompson River. The mid-Fraser area has more sites with carvings (n=10 vs. n=17), plus a more continuous distribution of carvings within its confines.

Temporal distribution A rather limited temporal distribution characterizes the carvings with most pieces dating to the last 1500 years. The oldest known carving is the zoomorphic hand maul from zone I at the Lehman site (EeRk 8) radiocarbon dated at 2185±150 years ago (Sanger 1970:90, 103). The possible anthropomorphic hand maul *(Fig. 9:6)* is also relatively old, originating from house pit #5 at the Bell site (EeRk 4), radiocarbon dated at 1380±65 years ago. At 1500±100 years ago there is the sudden appearance of small carvings in various media. The steatite carving complex originates at this time. Small anthropomorphic and zoomorphic steatite figurines, carved steatite pipes and pendants, small anthropomorphic antler figurines and carved antler hafts appear in the archaeological record, and the single carved zoomorphic antler comb with the incised decoration *(Fig. 9:7)* belongs to this time period. These carvings continue to be made until late prehistoric or ethnographic times although the steatite carving complex was on the wane in or before the historic period. A major addition to the carving tradition occurs around 1300±100 years ago when small steatite figurine bowls make their initial appearance. The vulviform bowl with two faces from house pit #13 at the Seton Lake site (EeR1 21) is dated at 1220±85 radiocarbon years ago. The seated human figurine bowls seem to be a somewhat later development, estimated to date from 800±200 years ago although no radiocarbon control is available. The seated human figuring bowls are probably the most recent form within the steatite carving complex and can be linked with Salish shamanism and ritualism (Duff 1956:114). Carved stone and whalebone clubs are added to the archaeological record between 1000 years and 600 years ago *(Figs. 9:8, 9:9, 9:10)*.

Although the evidence is scanty, it appears that Plateau carving including the steatite carving complex probably had its origin in first the decoration and then the carving of large stone implements including mauls and mortars or large non-steatite bowls. This development took at least 2000 years and may go back further, with the evolution of the smaller carving tradition spanning the last 1500 years.

Meaning. It is impossible in a paper of this length to even begin to deal with the question of meaning. Undoubtedly the carvings have meaning and were produced for more than just aesthetic reasons. Duff recently investigated meaning in Northwest Coast stone art and observed that many levels of meaning may exist for any one piece. If we are to gain any real understanding of the cultural significance of this art we must, it seems to me, be prepared to include the psychological in our paradigms as the ultimate meaning and purpose of this work appears to rest in that arena.

Decorated Objects

This category consists of all decorated objects, except those pieces which were partially carved and have already been described. A wide range of artifacts were decorated including utilitarian implements, toys and game items, and body and clothing ornaments. Thirty-two of the seventy-one sites in this study yielded decorated objects totalling 208 pieces. The private collections and museums of the southern interior contain many additional decorated artifacts but nearly all lack adequate provenience and contextual information. It appears that the 208 pieces of this study represent the range of decorated objects and decorative motifs in use in prehistoric times. Types of decorated objects are listed in Table 9:2.

The artifacts were embellished by several decorative techniques; the most common was inscribing a design onto the outer surface(s) and/or lateral margin(s) of the object. A gouging technique similar to incising was noted in association with incised decorations on a few specimens and one bark fragment exhibited a design of shallow "pin prick" holes *(Fig. 9:11)* which must have been made in a manner similar to tattooing, possibly with a porcupine quill. Some of the steatite pipes were decorated by one or more raised bands around the pipe bowl or stem. No other forms of decoration were observed. Presumably the ochre-stained pieces associated with burials were coloured

Table 9:2: Types of Decorated Objects from the Mid-Fraser Thompson River Region

Ornaments
Tubular beads of bone, steatite, and *Dentalium* shell
Pendants of bone, antler, red slate, steatite
Animal canine perforated pendants
Bone comb
Steatite ring

Game items and toys
Miniature bone bows
Rodent incisor dice
Gambling bones

Utilitarian objects
Antler digging stick handles
Antler splitting wedges
Bone creasers
Fixed bone and antler points
Antler harpoon valves
Antler awls and perforators
Bone and antler gadgets
Antler tine clubs
Antler hafts
Eyed bone needles
Bone pins
Antler tine flakers
Bone drinking tubes
Bone and antler sap scrapers
Antler "dagger"
Bone "head scratcher"
Wooden bow
Bark containers
Stone atlatl weight
Stone mortars
Tubular steatite pipes
Abrasive stone
Hand mauls of stone
Steatite spindle whorls
Miscellaneous bone and antler fragments

Illustrations of these artifacts will be found in Sanger (1968a, b; 1970); Wilson (1974); Smith (1900); Stryd (1973); Wyatt (1972).

as a result of the corpse being covered with ochre rather than representing a distinctive decorative technique. Of course some of the pieces may have been painted as they were in ethnographic times but no evidence of paint has been uncovered.

About eighty percent of all decorated objects are made of some organic media, notably antler or bone *(Figs. 9:12, 9:13)*. Bone artifacts comprise half of the non-lithic sample and are almost twice as frequent as decorated antler specimens. Dentalium shells, animal canines and incisors and a few pieces of wood were also decorated. Sanger (1968a:135) reported that at the Chase Burial site more than three-quarters of the antler items and less than one-tenth of the bone pieces were decorated but these frequencies are not supported by this study where

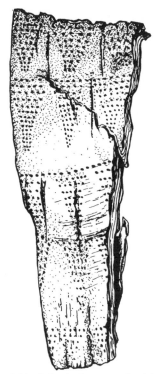

Fig. 9:11. Piece of birch bark decorated with a "tattooed" pattern from component 2 (?) at the plowed Fountain Site house pit village (EeR 119).

approximately thirty percent of both bone and antler artifacts were embellished. The decorated lithic objects are predominantly steatite, a not too surprising revelation considering how suitable this soft stone is for incising and for delicate, detailed work.

The steatite artifacts exhibit a better quality of incising than the non-lithic specimens, possibly because greater force and care was required to modify stone. The organic objects display a greater range of workmanship with quite a few examples of poor execution. Possibly some of these poorer specimens were not finished, but the majority appear to have been quickly incised with a rough design without concern for the quality of decoration. It should be noted that poor incising is most commonly found on ornaments and fragments of undeterminable function.

Burial and house pit sites yielded a similar number of decorated objects. Almost eighty percent of the burial sites contained embellished pieces whereas only twenty-five percent of the excavated house pit sites yielded decorated objects. It is apparent that decorated artifacts were selected as grave inclusions given the relatively small number of isolated burial and cemetary sites (n=13) and the high incidence of decorated artifacts (n=104).

The spatial distribution of decorated objects conforms to the pattern observed for the carvings. Two centres or nuclear areas can be identified: (1) the mid-Fraser region from Lytton to just north of Lillooet, and (2) the South Thompson River drainage with the Nicola valley as a minor sub-area. This distribution may, however, be indicative of the location of field work and the quality of preservation conditions rather than of the geographic extent of prehistoric artifact decoration. Excavations in areas such as the Okanagan Valley and the Thompson and North Thompson Rivers drainages will be required before the spatial boundaries of this decorative tradition can be delineated.

The temporal distribution of decorated objects is similar to that described for carvings except for a few considerably older specimens. Zone 7 at the Nesikep Creek site (EeRk 4) (Sanger 1970:Fig. 40a) yielded a bone bead with a series of deep cuts perpendicular to the long axis. This zone is dated at 5635±190 radiocarbon years ago (Sanger 1970:103-6) and this bead is the oldest known decorated artifact. Another piece of considerable antiquity is the fragment of a possible bone comb decorated by several short parallel lines from component 2 at the Moulton Creek site (EdQx 5) (Eldridge 1974:Fig. 33a). This specimen is older than 3800 years based on the age of the volcanic ash layer which caps component 2 (Eldridge 1974:51).

The practice of decorating utilitarian and ornamental objects can be seen as forming a 3000 year tradition which began sometime around 1000 B.C. and continued well into ethnographic times. The distinction between prehistoric and historic decorative art is, therefore, an heuristic device which has no meaning in terms of the art. The origin of this tradition may lie in the few pieces of older decorative art mentioned above but evidence is scanty and little can be said about its origin. It appears at present that the emergence of a true decorative art tradition did not take place until the first millenium B.C. The oldest assemblages—Bell site (EeRk 4), house pit #1; Mitchell site (EeR1 22), house pit #1, components 2 and 5; and Lochnore Creek site (EdRk 7), zone 1—primarily contain decorated bone and antler fragments which cannot be identified as to tool type although three decorated objects—one bone pendant, one stone pendant and a single bone needle—were recovered. Around 2000 B.P. there are several assemblages with decorated artifacts, notably the Guichon Slough site (EbRc 6) with a decorated abrasive stone (Wyatt 1972:78) and component 2 of house pit #22 at the Bell site (EeRk 4) (Stryd 1973: 287-8) which contained an incised steatite pipe, bone bead, one perforated bone pendant and a unilaterally barbed antler point. Between 2000 B.P. and the historic period there are many sites with decorated objects, presenting a continuity that leads directly to the ethnographies of Teit (1900, 1906, 1909) and others.

It is impossible in a paper of this length to adequately describe the various decorative motifs employed, their groupings and their placement on the artifacts. A few descriptive generalizations will have to suffice. Decoration invariably consists of various combinations of lines, dots and circles. No naturalistic representations were en-

Fig. 9:12. Decorated digging stick handles of antler from the Bell Site house pit village (EeRk 4) near Lillooet, B.C. *a* from house pit #8; *b* from house pit #23; *c* from house pit #21.

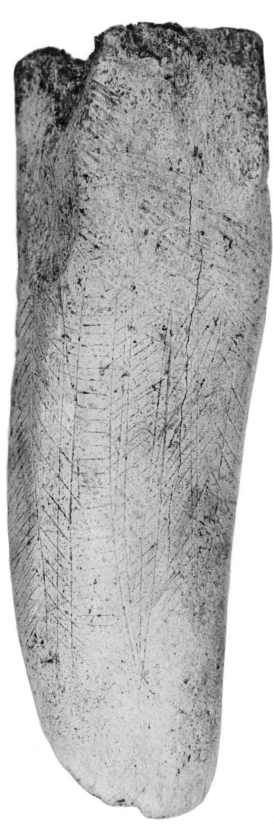

Fig. 9:13. Incised splitting wedge of antler from house pit #19 at the Bell Site house pit village (EeRk 4) near Lillooet, B.C. The poorly executed decorations consits primarily of the fir branch motif oriented longitudinally along the implement.

countered. Certain combinations are continually repeated and can be said to constitute decorative motifs. Boas (1900) has identified more than twenty of these motifs with their representational meaning from ethnographic sources and nearly all the motifs on the prehistoric specimens are included. Long parallel lines, short parallel lines, circles and dots, ticked lines, crossed lines, Xs, zigzags are some of the more common motifs (Boas 1900:Fig. 298; Sanger 1968a:Fig. 11).

Even a cursory inspection of the decorated objects will reveal that the distribution of the various motifs across the tool types as well as the association of motifs with one another is not random. Although no one motif appears to be restricted to a single artifact type, some motifs are found on only a limited range of tools. Long parallel lines, for example, are restricted to digging stick handles and a few other implements utilized by women (sap scrapers, mat creasers) although broad bands, a motif similar to and easily confused with the long parallel lines, have a wider distribution and are especially common in painted form on ethnographic implements (e.g., Teit 1900:Figs. 159, 160, 222). Other motifs, however, can be seen on nearly all artifact types, the ubiquitous short parallel line pattern being a good example. The well-known circle and dot motif is not as common, however, as might be anticipated and is found on less than one-third of the tool types.

Certain motifs are frequently associated with one another although no exclusive pairings were observed. Long parallel lines and long ticked lines are often found together as are parallel lines of medium length with triangles and partial triangles. Short parallel lines are often the only decoration on an object. Designs often occur in fours or multiples of fours probably because the number four was of mystic significance as it was in historic times (Teit 1900:337).

The placement of the various motifs both in terms of orientation and position on the artifacts also appears to be non-random. Designs are placed either along the lateral margins or on one of the broad surfaces of the tool but seldom are both the edges and the surfaces decorated. The major exceptions are digging stick handles and similar implements with oval cross-sections where the surface motif curves around the lateral margins and just onto the fringes of the opposite surface (Sanger 1968a:Plate VIII). Rarely is more than one surface decorated. Lateral margin decoration may be bilateral if the object is symmetrical but asymmetric forms usually display incising along only one margin. Artifacts with a circular cross-section such as tubular beads are decorated along their long axes although one bead exhibits short parallel lines perpendicular to both ends (Stryd 1973:Fig. 37e).

Designs on lateral margins are usually oriented at right angles to the long axis, that is, the motif is placed "across" the margin and "down" the length of the tool. This

Geographic Area	Number of Sites	Sites with Mobile Art		Sites with Decorated Objects		Sites with Carvings		Number of Decorated Objects		Number of Carvings	
		N	%	N	%	N	%	N	%	N	%
Lillooet	16	11	69	10	63	5	45	84	40	15	39
Lytton-Lochnore-Nesikep	10	8	80	5	50	5	62	28	14	6	16
Nicola Valley	11	6	55	6	55	0	0	12	6	0	0
Kamloops-Chase Shuswap	22	9	41	9	41	3	33	82	39	17	45
Williams Lake	7	1	14	1	14	0	0	2	1	0	0
Other Areas	5	1	20	1	20	0	0	0	0	0	0
Total	71	36	51	32	32	13	18	208	-	38	-

Table 9:3. Distribution of the mobile art included in this study by location within the mid-Fraser and Thompson River area.

placement is especially obvious with short parallel lines. When a surface is embellished, long motifs are normally oriented longitudinally whereas short designs have a transverse orientation. Diagonal placement is also quite common but is not restricted to either short or long motifs.

Meaning. The question of meaning of the decorative motifs and of motivation for such art is a complex one which can only be introduced at this time. Because of the continuity of decorative art into historic times, some information on the meaning of the various motifs is available from the ethnographic literature. Boas (1900) has summarized much of this data and Sanger (1968a) has applied it to a prehistoric context.

Boas (1900), Smith (1899, 1900), Teit (1900) and others have pointed out that most of the decorative motifs are really symbols utilizing realistic representations with conventionalized elements. That is, the motifs express ideas or convey messages through the use of simplified naturalistic representations, many of which have become conventionalized through time, presumably to avoid ambiguity of meaning although Boas (1900:377) attributes it to difficulties of execution. Conventional designs were usually understood (Boas 1900:377) whereas other motifs, including some conventional ones, depended on the function of the implement on which they were inscribed to provide meaning. Meaning could be modified by adding specific elements such as dots or short lines to the

standardized motif or by joining several distinct designs with connecting lines. Smith (1899:157) suggests that the grouping of designs also influenced meaning. Unlike much of Northwest Coast mobile art there appears to be little connection between the form of the implement and the decorative motifs and few designs are primarily decorative in purpose (Boas 1900:377). Smith (1899:154) reports that the incisions on small bird bone tubes may be notches or tally marks but, even if correct, this appears to be an exception to the primary symbolic function of the decorations.

If symbolic, what do the various motifs represent? Three major groups or kinds of representations are recognizable: (1) topographic features or weather phenomena such as mountains, creeks, the earth and lightning; (2) specific forms of man-modified ground, notable trails, crossing trails, trenches and trenches with earth piled to one side; and (3) animals, parts of animals and markings left by animals such as snake tracks, snake skins, rattlesnake tails, bats, wood worm tracks and eyes (which could also be human). Most of the symbolic designs found on artifacts can also be seen on pictograph panels, but the latter display a considerably greater range of representations including anthropomorphic, zoomorphic and "spirit" forms (Corner 1968:29) which, in my opinion, reflects the more varied purpose behind pictograph painting.

To simply leave the discussion of symbolic representa-

Site Type	Number of Sites	Sites with Mobile Art		Sites with Decorated Objects		Sites with Carvings	
		N	%	N	%	N	%
Cemeteries	13	10	77	10	77	5	39
House pit villages	49	23	47	19	39	8	16
Seasonal Camps	6	2	33	2	33	0	0
Cache Pits	1	0	0	0	0	0	0
Surface Chipping Locations	1	0	0	0	0	0	0
Other Sites	1	1	100	1	100	0	0
Total	71	36	51	32	45	13	18

Table 9:4. Distribution of the mobile art included in this study by site type.

tion at this point, would, I think, miss much of what is really being depicted. It is not the snake track or the mountain or the trench that is important *per se*; it is the power of the snake track, the mountain and the trench that is of concern and is the key to understanding the design. Boas (1900:379) mentions that young men rubbed wood worms on their arms in order to gain strength and that men decorated their clothing and implements with designs representing guardian spirits and dreams in order to endow those objects with supernatural powers. We may also note that trenches, crosses and other symbols were associated with female puberty ceremonies, a time when girls attained spiritual guardians and gained the power to give life.

The motifs may be viewed as symbols of power derived from animistic belief in the mysterious powers which pervade all nature (Teit 1900:344). Decorated artifacts may then become statements of power, expressions of the powers available to or desired by the owner/user, at least in the context of the activities represented by the object. This, I think, may account for the greater range of pictograph designs mentioned above, in that statements of power were but one purpose motivating pictograph painting, primarily as part of the guardian spirit quest.

To view a decorated object as a statement or message about power leads to two interesting questions: "who is making these statements?" and "to whom are they addressed?" The answer to the first question is probably the obvious one, namely, the user/owner of the decorated object. Presumably the statement is addressed to the animal, plant, person or object that is to be killed, collected, modified or in some other manner exploited by the owner/user with the aid of the decorated implement. The decorations transfer the supernatural powers of the owner to the tool and the tool uses that power to function better or to make a greater impact on its surroundings.

This is also true for non-utilitarian objects which function primarily in the social arena. Beads and pendants make statements about their owner's power and Smith (1899:157) has observed that pipes were decorated with designs representing the guardian spirit of their owners. These decorated objects are, in a sense, social announcements, statements of power addressed to the members of the community and, possibly, to all the animate and inanimate powers that permeate the Salish world view.

It is my opinion that the preceding discussion has only begun to explore the various levels of meaning which may underlie the decorative art tradition of the interior Plateau. Much of the significance of symbolic art appears to lie in its social and psychological genesis. If we are therefore, really interested in acquiring a more comprehensive understanding of the "Indian behind the artifact," the investigation of the more fundamental, subjective levels of meaning may be a worthwhile pursuit.

CHAPTER 10

An Introduction to Ozette Art

RICHARD DAUGHERTY AND JANET FRIEDMAN

Ozette was a large village located on the northern coast of Washington, perhaps the most important sea mammal hunting site on the entire west coast of North America, south of western Alaska. From Ozette, canoe-loads of hunters would pursue whales, fur seals, dolphins and other sea mammals. The many thousands of bones of these animals in the rich midden deposits of the site testify to the skill and success of the hunters. In addition to sea mammals, the Ozette environment provided a large variety of fish, shellfish and plant foods. Large land mammals, including deer and elk, either were not abundant in the area or were not hunted locally, for their remains are rare in the site deposits. Ozette was an excellent location for a village. In addition to its economic advantages, it was protected from the sea by offshore islands and a wide rocky reef that provided a quiet beach for launching and landing canoes. One of the five main villages of the Nootkan-speaking Makah, Ozette had a sizeable population which was increased substantially each spring by an influx of sea mammal hunters and their families from other villages.

The village extended nearly three-quarters of a mile along the coast, but nowhere except at the point opposite Cannonball Island was the level area above the beach wide enough to accommodate more than a double line of houses. At this point, where the remains of ancient sea terraces step gently up the hillside, these terraces have been widened to accommodate a random placement of houses. Cannonball Island, joined to the mainland by a sandy spit at low tide, is capped by nearly two metres of midden deposit. It, too, was occupied, perhaps as a defensive position in times of conflict, and as a lookout area for observers stationed there to watch for whales. There was one troublesome area near the centre of the

village. During periods of heavy rain, houses located here occasionally were subjected to sudden mud flows emanating from a small valley located immediately behind them. These flows deposited layers of mud on the floors of the houses, burying objects that happened to be lying there.

One particular rainy night in late spring about 450 years ago, a massive mud flow, perhaps triggered by an earth tremor, roared out of the valley, smashing and covering the houses in its path. Most of the roof planks and beams were carried out onto the beach, but the greater part of the houses and their contents were buried under from two to four metres of clay. The midden between the layers of clay has acted as a natural aquifer for the past hundreds of years, keeping the deposits wet. At least four houses are known to have been buried beneath this one massive flow, and additional ones may yet be discovered. Remains of other houses, both earlier in time and later, are known from below and above the four houses.

Archaeological excavations under the direction of the senior author were begun in the summers of 1966 and 1967, and continued on a year-round basis since the spring of 1970 until 1981. Emphasis was on the recovery of the buried houses and their contents. Preservation beneath the mud flow is such that nearly everything in the houses, including tools, containers, clothing, weapons, looms and art work, has remained in remarkably good condition. Items of wood and fibre, materials rarely found in an archaeological context, are here in abundance, however those of animal tissue, hair, fur or feathers are very rare. Over 40,000 specimens have been recovered thus far from the complete excavation of one house and parts of two others.

Excavation techniques employing water rather than the

Fig. 10.1. Effigy of whale fin carved from several pieces of western red cedar which have been sewn together. The fin is inlaid with approximately 700 sea otter teeth, some forming the outline of the mythical thunderbird.

customary tools of the archaeologist—shovels, trowels and brushes—have been perfect to remove the thousands of delicate items without damage. Preservation techniques, too, have had to be developed to accommodate the artifacts and house remains. Study of the houses reveals that art was a pervasive element in the lives of the prehistoric occupants of the village. Even with excavations continuing and additional discoveries being made almost daily, it is important now to examine the range of the art and its role in Ozette culture. This paper is introductory in nature and primarily descriptive.

Similarities of Ozette to the art of the other Nootkan-speaking peoples, to the art of the neighbouring Chemakuan-speaking Quileute to the south, and to a lesser extent to the art of the Salishan peoples of the Strait of Juan de Fuca, Puget Sound and the Gulf of Georgia to the east and northeast are obvious. The priorities in the development of these similarities remain to be determined, and no doubt reflect a complex set of interrelationships. We believe, however, that the Wakashan and Chemakuan-speaking sea mammal hunters at the entrance to the Strait of Juan de Fuca developed a distinctive art style with an antiquity of several thousand years that, while resembling in limited ways the art of the more northerly Northwest Coast, has its own style and vigor. This view, at least to a limited extent, is shared by others. Philip Drucker states, "The Wakashan speaking groups to the south [of the Haida, Tlingit, and Tsimshian] developed a simpler but more truly sculptural and vigorous style, which stressed mass and movement rather than conventionalization . . ." (1955:177-178). Based on unpublished ethnographic work that the senior author conducted with the Hoh and Quileute in the late 1940s, we are extending this statement to the Chemakuan speakers.

Materials

The Ozette people employed a wide range of materials in their artistic efforts, including wood, bone, antler, shell, stone, teeth and various types of fibres. Wood was the most important raw material in their culture and the one most often used in art, either alone or in combination with paint and inlay. The kinds of wood used depended primarily on the function of the various objects, rather than on artistic considerations such as ease of carving, texture or colour. For example, clubs used for killing seals often are carved in the likeness of a seal. They are made of yew (*Taxus brevifolia*) because this is a heavy, dense wood unlikely to split. Western red cedar (*Thuja plicata*) would be easier to carve but it would split in use. Studies by the junior author (Friedman 1975) demonstrate that the functional properties of wood largely dictated the choice of species in the manufacture of objects. Bowls are of red alder (*Alnus rubra*) or big leaf maple (*Acer macro phyllum*); whale harpoons and bows are of yew;

boxes are of western red cedar. All tend to be ornamented. Only where art objects were created for themselves or for ceremonial purposes did artistic considerations determine the selection of material. In these cases western red cedar was the dominant choice. It carves easily and is light weight.

Shells and teeth figure in Ozette art primarily as inlay materials. The opercula of the red turbins (*Atraea gibberosa*) are the shells most often used. They form inlay patterns along the front of sleeping platforms and in the shafts of whaling harpoons where they serve both decoratively and to provide a rough area for a hand grip. Sea otter (*Enhydra lutris*) teeth and pile perch (*Rhacochilus vacca*) teeth are inlaid into several boxes; the effigy of a whale fin carved of several pieces of cedar sewn together is decorated with 700 sea otter teeth (*Fig. 10:1*).

Bone and antler were used primarily for tool handles or, in the case of whalebone, for the manufacture of clubs. As with wood, these materials in their finished form were selected functionally rather than artistically. The Ozette people rarely used stone for artistic purposes. In fact they rarely used stone for any purpose other than as mauls, abraders, choppers, net and line weights and knives. Petroglyphs and a few carved boulders are exceptions to this statement.

Little can be said about the use of paint except to note that reds and blacks predominate. Where paint supplements carving and/or inlay work, it is now so faded that it is impossible to determine the original extent of the painting or the design.

Styles, Forms and Techniques

Ozette art can be characterized best as lively and realistic, dominated by zoomorphic and anthropomorphic forms. Conventionalized forms also are important. Sometimes they were used alone as on the heads of whalebone clubs, other times they augmented the realistic renditions of zoomorphic forms. Conventionalized elements seem to relate primarily, though not exclusively, to ceremonial-religious aspects of the culture, more often than to those of routine daily life. This perhaps helps explain the persistence of these elements through time and their widespread distribution among Wakashan, Chemakuan and Salishan peoples.

A strong element of geometric ornamentation also can be seen in the art of Ozette (*Fig. 10:2*). Zig-zag lines, parallel lines and patterns of triangles and crescents ornament combs, tool handles, the sides of boxes and the edges of bowls. Basketry was decorated in geometric designs patterned by the weave (*Fig. 10:3*), by changing the colour or material for certain segments of the basket or by false embroidery. A blanket of cattail fluff is woven in a plaid design.

Carving, whether in the round or by incising designs

Fig. 10:2. Wooden comb.

Fig. 10:3. Large bag used by whale hunters to carry their harpoon heads and other paraphernalia. The bag with its woven geometric designs is made of cedar bark.

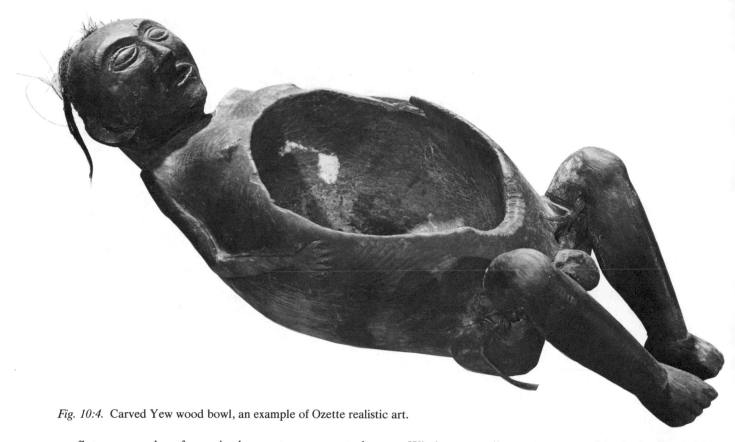

Fig. 10:4. Carved Yew wood bowl, an example of Ozette realistic art.

on flat or carved surfaces, is the most common technique of artistic expression, with the basic design often augmented by painting and/or inlay of teeth or shell. Tools were simple but effective: wedges of wood and bone; stone mauls, chisels with wood or bone handles fitted with shell, stone, beaver-tooth or metal bits; adzes with stone or metal blades and stone, metal or shell knives.

Realistic art is found throughout the Ozette collection, most notably on seal clubs and tool handles and on a bowl carved in the shape of a human *(Fig. 10:4)*. It is used in depicting humans, birds, seals, whales and canidae. Frequently, conventionalized symbols or decorative element were added to the realistic art, creating a mixture of two styles. Several traditional motifs are identifiable, and were applied in any of the styles of art mentioned— realistic, conventionalized or geometric.

One of these motifs, the thunderbird, is incised and painted on a wall panel, outlined by sea otter molars inlaid into the whale fin effigy *(Fig. 10:1)*, pecked into the dorsal portions of each of a pair of antler harpoon valves, carved in the round on two bone combs and carved two-dimensionally into a box side *(Fig. 10:5)*. Typically, the thunderbird is portrayed with wings outstretched and body and head profiled with an eagle-like beak. Triangular tufts of feathers on the head seem to be a distinguishing feature of the thunderbird. The feet, when included, are more conventionalized than realistic; legs simply terminate in circles or are shown as single lines.

Whales generally are represented by incised or inlaid designs on boxes and on house planks. In each case, they have a stylized dorsal fin. Often they are shown in x-ray technique, so that the vertebral column can be seen as a part of the body.

The human face is represented in both a very natural appearance *(Fig. 10:4)* and in a somewhat stylized form *(Fig. 10:6)*. It is found on spindle whorls, two-dimensionally on seal clubs and carved in-the-round on bowls, spools and tool handles *(Fig. 10:7)*. The back of the head seldom is represented. Rather, a carving in-the-round will have a face on both front and back *(Fig. 10:7)*; only the face itself will be present in two-dimensional incising. On many artifacts, the face is represented in a simplified and stylized manner. Within the circle representing the head, a single line curves to depict the nose and eyebrows; small circles or dots form the eyes and perhaps the mouth, if present *(Fig. 10:8)*. On others, the features of the face are carved realistically in bas relief.

An animal represented in a conventionalized manner is a generalized canidae, perhaps a dog or a wolf, which has been found carved in-the-round on the handles of weavers' swords *(Fig. 10:9)*, and incised on wall planks, combs and box sides. This animal is characterized by upright ears and an open mouth with sharp, pointed teeth or a closed mouth.

Mythical monsters, too, are represented in the Ozette materials, appearing as creatures with claws and often

Fig. 10:5. Side of box carved from western red cedar. The tufts above the eyebrows and the feathers formed by the use of the pinched, inverted V's identify the design as a Thunderbird.

teeth. An example is a sea monster carved in wrap-around fashion on a comb *(Fig. 10:10)*.

A single motif dominates all whalebone clubs in the collection *(Fig. 10:11)*. The top or handle is an elaborately carved rectangle, incised on both sides and carved in outline to represent the full head of a mythical being. It always is shown in profile with a large drooping mouth, and a complex eye formed of circles and triangles. On top of the head is a smaller, bird-like head, with a long beak which is slightly hooked and usually closed. This same design with modifications and alterations is pictured on nearly twenty clubs in the book *Primitive Art* by Franz Boas (1927), described as having come from Vancouver Island and Neah Bay. This is a motif of wide geographic distribution.

Conventionalized style entails the use of numerous formal elements, particularly in depicting parts of the body. Although these are less strictly conventionalized in the Ozette materials than on the northern Northwest Coast, they nonetheless are unmistakable.

A design element which appears as a pinched and elongated triangle or a V is variously manifested on the Ozette artifacts. Most frequently, it is used in combination with an ovoid as an element in an eye design *(Figs. 10:9 and 10:11)*, but it also may be used alone as a design element representing feathers *(Fig. 10:5)*, or more correctly, the space between feathers. This is the case with two spindle whorls, and a bowl rim.

Eye treatment in Ozette art is managed in a variety of ways. In clubs, combs, box parts, tool handles, spindle whorls and house planks, the eyes of humans, seals, canine forms, whales and birds often are simply incised circles or ovals *(Fig. 10:8)*. Alternatively, a compound incised eye, consisting of two or more concentric ovals may be used. This form most frequently depicts the human eye and may be seen, for example, on a bowl shaped like a human *(Fig. 10:4)* and on a tool handle *(Fig. 10:7)*. Compound ovals are used also for the eye of a monster on a comb *(Fig. 10:10)*, and on a small carving of a seal. Eyes may be inlaid with shells or teeth; on some artifacts a depression, presumably once holding an inlay, represents the eye. This is the case with the carved side of a box *(Fig. 10:5)*, a seal club and a bird on a carved plank. In one human representation, eyes are incised horizontal slits. In birds depicted on one particular bone comb and on several whalebone clubs, the face is in profile and the eye is a round drilled hole passing completely through the object. The hole may have served to hold a thong or strap, especially on the clubs. On an owl carved of wood, large, round eyes are raised in bas relief *(Fig. 10:12)*. Most common of all, eyes are represented as a complex combination of ovals and triangles. This is true for birds, canidae *(Fig. 10:9)* and stylized beings *(Fig. 10:5, Fig. 10:10)*, although seldom for the eyes of humans. The combination is found on harpoon valves, weavers' swords, box parts, whalebone clubs and house planks. The same

Fig. 10:6. Whalebone tool handle with a realistic, though somewhat stylized, representation of the human face.

Fig. 10:7. Human face on the handle of a carving tool. A nearly identical face appears on the reverse side.

Fig. 10:8. Handle of metal bladed knife, showing a simple, stylized human face.

design, as a decorative element away from the context of the face, is used to decorate the rim of a bowl, a box part, a comb and a spindle whorl. The design itself varies considerably from piece to piece. The ovoid portion may be a simple circle or oval, a combination of concentric ovals or a circle within an oval. There may be one triangle, two opposite each other or, in one case, three. On fifteen different artifacts, triangles are enclosed within an oval.

The brow ridge or eyebrow often is seen in Ozette art, particularly in representations of the faces of humans and owls *(Figs. 10:4, 10:6, 10:7, 10:12, 10:13 and 10:14)*. Frequently, the eyebrows are joined to the nose and appear as incised lines or in bas relief *(Fig. 10:8)*. A brow ridge of sorts on many seal cubs is a sharply sloping demarcation between the curve of the top of the head and the face. An incised line or one raised in bas relief depicting simplified arched eyebrows attached to a rectangular or triangular nose also is frequent. It is used to represent humans or tool handles *(Fig. 10:8)*, combs, spindle whorls and sculptures.

The treatment of the nose ranges from a complex shape, completely outlined and filled with inlay *(Fig. 10:5)*, to an absence of any representation whatsoever. Most commonly, whether in bas relief or in the round, a human nose, a seal rostrum or a bird beak is carved realistically, with incised dots to depict the nostrils. A realistic human nose is seen on a two-headed spool *(Fig. 10:13)*, on a bowl *(Fig. 10:4)* and on tool handles *(Figs. 10:6, 10:7)*. Figures 10:11 and 10:12 illustrate the realistic representation of a bird's beak.

The human mouth most commonly is represented open, with slightly prominent lips *(Figs. 10:4, 10:6, and 10:7)*. This is the case on tool handles, combs, sculptures and bowls; it also is true of seal heads on seal clubs, with the generalized canidae heads on tool handles and bowls, and with the carving of birds on combs. An alternate, and less frequently employed treatment of the mouth, depicts it open and with tongue or pointed teeth protruding. This usually is in carvings of seals and canidae *(Fig. 10:9)*, but it also is true of one seal club with a human face, several bowl sculptures, tool handles, a comb and a spindle whorl. The mouth, conveyed as a simple or compound oval, is a form restricted to human representations. The mouth is an open, hooked beak on most thunderbird depictions *(Fig. 10:1)*, including those on combs, harpoon valves, whalebone clubs *(Fig. 10:11)* and a plank.

Ears are represented only infrequently in either conventionalized or realistic art. The only instance in the Ozette collection of human ear characterization is on a very true to life representation on the human-shaped bowl. Here the ears are located in their natural position on either side of the head *(Fig. 10:4)*. Because human figures carved in-the-round most commonly have two faces and no back of the head, they rarely are given ears *(Fig.*

10:7). Animal ears are represented two basic ways. When a canidae is shown in profile incised into a flat surface, the ears are triangles, pointed and upright. This is the case on house planks, a comb, and on weavers' swords. On carvings done in-the-round, the ears appear as ridges on top of the head. Examples are some of the bowls, a mat creaser, a tool handle and a weaver's sword *(Fig. 10:9).*

The general absence of ears noted above is rather interesting in the case of the Ozette carved wooden seal clubs. Of the forty in the collection, none has external ears. This is surprising because the bones of northern fur seal *(Callorhinus ursinus)* comprise over eighty percent of the total faunal collection from the site thus far analyzed. This genus belongs to the eared seals. Since this feature also is usually absent on representations of humans, it may have been considered one to be stylized. Also, since these carvings were used as clubs, any carved projections soon would have been knocked off.

Feathers, often outlined by elongated triangles *(Fig. 10:5),* show most clearly as triangles hanging from the outstretched wings of birds. Examples are on a large, carved wall panel, a comb and house planks. Occasionally, open triangles or V's are incised over the body of the bird to represent feathers. Other designs used for this purpose are cross-hatching, parallel lines or randomly placed incised dots.

Hair rarely is shown in Ozette art, apparently for a variety of reasons. Often a face is incised as a circle enclosing stylized features, and neither hair nor ears is added to the simple outline. The human head also often is depicted as wearing a rain hat, which covers the hair at the top of the head. The only instance with hair clearly present is the bowl carved in the shape of a man *(Fig. 10:4).* On this piece, actual human hair has been fixed into a groove with pitch incised into the top of the head; the hair has been plaited into a single braid.

Very seldom is the body, especially the human body, represented in any detail in the Ozette collection. The only two pieces showing a complete human body are a small bone sculpture of a man in the fetal position *(Fig. 10:14)* and the wooden bowl carved in the shape of a man *(Fig. 10:4),* this latter previously noted for its unusual realism. Animal bodies generally are not represented. Human and other mammals usually appear as a head alone, generally incised on a flat surface such as a spindle whorl or box part. Or, a head, carved in the round, rests on an amorphous shaft or ovoid rather than on a body. This is seen in seal clubs, tool handles *(Fig. 10:7),* a spool *(Fig. 10:13)* and weavers' swords *(Fig. 10:9).* When the full body is shown, often it is stylized, carved in response to the function of the tool and the available design space rather than because of artistic considerations. A seal club may have flippers and tail carved onto its shaft, but even so the body of the seal is generalized. On a house plank

Fig. 10.9. Heads of generalized canidae (dog or wolf) carved on handle of weaver's sword.

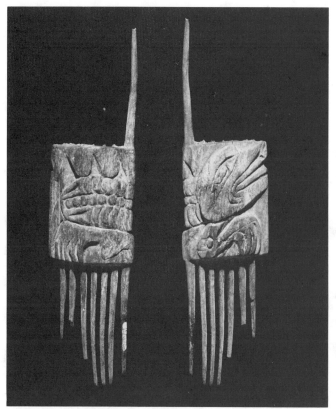

Fig. 10:10. Sea monster carved in wrap-around fashion on comb. Note the use of x-ray technique.

Fig. 10:11. Whalebone club of a type common throughout the northern region.

Fig. 10:12. Wooden club head depicting an owl.

Fig. 10:13. One end of a carved wooden spoon. A similar carved head ornaments the opposite end.

Fig. 10:14. Small bone sculpture of a man in a fetal position.

portraying entire canidae and birds, the bodies of the former are rounded and out of proportion to the rest. This may represent a mythical animal, or may simply display the lack of interest in, or lack of concentration upon, the body as compared with the head. Generally, the most realistically portrayed bodies are those of birds. These are seen in flight on a bone comb carved in-the-

round, in profile incised on a house plank and on harpoon valves and carved in-the-round at rest on a double-ended weaver's sword.

X-ray technique characterizes some pieces of Ozette art, notably a whale incised on a large wall panel, a small bone sculpture of a whale, a bird on a bird comb and a monster carved onto a wooden comb *(Fig. 10:10)*. In each instance, the spinal column and ribs are simplified and stylized, but are present along with the outline of the body.

Geometric designs often augment or supplement the representational and conventionalized art of the collection. This is seen, for instance, in the dots and circles which decorate a powder measure sculptured in the shape of a man's body found in the early historical level *(Fig. 10:15)*. It also is apparent in cross-hatching on the bird body of a bone comb, in a circle incised around the edge of a spindle whorl also decorated with human faces and in a series of triangular shapes on the blade of a weaver's sword. Often, geometric forms are the only decoration on a specimen. Parallel incised lines, the most frequently used geometric motif, are on box sides, bowl rims, spindle whorls and on a mat creaser. Zig-zag lines, crescents and combinations of triangles are less frequent, appearing on weavers' swords, a loom upright, a spindle whorl and a box side. Other geometric designs include concentric circles on one spindle whorl, radiating lines on another spindle whorl and dots on a bone comb. Complex combinations of lines and other geometric elements are on six of the wooden combs in the collection.

Another manifestation of geometric art, in addition to that incised on a flat surface, is the carving of grooves around a shaft. This may be seen on a number of tool handles and on cylindricl shafts of unknown function. In any society art may serve a variety of functions. At Ozette its primary purpose appears to be as decoration. The application of motifs to secular, functional artifacts that may be divided into three categories: those that are always decorated, those that are sometimes decorated and those that are never decorated. For instance, invaribly Ozette tool handles, spindle whorls, weavers' swords, combs and seal or fish clubs are decorated: the degree varies, but some motif is present on each of these items. The handles furnish a particularly good example of varying levels of decoration used to augment functional pieces. On some, the major decorative element consists simply of parallel incised lines or geometric shapes carved in-the-round. Others, usually handles for chisels or knives, are carefully executed sculptures of humans. The second category of artifacts—those optionally decorated—includes boxes, bowls, harpoon shafts and valves and loom uprights. The third—those that seem never to be decorated—includes wedges, awls, canoe paddles, canoe bailers, stone tools, bows, arrows and loom rollers.

Most frequently, the secular decoration applied to

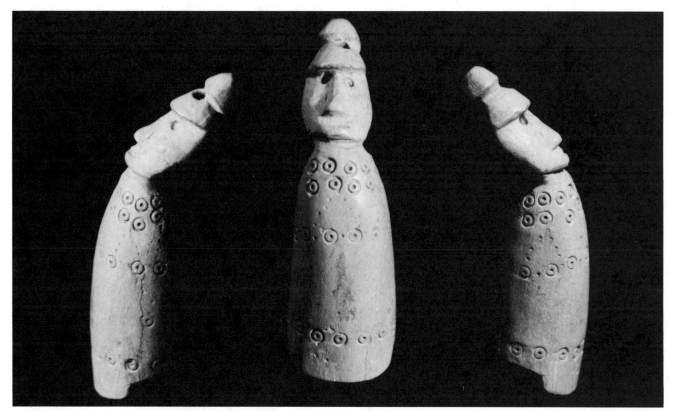

Fig. 10:15. Three views of small, carved human figure with dot and circle design for ornamentation. This object from the early historic level at Ozette appears to be a powder measure.

functional objects either is realistic or geometric. Animals, humans and geometric designs are carved in-the-round and incised on the appropriate surfaces of tools, bowls and combs. A few exceptions with conventionalized art applied to objects of secular use include a stylized creature on a weaver's sword, a sea monster on a comb, various motifs on box sides and stylized eye motifs possibly representing a human face on a spindle whorl.

Strictly ceremonial art is very difficult to isolate in the Ozette collection with the exception of carved whale fin inlaid with sea otter teeth *(Fig. 10:1)*. This piece represents the dorsal fin and the section of the back of the whale directly under it, said to have been given to the head whaler. As an art piece, the sculpture must have figured in a ritual of some sort.

Another excellent example of ceremonial art is a thunderbird on the side of a large box *(Fig. 10:5)*. This is identified as a thunderbird mainly on the basis of the tufts of feathers on the head and the feathers on the body. The face is carved carefully and is well finished with eyes and mouth stylized, and the whole inlaid with teeth of pile perch and sea otter. From these indications, it appears that the box may have had ceremonial functions, perhaps used for the storage of ritual paraphernalia. Or, it may have been one side of a box drum. A third example of ceremonial art is a club carved with owl faces on each end *(Fig. 10:12)*. This piece shows no evidence

of the bashing seen on utilitarian seal clubs; furthermore, it is finely and carefully smoothed and finished. The owl faces are a combination of realistic and conventionalized elements. The whalebone clubs in the collection *(Fig. 10:11)* all display the conventionalized representation of a mythical theme and, unlike the wooden seal clubs, probably had primarily ceremonial functions.

The unusually complete inventory of art work present at Ozette indicates a correlation between realistic representational art and secular functions on the one hand, and conventionalized art and ceremonial use on the other. The correlation is not perfect, however, for stylized themes also appear on objects of apparently secular function. Quite possibly items that seem intended for secular use may have performed a ceremonial function as well.

Excavations so far have not produced certain items of ceremonial use such as masks and drum frames. These may some day be found. Ozette offers an unparalleled opportunity for understanding the nature and role of art on the Northwest Coast at a time before the influences of Euro-American culture began to manifest itself and change both the art and the way of life of the people who produced it.

CHAPTER 11

Change and Continuity in Northwest Coast Art

ROY L. CARLSON

Where, when and why did Northwest Coast art originate, and what changes have taken place in it over the centuries? Instead of using this concluding chapter to summarize the preceding contributions, it seems more informative to attempt to answer this question by reviewing the information provided in the earlier chapters, and where possible adding to it. Form, meaning and style are all concepts which assist in responding to this query, and of these "meaning" is the most useful starting point. All art, or at least the kind of art found archaeologically, has form, and some has meaning. Form is obvious in that it can be seen and felt, and while it may be perceived differently by different people, it is nevertheless there visually and tactilely. Meaning, on the other hand, is more ephemeral and is relative to context. The "meaning" of an object to an art historian in the context of development of a particular art tradition is quite different from the "meaning" of such a piece in the context of the particular culture which produced it. There are also universal "meanings" such as the sexual meanings, the hidden agenda, as pointed out in Duff's analysis of Northwest Coast art. However, it is neither the art historical meanings, nor the universals, but the particular culturally specific meaning that I refer to here, and call symbolic meaning.

Symbolic meaning is actually a form of communication in which a form tells the viewer something more than that it is long and narrow or short and oval, something more specific than a universal reaction, something which relates to a system or sub-system of the culture from which stemmed this thing *we* classify as art. While it is possible to observe form, it is necessary to elicit symbolic meaning, and ask, "What does this mean?"

Discovery of symbolic meaning poses a problem for archaeologists studying the works of long dead peoples whose creations cannot be observed in use and who can't be asked about symbolic meaning. (Ethnologists have some of the same problems, but for different reasons.) There are some so-called psychic archaeologists who claim to be able to feel an object and find out what it was all about, or sit with it in a dark room until some "meaning" pops into their head. Such activities are best described as quackery except to the extent that meanings obtained in this manner are potentially universal meanings. Ethnographic analogy rather than psychic power is the normal method for drawing inferences concerning symbolic meaning, and even there some problems and limitations are present.

Art objects from nonliterate societies usually convey meaning, and are symbols which relate to the belief system. Ethnographic analogy is simply the method whereby prehistoric objects of the same or similar forms to those known ethnographically are assumed to have the same or similar meanings. It is one of the reasons why three of the chapters in this book (those by Holm, Duff and Suttles) describe the known ethnographic art in order to provide a basis for interpreting the unknown, the art found archaeologically. It is necessary to understand contexts and meaning of ethnographic art as a basis for analogy in interpreting prehistoric art. These chapters also point up one of the problems with ethnographic analogy which is understanding the complexities and potential multiple symbolism of the ethnographic art which in many cases such as Central Coast Salish (Suttles, Ch. 4) are poorly known and only partially understood. For this reason interpretations placed on archaeological artifacts are more likely to be valid on a general level, than on a highly specific one. In order to look for origins of Northwest Coast art it is necessary to look at those systems of belief in which art had meaning, and their origins.

Most Northwest Coast art objects were symbols of

power. This power was based on a spiritual encounter either by the current owner of the symbol or his ancestor. Spirits were potentially present in all natural phenomena including plants and animals, and it is the latter which were most commonly represented in art. Localized practices involving this basic belief in spirits were found in all coastal regions. Guardian spirits, shamanic spirits, secret society spirits and crest spirits constitute categories in which most spirits can be conceptualized and related to variations in belief and practice among different groups, even though these categories are not mutually exclusive, would probably not have been recognized by the bearers of ethnographic Northwest Coast culture, and do not include all Northwest Coast religious phenomena. We learn from ethnography that art communicated in these four areas, and that they were the stimuli to artistic production. The most economical hypothesis is that such was also the case in prehistoric times.

Collectors of museum specimens and ethnographers frequently did not bridge the gap between the art objects they collected and the belief systems behind them, and it has remained for later users of their data to try to put the two together. The fragments of ethnographic information collected over the years should be considered as just what they are, bits and pieces, and their interpretative value should be extended beyond the immediate specimen to other ethnographic objects of the same type. If the style of a prehistoric object is the same as that of the ethnographic analog, the case for continuity is considerably strengthened.

Style is that somewhat ephemeral quality of objects which is most easily recognized the more foreign it is. It refers to those recurrent combinations of attributes of form and content which cluster spatially and temporally. Hypothetically there are an infinite number of ways of depicting human and animal forms. Both guiding and restricting such depictions are the natural forms of the beings portrayed, the materials and tools used and the art tradition itself which defines the current or proper mode. The latter should be able to transcend both scale differences and differences in media, and thus along with content constitute the patterned forms in which the same elements are repeated from object to object and material to material and are basic to definitions of style.

Style is a function of art as a communicative device in nonliterate cultures. In order to serve as communication art must be culturally specific, and be maintained without radical alterations. In order to function as a way to communicate meaning, style must of necessity change only slowly and thus perpetuate meaning. There are really only two major styles on the Northwest Coast, a southern and a northern. Both illustrate spirits or ancestors manifested in human or animal form. The similarities between them are related in part to common materials and techniques and in part to the belief systems shared throughout the coast. The differences are less in actual content than in the forms of the motifs and their spatial inter-relationships on the field of design. Kwakiutl and Bella Coola areas partake of both styles. Borden's hypothesis (Ch. 8) that changes in the art tradition on the lower Fraser in the early historic period were the result of influences from the north would fit better with stylistic data if the direction, north, were changed to west. My impression is that what he calls "northern" is primarily Nootkan.

In the southern style the motifs are usually separate and do not interact or interlock in a meaningful manner. More than two creatures on a field of design are unusual, and ovoids and formlines are atypical. Both two-dimensional applied forms and sculptural forms are common as is asymmetry; eyebrows are frequently joined and there is considerable naturalism. Humanoids, the thunderbird, owls, wolf, snakes and small carnivores are commonly depicted. This style with some regional variations is typical of the Lower Columbia, Washington Coast, Straits of Juan de Fuca and Georgia, west coast of Vancouver Island, the lower Fraser and lower Thompson.

The northern style is characterized by a balanced symmetry and intricate interlocking of human and animal motifs modified to fit within natural spaces. Eagle, raven, bear, beaver, killerwhale, owl and humanoids are emphasized but many additional animals are shown. This style is typical of Tlingit, Haida and Tsimshian. Holm (Ch. 2) provides more detail on styles.

Guardian Spirits

Guardian spirits assisted their possessors in everyday tasks—canoe building, hunting, fishing or spinning and weaving. Such spirits were obtained through a dream or a vision either as a result of a specific quest or accidentally. Swan (1870:62) who studied the Makah in the early 1860's described the attitude concerning visions...

> what he sees he makes known to no one...
> whether in form of bird, beast or fish though
> the animal representing this guardian spirit
> is sometimes indicated by carvings or paintings
> made by the Indian.

Much the same situation prevailed among the adjacent Coast Salish peoples although information on spirit representations is not available for many groups. If this system were consistent throughout, then a bio-morphic design on a tool or other utilitarian object should represent the spirit power of the person owning and using the tool in question. Some ethnographic analogs and prehistoric examples are shown in Figure 11:1. The lightning snake, a powerful spirit for success in whaling, is depicted on the ethnographic harpoon valves. By analogy the prehistoric example shown by a wolf incised on the end of a point for a leister or fish spear should represent the guardian spirit of the owner of that implement. We do

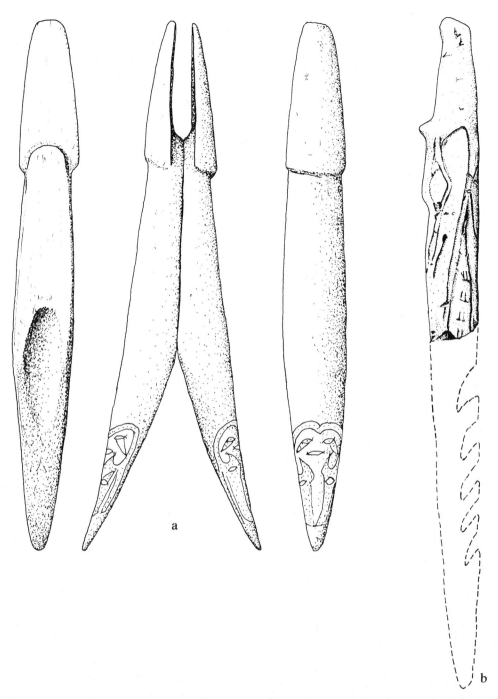

Fig. 11:1. Motifs on tools which may represent guardian spirits. *a* Valves from a whaling harpoon head depicting the lightning serpent, a powerful spirit for success in whaling. Southern Nootka, 19th century. *b* Butt end of a prehistoric leister or fish spear showing a wolf; Marpole phase, Cattle Point site, ca. 400 B.C.-A.D. 400.

learn that the wolf was a powerful spirit for success in hunting and fishing (Haeberlin and Gunther 1930:74). Another example shows a small bear carved on the end of an adze, a woodworking tool. One would assume that the bear was a guardian spirit who gave power for skill in woodworking. The earliest example of a tool bearing a potential spirit motif is the haft for a carving knife dating between 3500 and 4000 years ago (Matson 1976:182) which shows a bearded humanoid with his hands on his chest *(Fig. 8:6)*. This representation is not recognizable by ethnographic analogy, but the attributes of style—joined eyebrows and hands on the chest—place it clearly in the southern Northwest Coast art tradition

The Ozette material (Ch. 10), while barely prehistoric at best, shows a direct continuity into ethnographic Makah where Swan (1870:62) notes that the Thunderbird *(Figs. 10:5, 10:11)* took precedence over all other mythological beings, and that owls, bears and wolves were the most commonly represented guardian spirits. Owls in much the same style as those of Ozette occur as far south

Fig. 11:2. Fragment of a siltstone object, possibly a spindle whorl, incised on both sides with a representation stylistically similar to the Thunderbird. Garrison site, San Juan Islands, ca. A.D. 100.

as the Willamette Valley, Oregon (Murdey and Wentz 1975 Fig. 6u). On the southern Northwest Coast during the eighteenth century, the period to which most ethnographic information refers and from which most ethnographic art originated, it seems that Thunder was both a very widespread and powerful spirit, and that the Thunderbird is one of the most common motifs in art work. This fact is not generally understood. The centre of elaboration, as far as actual knowledge goes, was among the Makah largely because of Swan's study in the 1860's; unfortunately there were no comparable studies of Salish and other Nootkan groups at that time. The Makah possess the origin myth of the Thunderbird, and this spirit was fully integrated with concepts of whaling, wealth and war which explains his powerful nature. This power extended to Salish groups even though certain facets of the Nootkan complex such as whaling did not. The head on most whalebone clubs of this period is the Thunderbird which indicates power for war. One suspects that these ceremonial clubs all originated with a single Nootkan group such as the Makah, and that their widespread distribution came about through potlatching in connection with secret society dancing. The appearance of the Thunderbird on spindle whorls of the Central Coast Salish (Suttles, Ch. 4) could be related to spirit power necessary for spinning wool which was widely used on ceremonial regalia, and may mean that an inherited, possibly generalized power is represented. Barnett (1939: 271) reported Thunder as the strongest of all powers

among many Central Coast Salish groups, and Haeberlin and Gunther (1930:75) state it was a powerful spirit among Puget Sound Salish. The earliest representation in the same style as the Thunderbird is on a fragment of a siltstone object *(Fig. 11.2)* possibly a spindle whorl, from the Garrison site in the San Juan Islands. The earliest whalebone clubs (see Ch. 6) do not show the Thunderbird, but humanoids. The relationship between the Thunder spirit and Thunderbird is poorly known.

Shamanism

Shamanic spirits were those that enabled their possessors to undertake curing of the sick. Ritualists also undertook curing and ritual cleansing, but their power came by inheritance (Barnett 1939:273) rather than from encounters with spirits. Many of the same animals spirits were used for shamanism as well as everyday activities (Haeberlin and Gunther 1930), although reptilian forms—snakes and lizards—seem to be more often (if not exclusively) associated with shamanism. From the archaeological perspective, such representations on non-utilitarian paraphernalia are more likely to be shamanic spirits than other kinds of guardian spirits. Pendants, soul catchers, rattles and other objects bespeak more of shamanism than of other systems.

Ethnographic pendants of bone or stone are normally interpreted as shamanic charms depicting the shaman's spirit helpers. The ethnographic land otter pendants of the Tlingit (Jonaitis 1978) are the best known examples. The earliest prehistoric pendants are perforated or ringed animal teeth which may well have represented spirit power of their human owners, whether shamanic or guardian spirit. By 4500 B.P. fish pendants (Ch. 7) were known, and by 3500 B.P. MacDonald (Ch. 6) reports pendants conceptualized as "stylized figures hung upside down" from Prince Rupert Harbour sites.

A miniature skull *(Fig. 8:12a)* of the Locarno Beach phase about 2500 years ago has ethnographic counterparts in Hamatsa paraphernalia. The Hamatsa or Cannibal Dance is a Kwakiutl secret society which incorporated many elements of shamanism. Ribbed figures are also usually identified as having shamanic affiliations of which the earliest is the famous wolf (or land otter?) comb *(Fig. 2:1)* from the Prince Rupert Harbour sequence about A.D. 800. Animals depicted with ribs may actually symbolize transformed shamen.

The protruding tongue is probably the most significant shamanic element in Northwest Coast art, although very little specific information is known about it. Krause (1956:195) cites Veniaminof's report of 1840 in which he notes that the novice seeking spirit power is "lucky if he gets a land otter in whose tongue is contained the whole secret of shamanism." De Laguna (1954:175-176) notes that the novice shaman collects the tongues of those creatures that fall dead at his feet during the vision

Fig. 11:4. Antler figurine from Sucia Island. Such figurines were probably worn suspended on the chest, and suggest shamanic practices.

Fig. 11:3. Fragment of tubular soapstone pipe showing the protruding tongue. Pipes of this general type date between A.D. 400-1200, although the date of this particular pipe is unknown. From a water line excavation at Yale, B.C.

quest, and these become the source of his power. The numerous examples of ethnographic rattles which show the protruding tongue joining a human and an animal probably symbolically represent the transfer of spirit power, and the sexual connotations seen by Duff (Ch. 3) may not be there at all. Prehistoric examples of the protruding tongue are rare *(Fig. 11:3)*.

There are a number of figurines made of elk antler in the form of a human figure with perforated projections on the side of the head, a skirt, extended legs and arms either flat on the chest or at the sides *(Fig. 11:4)*. These figurines appear to date between A.D. 200 and A.D. 1200, and are found in interior Washington (Smith 1904, Strong 1959, Fig. 40), on Northern Puget Sound (Carlson 1954, Onat and Munsell 1970), and on the central coast of British Columbia (Ch. 7). Their size and the perforations indicate they were worn as pendants, probably on the chest. Only one has been found with a burial. The closest

analogies are with Siberian shaman's pendants (see Okaldnikov 1979:203), although the actual styles are not identical. This type is unknown from the historic period.

Another complex of prehistoric artifacts also strongly suggests shamanism. Prehistoric stone figures *(Fig. 11:5)* with bowls in their laps centre archaeologically along the Fraser and Thompson rivers and the adjacent coast. These bowls are not securely dated, but seem to belong in the period between 1 A.D. and A.D. 1000. They occur at Marpole (Ch. 8) about 1 A.D. and up river (Ch. 9) by A.D. 800. Duff (Ch. 3) attempts to relate these to girls' puberty ceremonies. The problem is that these bowls do not conform to Boas' (1890:90) descriptions of the bowls used in such rites. I suspect that they are actually tobacco mortars used in conjunction with pipes in the same style, and that both were employed in shamanic curing rituals involving smoking. Such practices are not known from the ethnographic period on the Northwest Coast, but are known from California, the direction from which the custom of smoking likely diffused. There is one example of a figure of the same style which is actually a pipe *(Fig. 8:29a)*.

Whatever speculations one wishes to make regarding their specific use, it can be said with high probability that these bowls relate to shamanic practices. The depictions

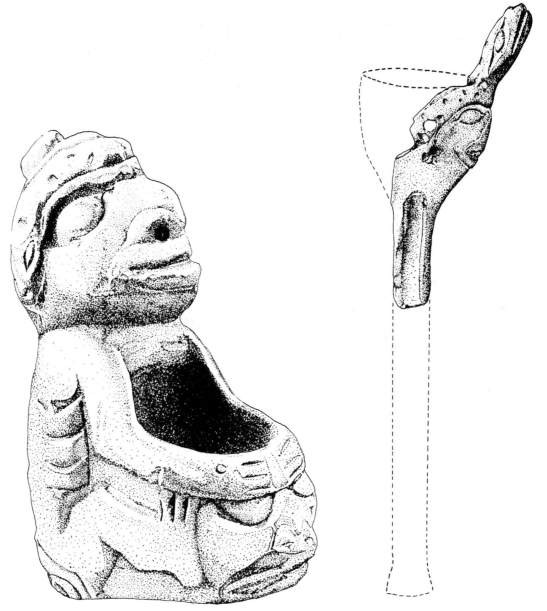

Fig. 11:5. Soapstone bowl and tubular pipe suggesting use in shamanic curing ceremonies. The bowl or tobacco mortar is from a pit house village near Lytton, N.B., and the pipe fragment from the beach near Sidney, B.C. Both pieces probably date 400-1200 A.D.

of ribbed humans in conjunction with rattlesnakes, toads and frogs and other reptilian forms is strongly indicative of shamanism and curing. The human depicted is probably the shaman himself, and other creatures his spirit helpers. Snakes are frequently found depicted on these bowls. Among the Puget Sound Salish a shaman demonstrated his power by making a stone or belt or other object turn into a snake which moved, and powerful shamans had a snake or lizard which they shot into people (Haeberlin and Gunther 1930:78-79). The "O" mouth form which appears on several of these bowls has been likened to that of Tsonoqua, the cannibal woman of the Kwakiutl. Similarities in form are indeed there, but in total configuration the prehistoric pieces suggest shamanic curing practices in which case the mouth form

could represent the blowing of smoke rather than the "Hu! Hu!" of the cannibal woman.

Secret Societies

Drucker (1940:227) described the secret societies of initiation of the Kwakiutl as "a dramatic re-enactment of the legendary encounter of the novices ancestor with a spirit and a display of the gifts (names, songs masks, carvings and other 'privileges') bestowed by the supernatural benefactor." He also noted the similarities between the secret societies and shamanic practices, and suggests that the former were derived from shamanism. Masks, puppets and other items of stagecraft were employed in these performances. The sxwayxwey among

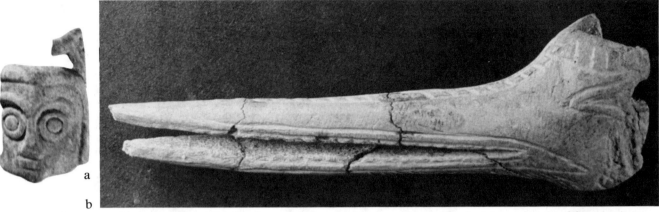

Fig. 11:6. Minature prehistoric masks made of antler. *a* found on the beach on Mayne Island; style suggests late Marpole phase, 800-1200 A.D.; *b* from excavations at Crescent Beach, 500-1000 B.C.

the Salish (Suttles, Ch. 4) and the Duckwally of the Makah are similar performances which also employ masks and rattles. No prehistoric rattles have been found, and no masks except for several small effigies *(Figs. 11:6, 8:9)* all from the Coast Salish region. The earliest is a miniature long beaked mask of antler dating to about 2500 years ago which resembles historic masks. The other *(Fig. 8:9)* is of stone, dates to about A.D. 1, and has a nasal cavity like the sxwayxwey ghost mask. A third *(Fig. 11:6)* , also of antler, is undated but stylistically suggests late Marpole phase (ca. A.D. 800) and a link to the sxwayxwey complex of ethnographic times. The small skull *(Fig. 8:12a)* dating to about 500 B.C. analogous to Hamatsa paraphernalia has already been mentioned.

Crests

Crests are graphic portrayals of power or privileges which were inherited from ancestors who "earned" them, rather than their being "earned" through spirit encounters by their immediate possessors. Crests and ancestors are what one sees on the "totem" poles of the northern groups (Tlingit, Haida, Tsimshian) on the feast dishes, house posts and some masks used by them and the Kwakiutl and on some Coast Salish house posts and possibly ritual paraphernalia. Crests are emblems of status and prestige and emphasize family or lineage connections. Wolf, raven, bear, eagle, beaver, frog, killer whale and other animal representations served as crests. The emphasis in studies of Northwest Coast art has long been on the crest system and its relationship to social rank. This emphasis has tended to obscure the basic concept of spirit power which is fundamental to the crest system as well as to guardian spirits and shamanism. Crests have cosmological or spiritual contexts as well as those of social rank, and it seems likely that the system of inheritance of crests developed from an earlier system of seeking spirit power. The problem the archaeologist faces is how to tell from

an art object whether the figure depicted was earned or inherited particularly since there was probably a developmental progression from the former to the latter.

The most obvious examples of crests are some of the red paint pictographs placed in prominent positions on cliff faces on the central coast of British Columbia. They are analogous to the totem poles of other regions, and likely proclaimed the inherited privileges of local chieftains. These pictographs are probably not very old. Figures on stone bowls such as the frog on the bowl from Kwatna *(Fig. 7:8)* could also be crest symbols.

Conclusions

Where, when and why did Northwest Coast art originate and what changes have taken place over the centuries? The empirical evidence indicates the initial appearance of simple life forms in the archaeological record some 4500 years ago followed by considerable elaboration of the tradition in the period between 2000 and 2500 years ago. The earliest piece in the southern style is the haft from the Glenrose site dating between 3500 and 4000 years ago. The archaeological data do not provide a clear picture of the development of the northern style with its form lines and interlocked parts. The spoon handle *(Fig. 8:10c)* dated 2500 years ago is certainly approaching Northern style, and a zoomorphic concretion *(Fig. 2:22)* with rudimentary joint marks dates about 2000 years ago. An early T-form, one of Holm's (Ch. 2) "holes in the donut", is on a pendant *(Fig. 11:7)* from a burial at the Garrison site in the San Juan Islands (Carlson 1960). The site is Marpole phase and has radiocarbon dates of 150 B.C. for the lowest strata and A.D. 370 for the most recent one. The pendant comes from the middle strata so a date of about A.D. 100 would be appropriate. A bone object *(Fig. 6:15c)* with classic eye elements dates to about A.D. 1100 and suggests northern style was full blown by then. The best prehistoric example of northern

Fig. 11:7. Antler pendants made from brow bands. Marpole phase, Garrison site. ca. A.D. 100.

style *(Fig. 6:13c)* is not satisfactorily dated. All in all, current archaeological information suggests that classic northern style resulted in part from the interaction created by the influence of southern art on an originally simple rendering of life forms on the Northern Coast.

The Ozette material points up what has been lost through decay at other sites, and behooves us to search for earlier waterlogged deposits where perishables have been better preserved. A more complete archaeological record might also help place idiosyncratic forms which presently constitute some of the discontinuities in the Northwest Coast art traditions. Such forms as that in Figure 11:8, which presently stand alone in style and content, could be the result of experimental or innovative behavior or could be related to styles yet to be discovered.

The preceding paragraphs describe some of the continuities in the archaeological record in terms of fitting various artifacts into the ethnographic belief systems by analogy, and at the same time projecting those belief systems into the past. This method worked best on the general level for inferring a 4000 year belief in spirits, reasonably well for guardian and shamanic spirits, and less well for secret societies and crests because of the difficulty in differentiating symbols associated with these practices from the more general ones.

Why specific art traditions originate is always conjectural, although evidence from nonliterate cultures the world over is that such art usually relates to the belief system which in turn arose as part of man's attempts to explain and control his world. A basic belief in spirit power and control through shamanistic practices were probably part of the belief system of the earliest inhabitants of the Northwest Coast. As populations and food surpluses grew and life became patterned around intensive food gathering in spring, summer and fall, the winter became free for shamanic performances, dances and potlatches which integrated belief with art and fostered the development of the art tradition. The masterpieces of historic times came from simple beginnings. Only further archaeological research will provide more definite glimpses of the intervening steps.

Fig. 11:8. Stone figure from "between Vancouver Island and the Mainland." This figure is idiosyncratic and does not closely conform to any known Northwest Coast style.

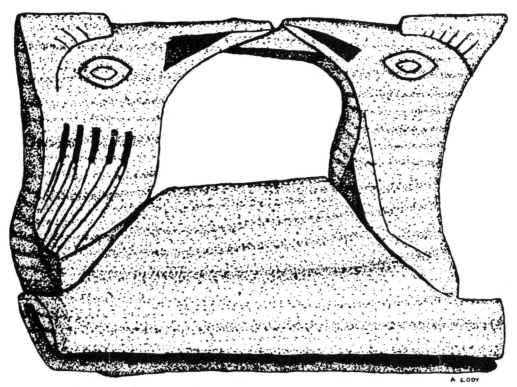

Fig. 11:9. The oldest wood carving known from the Northwest Coast. Mat creaser made of cedar recovered in July, 1983 in waterlogged deposits at the Hoko River site which date to 2750 C-14 years ago. This artifact indicates nearly three millenia of continuity for the southern Northwest Coast art style. Illustrations and information courtesy of Dale Croes, director of the Hoko River Archaeological project. Length 14 cm.

REFERENCES

Ackerman, Robert E.
1968   The archaeology of the Glacier Bay Region, south-eastern Alaska. *Report of Investigations, No. 44. Laboratory of Anthropology, Washington State University,* Pullman.

Ackerman, R.E., T.D. Hamilton and R. Stuckenrath
1979   Early culture complexes on the northern *Northwest Coast. Canadian Journal of Archaeology* 3:195-209.

Allely, J.
1975   A Clovis point from the Mohawk River Valley, western Oregon. In Archaeological Studies in the Willamette Valley, Oregon, edited by C.M. Aikens: *Anthropological Papers of the University of Oregon* No. 8. Eugene.

Barbeau, Marius
1950-51   *Totem Poles.* National Museum of Canada, Bulletin 119.
1951   The Old-World dragon in America. In *Indian Tribes of Aboriginal America.* Selected Papers of the XXIX Internationa Congress of Americanists, edited by Sol Tax, pp. 115-122.
1957   *Haida myths Illustrated in Argillite Carvings.* National Museum of Canada Bulletin No. 139, Anthropological Series No. 38, Ottawa.
n.d.   Tsimshian manuscripts on file with the Canadian Centre for Folk Culture Studies, National Museum of Man. Ottawa.

Barnett, H.G.
1938   The Coast Salish of Canada. *American Anthropologist* 40:118-41.
1939   Culture element distributions: IX: Gulf of Georgia Salish. *Anthropological records* 1:5. University of California Press, Berkeley.
1955   *The Coast Salish of British Columbia.* University of Oregon, Eugene.

Boas, Franz
1891a   The Shuswap. *Sixth Annual Report on the Northwestern Tribes of Canada, British Association for the Advancement of Science for 1890,* pp. 633-647
1891b   The LkungEn. *Sixth Annual Report on the Northwestern Tribes of Canada, British Association of the Advancement of Science for 1890,* pp. 563-582.
1897   The social organization and secret societies of the Kwakiutl Indians. *Annual Report of the United States National Museum for 1895,* pp. 311-378.
1900a   Art. In The Thompson Indians of British Columbia, by James Teit. *Memoirs of the American Museum of Natural History,* Vol. 2, Part 4:387-390.

1900b   The mythology of the Bella Colla Indians. *Memoirs of the American Museum of Natural History,* Vol. 2.
1905-1909 The Kwakiutl of Vancouver Island. *Memoirs of the American Museum of Natural History,* Vol. 8:307-515.
1932   Bella Bella Tales. *Memoirs of the American Folklore Society,* No. 25.
1955   *Primitive Art.* Dover Publications, New York.

Boehm, Sheila Gay (nee Calvert)
1973   *Cultural and non-cultural variation in the artifact and faunal samples from the St. Mungo Cannery site, B.C. DgRr 2.* Unpublished M.A. Thesis, Department of Anthropology, University of Victoria.

Borden, Charles E.
1950   Preliminary report on archaeological investigations in the Fraser Delta region. *Anthropology in British Columbia* No. 1:13-26.
1951   Facts and problems in Northwest Coast prehistory. *Anthropology in British Columbia* No. 2:35-57.
1954   Some aspects of prehistoric coastal-interior relations in the Pacific Northwest. *Anthropology in British Columbia* No. 4:26-32.
1960   DjRi3, an early site in the Fraser Canyon, British Columbia. *National Museum of Canada Bulletin* No. 162:101-118
1961   Fraser River Archaeological Project, progress report. *National Museum of Canada, Anthropology Papers* No. 1.
1965   Radiocarbon and geological dating of the Lower Fraser Canyon Sequence. *Proceedings Sixth International Conference on Radiocarbon and Tritium Dating:* 165-178. Pullman, Washington.
1968a   A late Pleistocene pebble tool industry in south-western British Columbia. *Eastern New Mexico University Contributions in Anthropology* Vol. 1, No. 4:55-69.
1968b   Prehistory of the lower mainland. In: *Lower Fraser Valley: evolution of a cultural landscape.* B.C. Geographical Series No. 9, edited by A.H. Siemens, pp. 9-26. Department of Geography, University of British Columbia.
1969a   The Skagit River atlatl: a reappraisal. *B.C. Studies* No. 1:13-19.
1969b   Excavations at old Musqueam 1967-1968. *Newsletter, Archaeological Society of British Columbia,* Vol. 1, No. 2:2-4.
1970   Culture History of the Fraser Delta region. In Archaeology in British Columbia, New Discoveries, edited by R.L. Carlson. *B.C. Studies* No. 6-7:95-112.
1975   Origins and development of early Northwest Coast culture to about 3000 B.C. *National Museum of Man Mercury Series, Archaeological Survey of Canada Paper* No. 45.
1976   A water-saturated site on the southern mainland coast of British Columbia. In: The excavation of

water-saturated archaeological sites (wet sites) on the Northwest Coast of North America, edited by Dale Croes. *National Museum of Man Mercury Series, Archaeological Survey of Canada Paper* No. 50:233-260.

Borden, Charles E. and David Archer
1975   Musqueam northeast archaeological salvage project. In Archaeological salvage projects 1974, edited by R. Wilmeth. *National Museum of Man Mercury Series, Archaeological Survey of Canada Paper* No. 36:57-65.

Burley, D.V.
1980   Marpole. Anthropological reconstructions of a prehistoric Northwest Coast culture type. *Department of Archaeology, Simon Fraser University Publication* No. 8. Burnaby.

Butler, B. Robert
1957   Art of the Lower Columbia Valley. *Archaeology* 10:158-165.

Calkins, Harry J.
1977   Art legacy of the Coast Salish. *Puget Soundings,* April 1977:26-29.

Calvert, Gay
1970   The St. Mungo Cannery site: a preliminary report. *B.C. Studies,* No. 6-7:54-76.

Carlson, Catherine
1979   The early component at Bear Cove. *Canadian Journal of Archaeology* 3:177-209.

Carlson, R.L.
1954   *Archaeological investigations in the San Juan Islands.* M.A. Thesis. University of Washington, Seattle.
1960   Chronology and culture change in the San Juan Islands, Washington. *American Antiquity* Vol. 25 (4):562-586.
1972   Excavations at Kwatna. In Salvage '71, edited by R.L. Carlson, pp. 44-58. *Department of Archaeology, Simon Fraser University Publication* No. 1. Burnaby.
1979   The early period on the central coast of British Columbia. *Canadian Journal of Archaeology* 3:211-228.

Carlson, R.L. and Philip M. Hobler
1972   Radiocarbon dates from sites excavated by Simon Fraser University. *The Midden.* Vol. IV, No. 5. The Archaeological Society of British Columbia. Vancouver.

Chapman, M.W.
1982   Archaeological Investigations at the O'Conner Site, Port Hardy. In Papers on central coast archaeology, edited by P.M. Hobler, pp. 65-132. *Department of Archaeology, Simon Fraser University Publication* No. 10. Burnaby.

Codere, Helen
1948   The Swaixwe myth of the Middle Fraser River: the integration of two Northwest Coast cultural ideas. *Journal of American Folklore* 61:1-18

Collins, Henry et al.
1973   *The Far North: 2,000 Years of American Eskimo and Indian Art.* National Gallery of Art, Washington.

Collins, June M.
1974   Valley of the Spirits: The Upper Skagit Indians of western Washington. *American Ethnological Society Monograph* 56. University of Washington, Seattle.

Conover, Kathryn J.
1972   Archaeological samplings at Namu: A problem in settlement reconstruction. Ph.D. Dissertation, University of Colorado, Boulder.

Corner, John
1968   *Pictographs in the interior of British Columbia.* Wayside Press, Vernon, B.C.

Cowan, Ian McT.
1940   Distribution and variation in the native sheep of North America. *American Midland Naturalist* 24:505-508.

Cowan, Ian McT. and Charles J. Guiguet
1965   The mammals of British Columbia. *British Columbia Provincial Museum Handbook* No. 11. Victoria.

Cressman, L.S., D.L. Cole, W.A. Davis, T.M. Newman and D.J. Scheans
1960   Cultural sequences at the Dalles, Oregon. *Transactions of the American Philosophical Society* 50(10).

Croes, D.R., editor
1976   The excavation of water-saturated sites (wet sites) on the Northwest Coast of North America. *National Museum of Man Mercury Series, Archaeological Survey of Canada Paper* No. 50.
n.d.   Lachane basketry and cordage. Ms. on file (1976), Archaeological Survey of Canada, National Museum of Man. Ottawa.

Crowe-Swords, D.
1974   *The Carruthers Site, a late prehistoric site in the lower Fraser Valley.* Unpublished M.A. Thesis on file at the Department of Archaeology, Simon Fraser University, Burnaby, B.C.

Cybulski, Jerome
1974   Tooth wear and material culture: precontact patterns in the Tsimshian area, British Columbia. *Syesis,* 7:31-35. Victoria.
n.d.   Human remains from the Boardwalk Site (GbTo 31), Prince Rupert, B.C. Ms. in preparation.

Davis, S.
1979   *The Hidden Falls site.* Paper presented at the Northwest Anthropology Conference 1979, Eugene, Oregon.

Dewhirst, J.
1980   The indigenous archaeology of Yuquot, a Nootkan Outside village. *National Historic Parks and Sites Branch, History and Archaeology* No. 39. Ottawa.

Dikov, N.N.
1979   *Ancient Cultures of Northeast Asia.* Nauka Publishing House, Moscow.

Drucker, Philip
1940   Kwakiutl dancing societies. *Anthropological Records:* II. University of California, Berkeley.
1943   Archaeological survey on the northern Northwest Coast. *Bureau of American Ethnology. Bulletin* 133, *Anthropological Paper* No 20:17-132. Washington, D.C.
1955a   Indians of the Northwest Coast. *American Museum of Natural History Anthropological Handbook* No. 10. McGraw-Hill, New York.
1955b   Sources of Northwest Coast culture. In New Interpretations of aboriginal American culture history, *75th Anniversary Volume of the Anthropological Society of Washington, D.C.:* 59-81.

Duff, Wilson
1952   The Upper Stalo Indians of the Fraser Valley, British Columbia, *British Columbia Provincial Museum Memoir* No. 1, Victoria.
1955   Unique stone artifacts from the Gulf Islands, *British Columbia Provincial Museum, Annual Report* (1955):45-55.
1956a   Prehistoric stone sculpture of the Fraser River and Gulf of Georgia. *Anthropology in British Columbia* No. 5:15-151.
1956b   An unusual burial at the Whalen Site. *Research Studies of the State College of Washington,* Vol. 24, No. 1:67-72
1963   Stone clubs from the Skeena River area. *Provincial Museum Annual Report for 1962,* pp. 2-12. Victoria.
1969   The Northwest Coast. In *Masterpieces of Indian and Eskimo Art from Canada.* Musée de l'Homme, Paris.
1975   Images Stone B.C.: Thirty centuries of Northwest Coast Indian sculpture. *Art Gallery of Greater Victoria, B.C.* Hancock House.

Eldridge, Morley
1974   Recent archaeological investigations near Chase, B.C. *Cariboo College Papers in Archaeology* 4. Kamloops.

Elmendorf, W.W.
1960   The structure of Twana culture. *Research Studies, Monographic Supplement* No. 2. Washington State University, Pullman.

Emmons, George T.
1907   The Chilkat Blanket. *Memoirs of the American Museum of Natural History.* Vol. III, Part IV, New York.

n.d.   Notes, photos, etc. on the Schwy-Why legend. On file in the British Columbia Provincial Archives.

Fladmark, Knut
1970a   A preliminary report on lithic assemblages from the Queen Charlotte Islands, B.C. In *Early Man and Environments in Northwestern North America,* edited by J.W. Smith and R.A. Smith, pp. 118-136, University of Calgary. Calgary.
1970b   Preliminary report on the archaeology of the Queen Charlotte Islands: 1969 Field Season. *B.C. Studies* No. 6-7:18-45. Vancouver.
1973   The Richardson Ranch site: A 19th century Haida House. In *Historical Archaeology in Northwestern North America,* edited by Donald M. Getty and Knut R. Fladmark, University of Calgary. Calgary.
1974   *A paleoecological model for Northwest Coast prehistory.* Ph.D. dissertation. University of Calgary.
1979   The early prehistory of the Queen Charlotte Islands. *Archaeology* 32(2):38-45.

Friedman, Janet P.
1975   *The prehistoric uses of wood at the Ozette archaeological site.* Ph.D. dissertation, Washington State University.

Gessler, Nicholas and Trisha Gessler
1974   Petroglyphs on the Queen Charlotte Islands. In The Charlottes: a journal of the Queen Charlotte Islands. *The Queen Charlotte Islands Museum Society* Vol. 3, pp. 17-18.

Grant, Campbell
1967   *Rock Art of the American Indian,* Thomas Y. Crowell Company, New York.

Gunther, Erna
1966   *Art in the Life of the Northwest Coast Indians.* Superior Publishing Co., Seattle.

Gustafson, C.E., D. Gribow and R.D. Daugherty
1979   The Manis Mastodon site: early man on the Olympic Peninsula. *Canadian Journal of Archaeology* 3:157-164.

Haeberlin, Hermann K.
1918   Principles of Esthetic Form in the Art of the North Pacific Coast, *American Anthropologist,* n.s., Vol. XX:258-264.

Haeberlin, H.K. and Erna Gunther
1930   Indians of Puget Sound. *University of Washington Publications in Anthropology* Vol. IV.

Hansen, Gordon W.
1973   *The Katz site: a prehistoric pithouse settlement in the lower Fraser Valley, British Columbia.* Unpublished M.A. Thesis, Department of Anthropology and Sociology, University of British Columbia.

Harper, J. Russell, editor
1971   *Paul Kane's Frontier.* University of Texas, Austin.

Hawthorn, Audrey
1967   *Art of the Kwakiutl Indians and Other Northwest Coast Tribes.* University of Washington, Seattle.

Heizer, R.F. and J.E. Mills
1952   *The Four Ages of Tsurai.* University of California Press, Berkeley.

Hess, Thom
1974   *Dictionary of Puget Salish.* University of Washington, Seattle.

Hester, James and Sarah Nelson, editors
1978   Studies in Bella Bella prehistory. *Department of Archaeology, Simon Fraser University Publication* No. 5. Burnaby.

Hill, Beth and Roy Hill
1974   *Indian Petroglyphs of the Pacific Northwest.* Hancock House. Saanichton, B.C.

Hill-Tout, Charles
1902   Ethnological studies of the mainland Halkomelem. *British Association for the Advancement of Science, Report for 1902:* 355-490.

Hobler, Philip M.
1970   Archaeological survey and excavation in the vicinity of Bella Coola. In Archaeology in British Columbia:new discoveries, edited by R.L. Carlson. *B.C. Studies* 6-7:77-94.

Hobler, Philip M. editor
1982   Papers on Central Coast archaeology. *Department of Archaeology, Simon Fraser University, Publication* No. 10. Burnaby.

Hobler, P.M. and R.L. Carlson
1975   Archaeology of the Central Coast of British Columbia. Ms. prepared for *Handbook of North American Indians,* Vol. VII, Northwest Coast.

Holm, Bill
1965   *Northwest Coast Indian Art: An Analysis of Form.* University of Washington Press, Seattle.
1972   *Crooked Beak of Heaven: Masks and Other Ceremonial Art of the Northwest Coast.* University of Washington, Seattle.

Holm, Bill and William Reid
1975   *Form and Freedom, A Dialogue on Northwest Coast Indian Art.* Institute for the Arts, Rice University, Houston.

Hopkins, D.M.
1979   Landscape and climate of Beringia during the late Pleistocene and Holocene time. In *The First Americans,* edited by W.S. Laughlin and A.B. Harper. Gustav Fischer, New York.

Inglis, Richard I.
1974   Contract salvage 1973: a preliminary report on the salvage excavations of two shell middens in the Prince Rupert Harbour, B.C. GbTo 33/36. *The Midden,* Vol. VI, No. 1:11-14. The Archaeological Society of British Columbia.
1976   Wet site distribution — the northern case GbTo 33, the Lachane Site. In: The excavation of water-saturated archaeological sites (wet sites) on the Northwest Coast of North America, edited by Dale Croes, pp. 158-185, *National Museum of Man Mercury Series, Archaeological Survey of Canada Paper* No. 50. Ottawa.

Inverarity, Robert Bruce
1950   *Art of the Northwest Coast Indians.* University of California Press. Berkeley and Los Angeles.

Jacobs, Melville
1959   *The Content and Style of an Oral Literature: Clackamas Chinook Myths and Tales.* University of Chicago.

Jenness, Diamond
1955   The faith of a Coast Salish Indian. *Anthropology in British Columbia Memoir* 3. British Columbia Provincial Museum, Victoria.
n.d.   The Saanich Indians of Vancouver Island. MS in the collection of the National Museum of Man, Ottawa.

Jonaitis, Aldona
1978   Land otters and shamans: some interpretations of Tlingit charms. *American Indian Art,* Vol. 4, No. 1. Scottsdale.

Kidd, Robert S.
1968   Archaeological survey in the lower Fraser River Valley, British Columbia, 1963. *National Museum of Canada, Bulletin 224, Contributions to Anthropology VI, Paper* No. 5:208-247.

Krause, A.
1956   *The Tlingit Indians.* Translated by E. Gunther. University of Washington Press. Seattle.

Kroeber, A.L.
1939   *Cultural and Natural Areas of Native North America.* University of California, Berkeley.

de Laguna, Frederica
1934   *The Archaeology of Cook Inlet, Alaska.* The University of Pennsylvania Press, Philadelphia.
1954   Tlingit ideas about the individual. *Southwest Journal of Anthropology,* 10(2):172-191
1958   Geological confirmation of native traditions, Yakutat, Alaska. *American Antiquity,* 23(4):434.
1960   The story of a Tlingit community. *Bureau of American Ethnology Bulletin* 172. Washington.

Lamb, W. Kaye
1960   *The Letters and Journals of Simon Fraser, 1806-1808.* MacMillan, Toronto.

Lane, Barbara S.
1951   The Cowichan knitting industry. *Anthropology in British Columbia* No. 2:14-27.

LeClair, Ronald
1976   Investigations at the Maurer Site near Agassiz,
            *Current Research Reports, Department of
            Archaeology, Simon Fraser University
            Publication* No. 3:33-42.

LeRoi-Gourhan, A.
1946   *Archaeologie du Pacific-Nord.* Paris.

Lévi-Strauss, Claude
1969a   *The Raw and the Cooked: Introduction to a
            Science of Mythology:* I. Translated from the
            French by John and Doreen Weightman. Harper
            and Row, New York.
1969b   Quotation from "Splendor from the past."
            Article in *Time Magazine* (Canadian Edition),
            April 4, 1969, p. 16.
1975   *La Voie des Masques* (2 tomes). Skira.
            Genève, Switzerland.

Luebbers, R.A.
1971   Archaeological sampling at Namu. Manuscript
            Bella Bella research project, University of
            Colorado, Boulder.

Lundy, Doris
1974   *The rock art of the Northwest Coast.*
            M.A. Thesis, Department of Archaeology,
            Simon Fraser University.

MacDonald, George F.
1969   Preliminary culture sequence from the Coast
            Tsimshian area, B.C. *Northwest Anthropological
            Research Notes* 3(2):240-254.
1970   Preliminary report for the National Museum of
            Man on the excavations at Prince Rupert
            Harbour.
1971   Description of cover illustration. *Research
            Report No. 1, Archaeology Division, National
            Museum of Man,* p. ii. Ottawa.
1976   Masterworks of Haida art: George Mercer
            Dawson and the McCord Museum Collection.
            Apollo Magazine, Vol. CIII, No. 171, May,
            1976, pp. 90-94.

Masson, L.F.R., editor
1889-90   *Les Bourgeois de la Compagnie du Nord-Ouest.*
            V. 1. Quebec.

Matson, R.G.
1976   The Glenrose Cannery Site. *National Museum of
            Man Mercury Series, Archaeological Survey of
            Canada Paper* No. 52. Ottawa.

McIllwraith, T.F.
1948   *The Bella Coola Indians.* 2 vols. Toronto.

McKenzie, K.
1974   *Ozette prehistory: prelude.* M.A. Thesis,
            Department of Archaeology, University
            of Calgary.

Mitchell, Donald H.
1971   Archaeology of the Gulf of Georgia area, a
            natural region and its culture types. *Syesis*

            vol. 4, supplement 1.
1981   Test excavations at randomly selected sites in
            eastern Queen Charlotte Strait. *B.C. Studies*
            No. 48. Vancouver.

Mooney, James
1928   The aboriginal population of America north
            of Mexico. *Smithsonian Miscellaneous
            Collections* 80:7:1-40.

Murdy, C.N. and W.J. Wentz
1975   Artifacts from Fanning Mound, Willamette
            Valley, Oregon. In Archaeological studies in the
            Willamette Valley, Oregon, edited by
            C.M. Aikens, pp. 349-374. *Anthropological
            Papers of the University of Oregon,* No. 8.

Nelson, E.W.
1899   The Eskimo about Bering Strait. *Eighteenth
            Annual Report, Bureau of American Ethnology,*
            Part 1, Washington D.C.

Newman, T.M.
1959   *Tillamook prehistory and its relation to the
            Northwest Coast culture.* Ph.D. dissertation,
            University of Oregon, Eugene.
1966   Cascadia Cave. *Occasional Papers of the Idaho
            State University Museum* No. 18. Pocatello.

Nordenskiold, A.E.
1882   *The Voyage of the Vega.* New York.

Okladnikov, A.P.
1971   Petroglyphs of the Lower Amur River,
            Publications of Science, Leningrad Division,
            Leningrad.
1979   *Sibirien: Archaeologie und Alte Geschichte.*
            Akademie der Wissenschaften der U.D.S.S.R.

Olson, Ronald L.
1936   The Quinault Indians. *University of Washington
            Publications in Anthropology* 6:1-190.

Onat, Astrida and D. Munsell
1970   Skagit art: descriptions of two similarly carved
            antler figurines. *The Washington
            Archaeologist.* Vol. XIV, No. 3. Seattle.

Orchard, William C.
1926   A rare Salish blanket. *Leaflets of the Museum
            of the American Indian, Heye Foundation,*
            New York, No. 5.

Osborne, D.
1956   Early lithic in the Pacific Northwest. *Research
            Studies of the State College of Washington*
            24(1). 38-44. Pullman.

Panofsky, Erwin
1939   *Studies in Iconology.* Oxford University Press,
            New York.

Pettigrew, Richard M.
1975   *Progress report on the Lower Columbia cultural
            sequence.* Paper given at the Northwest
            Anthropological Conference, Seattle, March

27-29, 1975.

1976   *Lower Columbia archaeology.* Paper read at the Public Archaeology Conference, Oregon Museum of Science and Industry, January 10 1976.

Pomeroy, J.A.
1976   Stone fish traps of the Bella Bella region. In Current Research Reports, R.L. Carlson (editor), pp. 165-173. *Department of Archaeology Simon Fraser University, Publication* No. 3.

Rice, David G.
1972   The Windust Phase in Lower Snake River region prehistory. *Washington State University Laboratory of Anthropology Report of Investigations* No. 50. Pullman.

Sanger, David
1968a   The Chase burial site, EeQw l, British Columbia *National Museums of Canada, Bulletin* 24:86-185.
1968b   The Texas Creek burial site assemblage, British Columbia. *National Museums of Canada, Anthropology Papers,* No. 17.
1970   The archaeology of the Lochnore-Nesikep locality, British Columbia. *Syesis* 3:1-129, Supplement 1.

Severs, Patricia D.S.
1974   Archaeological investigations at Blue Jackets Creek, FlUa 4, Queen Charlotte Islands, British Columbia, 1973. *Canadian Archaeological Association Bulletin,* No. 6, pp. 163-205.

Silverstein, Michael
n.d.   Chinookans of the Lower Columbia. Ms. prepared for the Handbook of North American Indians, vol. VII.

Smith, H.I.
1899   Archaeology of Lytton, British Columbia. *American Museum of Natural History Memoirs,* Vol. 1, part 3:129-162.
1900   Archaeology of the Thompson River region, British Columbia. *American Museum of Natural History Memoirs,* Vol. 2, part 6:401-442.
1903   Shell-heaps of the Lower Fraser River, British Columbia. *Jesup North Pacific Expedition, American Museum of Natural History Memoirs,* Part 4:133-191.
1904   A costumed human figure from Tampico, Washington. *American Museum of Natural History Bulletin,* Vol. 20. New York.
1907   The archaeology of the Gulf of Georgia and Puget Sound. *The Jesup North Pacific Expedition, Memoir of the American Museum of Natural History,* Vol. II, Part VI, pp. 300-441.
1913   The archaeological collection from the southern interior of British Columbia. *Museum of the Geological Survey,* Canada.
1936   The man petroglyph near Prince Rupert, or the Man Who Fell From Heaven. In *Essays in Anthropology presented to A.L. Kroeber,* edited by R.H. Lowie, pp. 309-312. Berkeley.

Smith, Marian W.
1940   The Puyallup-Nisqually. *Columbia University Contributions to Anthropology* 32.
1941   The Coast Salish of Puget Sound. *American Anthropolgist* 43:197-211.

Snyder, W.
1956   "Old Man House" on Puget Sound. *Research Studies of the State College of Washington,* 24(1):17-37. Pullman.

Stenzel, Franz
1975   *James Madison Alden: Yankee Artist of the Pacific Coast, 1854-1860.* Amon Carter Museum, Fort Worth.

Stern, Bernhard J.
1934   *The Lummi Indians of Northwest Washington.* Columbia University, New York.

Stewart, Hilary
1973   *Artifacts of the Northwest Coast Indians.* Hancock House, Saanichton, B.C.
1974   Missing statue located. *The Midden* 6(4):10-11. The Archaeological Society of British Columbia.

Strong, E.
1959   *Stone Age on the Columbia River.* Binfords and Mort, Portland.

Strong, William D.
1945   The occurrence and wider implications of a "Ghost Cult" on the Columbia River suggested by carvings in wood, bone, and stone. *American Anthropologist,* 47:244-261.

Strong, W.D., W.E. Schenck and J. Steward
1930   Archaeology of the Dalles-Deschutes region. *University of California Publications in American Archaeology and Ethnology,* Vol. 29, Berkeley and Los Angeles.

Stryd, A.H.
1972   Housepit archaeology at Lillooet, British Columbia: the 1970 field season. *B.C. Studies* 14:17-46.
1973   *The later prehistory of the Lillooet area, British Columbia.* Ph.D. dissertation, University of Calgary.

Suttles, Wayne
1951   *The economic life of the Coast Salish of Haro and Rosario Straits.* Ph.D. dissertation, University of Washington.
1957   The Plateau Prophet Dance among the Coast Salish. *Southwestern Journal of Anthropology* 13:352-396.
1960   *Spirit dancing and the persistence of native culture among the Coast Salish.* Paper read at the 5th International Congress of Anthropological and Ethnological Sciences, Paris.
1968   Coping with abundance: subsistence on the Northwest Coast. In *Man the Hunter,* edited by R.B. Lee and I. DeVore. pp 55-68. Aldine, Chicago.
1972   On the cultural track of the sasquatch.

Northwest Anthropological Research Notes 6(1)65-90. Moscow: University of Idaho.

Swan, J.G.
1870   The Indians of Cape Flattery. *Smithsonian Contributions to Knowledge,* Vol. 16. Washington.

Swanton, J.R.
1909   Tlingit myths and texts: *Bureau of American Ethnology Bulletin* 39. Washington.

Teit, James
1900   The Thompson Indians of British Columbia. *American Museum of Natural History Memoirs,* Vol. 2, part 4:163-392.
1906   The Lillooet Indians. *American Museum of Natural History Memoirs,* vol. 2, sect. 5:195-292.
1909   The Shuswap. *American Museum of Natural History Memoirs,* Vol. 2, part 7:447-789.

Voegelin, C.F. and F.N. Voegelin
1966   *Map of North American Indian Languages.* American Ethnological Society.

Warren, Claude
1968   The view from Wenas. *Occasional Papers of the Idaho State University Museum* No. 24. Pocatello.

Waterman, T.T.
1924   The Shake religion of Puget Sound. *Annual Report of the Smithsonian Institution for 1922,* pp. 499-507.

Willey, Gordon R., and Philip Phillips

1958   *Method and Theory in American Archaeology.* University of Chicago Press.

Wilson, Charles
1865   Report on the Indian tribes inhabiting the country in the vicinity of the 49th Parallel of North latitude. *Ethnological Society of London, Transactions,* Vol. 6, n.s., pp. 275-332.
1970   *Mapping the Frontier.* Edited by George F.G. Stanley. Macmillan, Toronto.

Wilson, Robert L.
1974   A report on salvage archaeology conducted in the vicinity of Kamloops, British Columbia, in 1973. MS on file with the Archaeological Sites Advisory Board of British Columbia, Victoria.

Wingert, Paul
1949a   *American Indian Sculpture, A Study of the Northwest Coast.* J.J. Augustin, New York.
1949b   Coast Salish painting. In *Indians of the Urban Northwest,* edited by Marian W. Smith, pp. 77-91. Columbia University Press, New York.
1951   Tsimshian Sculpture. In The Tsimshian: their arts and music. *Publications of the American Ethnological Society,* Vol. XVIII. University of Washington Press, Seattle.
1952   *Prehistoric Stone Sculpture of the Pacific Northwest.* Portland: Portland Art Museum.

Wyatt, David
1972   *The Indian history of the Nicola Valley, British Columbia.* Unpublished Ph.D. dissertation. Department of Anthropology, Brown University.

CREDITS AND ACKNOWLEDGEMENTS

The final appearance of this volume is the result of the efforts of a great many people. Other than to the contributing authors, thanks go first to Barbara Hodgson whose skills in graphics and layout brought order out of chaos in the design of this book. Funding for typesetting and layout was covered in part by a grant from the British Columbia Heritage Trust for which we thank them. Printing and other costs were borne by the Department of Archaeology publications fund at Simon Fraser University.

Particular thanks go to Donald Abbott and Philip Hobler for help in getting some of the photographs together. Many other individuals also contributed in everything from typing to illustrations to advice as this book gradually came into being, and I thank them all for their help: Brenda Baker, Ingrid Bell, Helga Borden, Bob Brown, Eddy Chan, Monica Deutsch, Bernice Ferrier, Knut Fladmark, Richard Inglis, Doe Kennedy, Rick Percy, Mary Quirolo, Sheila Roberts, Penny Scharf, Audrey Shane, Richard Shutler, Jr., Mary Lee Stearns and Hilary Stewart.

The fluted points in Figure 1:3 are re-drawn from Alley (1975) and Osborne (1956). Other artifacts in Chapter 1 are in the archaeological collections of Washington State University, the Burke Museum, the Museum of Man, the University of British Columbia and Simon Fraser University.

Thanks also go to the institutions and individuals who allowed authors to research and photograph materials in their collections, and who in some instances provided the photographs. In the Chapter by Duff it was not always possible to determine exact location of the specimen, some of which we know only from slides in his collection. The following institutions or individuals have artifacts or photographs used in this volume:

American Museum of Natural History, New York
Figs. 2:2; 2:19; 2:23; 3:4; 3:5 drawing by Bill Reid; 3:6; 4:4 d, D. Kennedy photo; 4:11; 4:12.

British Columbia Provinicial Museum, Victoria
Figs. 2:21; 2:25; 3:14 photo; 3:17; 3:27; 3:31 photo; 3:32 photo; 4:3; 4:4b; 4:5a photo; 4:6, A. Hoover photo; 4:8; 4:14 b, d, e, f, g, k, i; 5:2 photo; 5:4; 5:6; 5:8; 5:11; 8:30a; 8:35; 9:1-9:13; 11:6a.

Brooklyn Museum
Fig. 4:14j D. Kennedy photo.

Burke Memorial Washington State Museum, Seattle
Figs. 2:3-2:8; 2:10; 2:13; 2:14; 2:17; 2:18; 4:2a, b; 11:1b; 11:2; 11:4; 11:7; 11:8.

Indiana University
Fig. 2:12.

'Ksan Association
Fig. 2:24.

Makah Tribal Museum, Neah Bay
Figs. 10:1-10:15.

McCord Museum, Montreal
Figs. 2:23; 3:18.

Museum of the American Indian, New York
Figs. 3:11; 3:12; 3:13; 8:25; H. Stewart Photos.

Museum of Anthropology, University of British Columbia, Vancouver.
Figs. 3:8 photo; 3:20 photo; 3:21 photo; 3:22; 3:23; 3:25 photo; 3:33; 4:4a, c, D. Kennedy photo; 8:4; 8:6-8:11 N. Cheney drawing; 8:12; 8:13, 14 N. Cheney drawings; 8:15-8:21; 8:23; 8:26-8:27; 8:28 drawing by C.M. Irvine; 8:29-8:34.

Museum of Man, Ottawa
Figs. 2:1; 3:3; 3:30; 3:34 H. Stewart photo; 4:8-4:10; 4:13; 6:2-6:31; 6:33-6:36.

Museum of Northern British Columbia, Prince Rupert
Fig. 6:32

Museum fur Volkerkunde, Berlin
Fig. 2:22.

Peabody Museum, Harvard University
Figs. 2:9; 2:11.

Simon Fraser University, Museum of Archaeology and Ethnology, Burnaby
Figs. 3:1 photo; 3:2; 3:10 photo; 7:1-7:4; 7:5 photo; 7:6; 7:7; 7:8b; 8:2; 11:1; 11:3 photo; 11:5; 11:6b.

University Museum, University of Pennsylvania, Philadelphia.
Fig. 4:2c, d.

Vancouver City Museum
Figs. 3:9; 3:15; 3:16; 4:4c, d; 4:5b; 8:5; 8:6c, d.

Whatcom County Museum of History and Art, Bellingham.
Fig. 4:7.

Private Collections
de Menil collection, 4:14a, 2:30; Mikelson collection, 7:8c; W.H. Cross collection, 3:26, 3:8; Gore-Langton collection, 3:7; Ruddick collection, 3:25; Hauberg collection, 2:15, 2:27; Sosland collection, 2:16.